**Languaging**

Reconceptualising language as a dynamic, relational, and embodied practice, this book explores the concept of languaging. Moving beyond static, standardised, and purified understandings of languages, it traces how communication is lived, contested, and embodied across urban, rural, and remote mobility, everyday encounters, classroom pedagogies, and digital platforms. Through critical analyses of First Knowledging and First Languaging, nomadic languaging and knowledging, racialised and AI-mediated communication, it highlights how languaging is both playful and precarious. It entails creativity and resistance, while also exposing language users to inequality and surveillance, and is deeply entangled with histories of colonialism, racial hierarchies, and displacement. Concluding with the concept of pedagogical languaging, the book calls for a reimagining of education as interactional design, rather than the delivery of standardised curricula, with learning environments where diverse semiotic repertoires – linguistic, embodied, cultural, and digital – are recognised as epistemic resources rather than treated as deficits.

SENDER DOVCHIN is Professor of Applied Linguistics at Curtin University, Australia. She has been recognised three times by *The Australian Research Magazine*, in 2021, 2024, and 2025, as the top linguist in the nation.

KEY TOPICS IN APPLIED LINGUISTICS

Series Editors

Claire Kramsch (University of California, Berkeley)
and Zhu Hua (UCL Institute of Education, London)

Books in this series provide critical accounts of the most important topics in applied linguistics, conceptualised as an interdisciplinary field of research and practice dealing with practical problems of language and communication. Some topics have been the subject of applied linguistics for many years and will be re-examined in the light of new developments in the field; others are issues of growing importance that have not so far been given a sustained treatment. The topics of the series are nuanced and specialised, providing an opportunity for further reading around a particular concept. The concept examined may be theoretical or practice-oriented. Written by leading experts, the books in the series can be used on courses and in seminars, or as succinct guides to a particular topic for individual students and researchers.

# Languaging
## Playfulness and Precarity

SENDER DOVCHIN
*Curtin University*

## CAMBRIDGE
UNIVERSITY PRESS

Shaftesbury Road, Cambridge CB2 8EA, United Kingdom

One Liberty Plaza, 20th Floor, New York, NY 10006, USA

477 Williamstown Road, Port Melbourne, VIC 3207, Australia

314–321, 3rd Floor, Plot 3, Splendor Forum, Jasola District Centre, New Delhi – 110025, India

Cambridge University Press is part of Cambridge University Press & Assessment, a department of the University of Cambridge.

We share the University's mission to contribute to society through the pursuit of education, learning and research at the highest international levels of excellence.

www.cambridge.org
Information on this title: www.cambridge.org/9781009526937

DOI: 10.1017/9781009526883

© Sender Dovchin 2026

This publication is in copyright. Subject to statutory exception and to the provisions of relevant collective licensing agreements, no reproduction of any part may take place without the written permission of Cambridge University Press & Assessment.

When citing this work, please include a reference to the DOI 10.1017/9781009526883

First published 2026

Cover image: Mongolian nomadic camel herders | Photo by Sender Dovchin

Emojis used under a creative commons licence, © X Corp. Full details: Copyright 2026 X Corp and other contributors.

Code licensed under the MIT Licence: http://opensource.org/licenses/MIT

Graphics licensed under CC-BY 4.0: https://creativecommons.org/licenses/by/4.0/

*A catalogue record for this publication is available from the British Library*

*A Cataloging-in-Publication data record for this book is available from the Library of Congress*

ISBN 978-1-009-52693-7 Hardback
ISBN 978-1-009-52692-0 Paperback

Cambridge University Press & Assessment has no responsibility for the persistence or accuracy of URLs for external or third-party internet websites referred to in this publication and does not guarantee that any content on such websites is, or will remain, accurate or appropriate.

For EU product safety concerns, contact us at Calle de José Abascal, 56, 1°, 28003 Madrid, Spain, or email eugpsr@cambridge.org.

# Contents

*List of Figures and Tables*   *page vi*
*Acknowledgements*   *viii*

1 From Languages to Languaging: Playful Voices, Precarious Grounds   1
2 First Languaging, First Knowledging   35
3 Nomadic Languaging and Nomadic Knowledging   63
4 Racialised Languaging   92
5 AI-mediated Languaging   117
6 Pedagogical Languaging and the Future of Applied Linguistics   145

*References*   158
*Index*   182

# Figures and Tables

**Figures**
1.1 David is drawing  *page 10*
1.2 David's artwork  *11*
1.3 Headless sheep  *18*
1.4 Mongol School  *19*
2.1 Reindeer and Urts (teepees)  *36*
2.2 Reindeer and Uvugdorj, a Tsaatan elder from the Eastern Taiga, moving to his spring camp. Uvugdorj was renowned for his intellect and wisdom  *39*
2.3 Humans and reindeer: The Eastern Taiga, the fourth-generation shaman from Soyon tribe, D. Yesun Erdene, in his autumn camp  *42*
2.4 Creating Aboriginal artworks  *48*
2.5 The girls  *49*
2.6 Writing a letter  *52*
2.7 Kaarda friend!  *56*
3.1 Nomadic reminiscing circle  *64*
3.2 Before the horse race  *75*
3.3 Mongolian nomadic herders  *78*
3.4 Ингэ хөөслөх Demonstrating *khoos-ing the camels*  *81*
5.1 Learning Mongolian  *123*
5.2 Russianised Mongolian  *126*
5.3 Playing with ChatGPT  *129*
5.4 Languaging through ChatGPT  *134*
5.5 What language is it?  *136*
5.6 *Sevleg Urgeeh*  *138*
5.7 Chinggis Khan  *140*

**Tables**
1.1 Code-switching versus languaging  *16*
2.1 Miriwoong Dawang  *46*

2.2  Tell us something in your language!  48
2.3  Darren  52
3.1  *Giingoo*  74
3.2  Teasing  77
3.3  *Khoos*  79
3.4  English is nomadic  84
4.1  My name  *102*
4.2  I use Aboriginal English  *108*
4.3  It's awful!  *114*

# Acknowledgements

I pay my respect to the Whadjuk peoples of the Noongar nation on whose lands I live, work, and where I wrote this book. I acknowledge the Noongar Elders, past and present, whose language was suppressed due to past government policies, and I thank them for continuing to share their knowledge with the generations so we can continue using Noongar language now and into the future.

I use the terms Aboriginal, First Nations, and Indigenous interchangeably and do so respectfully and with recognition of the diversity of Aboriginal and Torres Strait Islander peoples of Australia, knowing that such terms are not universally accepted. Various data examples in this book obtained ethical approval from Curtin University's Human Research Ethics Committee.

This book could not have come into being without the love, guidance, and support of many people. First and foremost, I owe my deepest gratitude to my family – my son, Wilson Dring, and my partner, Elliot Gane; my father, Dovchin Yondon, and my sister, Ulemj Dovchin; and my late mother, Erdenechimeg Perliijantsan – whose unwavering love, patience, and encouragement have sustained me throughout this journey. Your belief in me has been both my anchor and my inspiration.

I am profoundly grateful to my mentors, whose wisdom and generosity of spirit have shaped not only this book but also my growth as a scholar and a human being. Your guidance has lit the path forward in ways that words cannot fully capture. To my colleagues, thank you for your collaboration, insights, and friendship. Working alongside you has enriched my thinking and reminded me of the value of shared intellectual and personal journeys. I am indebted to the research participants who trusted me with their stories and experiences. This work is grounded in your voices, and it is my hope that it does justice to the courage and resilience you embody. This is a book that I have had the privilege of exploring alongside my wonderful research team, who have contributed across various

## Acknowledgements

projects: Rhonda Oliver, Graeme Gower, Lissy Jackson, Libby Lee-Hammond, Sophie Mung, Tamara Tucker, Debra Hannagan, Ana Tankosić, Stephanie Dryden, Qian Gong, Bolormaa Shinjee, Toni Dobinson, and Carly Steele.

I would like to sincerely acknowledge the many community partners who walked alongside me in this project, particularly Purnululu Aboriginal School, Kadidjiny Aboriginal Playgroup, William Langford Community House, Yalkarang Consulting, Wongutha Aboriginal Boarding School, Tsaatan Reindeer Photography, and many others. Your commitment, collaboration, and care made this work possible, and I am deeply humbled by the opportunity to learn with and from you. Finally, I would like to thank the series editors, Zhu Hua and Claire Kramsch, for their generous support and insightful feedback, as well as Rebecca Taylor and Isabel Collins for their guidance and support throughout the complex publishing process.

To each of you – family, mentors, colleagues, participants, and communities – I offer my heartfelt thanks. This book is as much yours as it is mine.

# 1 From Languages to Languaging
## Playful Voices, Precarious Grounds

### 1.1 FROM LANGUAGE/S TO LANGUAGING

You might assume that I speak, write, and use Mongolian fluently, since I am Mongolian by birth, raised in Mongolia, and spent most of my childhood there. I do consider Mongolian as my first language – the language of my homeland and my mother tongue. However, I must admit, somewhat reluctantly, that I am not able to produce "pure" academic written Mongolian system, as I have not been immersed in that system for the past two decades due to my migration to Australia. This long-term separation from formal Mongolian academic contexts has limited my ability in its academic conventions. In contrast, I have been more actively engaged with academic English, having had direct access to it since I settled in Australia. However, I still speak English with my own accent – *nonstandard* and not so perfect Mongolian-accented English (Dovchin, 2024a). I have also had direct access to and exposure to the Russian language since childhood, due to Mongolia being under Soviet rule for seventy years until the collapse of the Soviet Union in 1990. This historical context allowed me to learn Russian early on, but since my connection with the language was disrupted after the Soviet Union's collapse, I do not consider myself a fluent Russian speaker, even though I can understand Russian movies or news. Later in life, I worked in Japan and learned some Japanese, but not at a level of fluency or native-like proficiency – just a few phrases and expressions here and there (Dovchin, 2024b). From this perspective, it makes little sense to classify myself as a "pure" language user in either Mongolian or English, or in Japanese or Russian. My linguistic practice is shaped by complex indexicalities, drawing on all available linguistic resources – language contact, accessibility, and contextual availability. What I *do* with what languages I *have* is not a reflection of linguistic purity, but rather a response to the conditions under which I live, work, and communicate. My birthright to Mongolian language does not guarantee mastery across all its registers. Similarly, my direct exposure to English coexists with an accent that conflicts with dominant standard English norms. My case here somewhat illustrates that real-life language use is not merely about purity or proficiency but more about access, contact, exposure, and the evolving contexts of its use over time.

Mainstream applied linguistics has traditionally adopted an ontological stance that treats language as a bounded and self-contained entity with clear rules, purity, and internal structured organisation. This structuralist perspective has had far-reaching implication for how languages are understood, taught, and studied – particularly in relation to standardisation, grammar, and the construction of so-called legitimate or true languages (Gramling, 2016, 2021; Lee, 2022; Makoni & Pennycook, 2005; Matras, 2025; Pennycook, 2024). Language is often viewed as a biological trait we *have* – humans' innate capacity for language – our brains are wired for acquiring and processing language. This includes abilities like hearing sounds, producing speech, and understanding grammar, which are rooted in our biology (Millikan, 2005). Viewing language as a single, unified system that humans have inherently implies perceiving it as a fixed, autonomous entity that exists independently of its users – akin to a ready-made set of rigid rules or structures that precede and govern actual communication. Within this ontological position, language is seen as something fixed and separable – something that can be named, fixed, purified, and measured (Otheguy et al., 2015). Often, language is thought of as a static, pre-existing entity – a system with clearly defined boundaries, grammar, vocabulary, and rules that are established independently of how people actually speak or interact. This view imagines language as something complete and unchanging, waiting to be used by speakers who simply apply these preset rules when communicating. This conception assumes that language is a completed, unchanging system, passively waiting for speakers to merely activate and reproduce it with precision and fidelity. These elements are regarded as objective and universal truths, existing outside and regardless of the dynamic realities of human interaction.

The languages I have in me, from this perspective – Mongolian, English, Japanese, and Russian – could be seen as belonging to four distinct, bounded language systems, each judged against idealised notions of linguistic "purity" and "correctness." Whenever I switch between languages or blend them, it has sometimes been perceived as a deviation from these norms. In my own experience, I have always felt the pressure to demonstrate my strongest multilingual competence precisely by aligning my use of Mongolian or English, by

## 1.1 From Language/s to Languaging

extension Russian and Japanese, with established monolingual norms – emphasising purity and correctness – especially in formal or professional settings. Whether in meetings, presentations, or official communications, I found myself consciously adjusting my language to fit dominant expectations. This pressure reveals the persistent power of dominant monolingual frameworks that continue to shape what is considered appropriate and legitimate language use. As a result, like many multilingual individuals, I often strategically adopt monolingual behaviours to navigate social expectations, gain acceptance, and enhance my credibility or effectiveness. This personal negotiation has made me keenly aware of how rigid, essentialist views of language obscure the flexible, hybrid, and deeply contextual nature of multilingual communication as it unfolds in real life.

In everyday contexts – as I mentioned earlier and reiterate here – "what I *do* with the languages I *have* is not a reflection of linguistic purity," because English, Mongolian, Russian, Japanese, and so on that I have in me are certainly not "pure" in any prescriptive sense. Rather, what I *do* with these languages shapes the nature of my everyday communication. For instance, when chatting with a friend, I might ask a question in Mongolian, with some integration of English expressions to describe something technical like a phone app and then finish with a Russian phrase to capture the exact emotional feeling – each shift happening naturally as part of the flow of conversation. This insight fundamentally challenges the traditional ontological position that views language as a fixed, bounded, and pure system. Such a view not only reduces language to a mechanical code to be mastered but also enforces an illusion of linguistic purity and homogeneity. It overlooks the profound complexity and variability inherent in real-world language use, where meaning is continuously negotiated, reshaped, and reinvented within social contexts. It denies the creative, adaptive, and fluid nature of language as a living practice – one that evolves with culture, identity, and power relations.

This traditional ontological position, which views language as a fixed, bounded, and pure system, is itself a constructed invention (Gramling, 2016, 2021; Makoni & Pennycook, 2005; Reagan, 2004). Reagan (2004, p. 42) provocatively suggested a decade ago, "there may not actually be such a thing as English. In fact, my argument goes further – not only does English not truly exist as a fixed entity, but neither do Russian, French, Spanish, Chinese, Hindi, or any other language" (p. 42). To support this bold assertion, Reagan (2004) highlighted that the concept of languages as stable, bounded entities is problematic from both historical and social perspectives. Historically, language has always been evolving and changing, meaning any attempt to define the boundaries of a language only captures it at a specific moment in time and place (Reagan, 2004, p. 44). Socially, language varies depending on context, individual speakers, social class, gender, and other factors. Reagan (2004, pp. 44–46) proposed that a language is essentially a collection of individual speech varieties – or idiolects – that have been grouped together for reasons beyond purely linguistic criteria. He concluded by advocating for a critical awareness of language that adopts a constructivist approach, rejecting the positivist tendency to treat language as a fixed object, in favour of a more complex, nuanced, and sophisticated understanding of language (Reagan, 2004, p. 56). Building on Reagan's claim, Makoni and Pennycook (2005) asserted that while it is notable that new linguistic categories have been given invented names, the more important issue goes beyond just naming. Many languages were constructed and named within the context of colonial and missionary activities. At the same time, a system of classification – a metalanguage or overarching discourse – was also created to organise languages into distinct, countable units. This classification system promoted the idea that languages are fixed, separate entities, an idea reinforced by the existence of grammars and dictionaries that treated languages as institutionalised objects. These inventions had tangible consequences: they influenced how people understand languages, shape language policies, impact educational practices, and affect individual and group identities linked to linguistic labels. A critical approach to language studies, therefore, must involve questioning and deconstructing these invented categories. This *"disinventing"* process requires recognising the historical origins of these concepts and reimagining how languages relate to identity, place, and social life today. Their goal was not to romanticise a return to a pre-colonial linguistic landscape but to find new, critical ways of understanding language in the modern world.

More recently, David Gramling (2016, 2021), in his works *The Invention of Monolingualism* and *The Invention of Multilingualism*, has presented a critical rethinking of how language in relation to the concepts of monolingualism and multilingualism was understood. He has argued that neither language nor multilingualism exist as fixed, natural, or purely linguistic entities. Instead, these concepts were socially and politically constructed, deeply embedded within power dynamics and historical contexts. Gramling, in this sense, challenges traditional essentialist and structuralist perspectives that view languages as pure, bounded systems with clear-cut boundaries. Instead, he insists that

## 1.1 From Language/s to Languaging

what counts as a "language" or as "multilingual competence" is always defined and regulated through social practices, prevailing ideologies, and institutional policies. A key focus of Gramling's analysis is how multilingualism, rather than being an organic reflection of people's everyday linguistic realities, is often deliberately "invented" or framed in particular ways to serve nationalist agendas or reinforce existing social hierarchies. Official definitions and institutional categorisations tend to impose rigid boundaries on what qualifies as a language or legitimate multilingual ability. These boundaries privilege certain languages – usually those associated with political and economic power – while marginalising others, thus denying the hybrid, fluid, and dynamic linguistic repertoires that many individuals and communities actually use in daily life. Furthermore, Gramling has shown how languages have increasingly been treated as standardised, monolithic codes designed primarily to serve the interests of dominant elites. This institutionalised vision of language as a fixed system has become deeply entrenched in educational systems, government policies, and social norms. As a result, individuals and entire communities are often judged and marginalised based on their perceived deficiencies in adhering to these dominant language standards. This can perpetuate exclusion, discrimination, and linguistic injustice, as the diversity and hybridity of real-world language use are disregarded or devalued. Ultimately, Gramling's work has revealed how language ideologies are not merely abstract theories but have concrete consequences for how people experience identity, social inclusion, and access to resources. By exposing the invented nature of monolingualism and multilingualism, he calls for a more critical and inclusive approach to understanding language – one that recognises linguistic diversity as dynamic, fluid, and inseparable from social and political realities.

By clinging to this narrow, prescriptive, and invented model, we risk perpetuating rigid linguistic hierarchies that marginalise dialects, hybrid forms, and fluid linguistic practices. This perspective not only limits academic understanding but also influences education, policy, and societal attitudes in ways that stifle linguistic diversity and the rich, dynamic realities of how people actually communicate. For example, Moyer (2023, p. 98) argues that nationalist discourses have emerged, relying on "a homogenous language system based on linguistic criteria to define belonging to a community of speakers but also as a source of identity and nation-state building." The myth of monolingualism has remained as the norm in many spheres of linguistics as well as in popular thinking (Moyer, 2023, p. 98). This is because "the idea of a single nation with one language system has been promoted at the expense of negating variation and language diversity existing within a given nation or state" (Moyer, 2023, p. 98). Aligning with Moyer's idea, Nystrom's (2025) recent study also highlights how Canada's multicultural image is, in fact, creating monolingual realities within multilingual families. Its official bilingual policy privileges English and French, effectively marginalising other languages, actively constructing linguistic boundaries. This privileging of English and French creates an uneven linguistic landscape that marginalises the rich diversity of other languages spoken by immigrant communities across the nation. These national language policies do much more than merely regulate communication at the societal level. They actively construct and reinforce linguistic boundaries that influence how families use language in everyday life. These policies shape parental language choices and children's language learning environments, and ultimately drive intergenerational language shifts – where heritage languages are displaced by dominant official languages. In doing so, these policies contribute to creating monolingual realities inside families that were once multilingual, leading to significant cultural and identity implications for future generations.

Similarly, in Australia, clinging to invented models of language has had profound implications for education and policy, particularly within the Australian schooling system's approach to First Nations children (Steele & Oliver, 2024). The prevailing single-minded emphasis on English language and literacy skills has largely overlooked the linguistic identities of these learners, as well as the broader social, cultural, and political contexts that shape their language practices. This approach failed to recognise that First Nations children navigate complex multilingual realities deeply intertwined with the ongoing processes of colonisation. By prioritising literacy narrowly defined in terms of English proficiency and correctness, educational policy effectively sidelined the rich linguistic and cultural knowledge these children bring to the classroom. The authors go on to argue that this singular focus on English-only policy represents more than a pedagogical oversight; it functions as a policy of distraction that serves as a mechanism of colonial control. Rather than fostering genuine inclusion or linguistic justice, such policies reinforce colonial structures by marginalising Indigenous languages and epistemologies. This perpetuation of dominant language ideologies sustains existing power asymmetries within Australian society, maintaining systemic inequities between settler and First Nations peoples. In effect, educational policies that insist on English literacy as the sole

## 1.1 From Language/s to Languaging

marker of success contribute to the erasure of Indigenous linguistic identities and uphold a colonial status quo that restricts First Nations children's agency and full participation in their own education (Steele et al., 2025).

So, moving forward, how can we actively, as Makoni & Pennycook (2005) note, "disinvent" this essentialist view of language – recognising the real risks it poses – and instead cultivate more inclusive, dynamic understandings that reflect lived linguistic realities? Jerry Lee's *Locating Translingualism* (2022) opens with a compelling metaphor: a bird soaring high above the earth, surveying the landscape for sustenance. It spots a caterpillar – yet something seems amiss. This caterpillar has evolved to mimic a snake, complete with eyespots and movements that deceive even the most vigilant predator. The bird hesitates, uncertain whether it faces prey or a threat. This image aptly introduces Lee's investigation into the complexities of language and culture in a globalised world. Just as the bird must interpret ambiguous signs to survive, humans continuously decode cultural and linguistic cues to navigate social realities. Yet, these signs – like the caterpillar's eyespots – can be misleading, partial, and deeply dependent on context. Building on this metaphor, Lee urges us to reconsider how we conceptualise language and cultural interaction. He cautions against limiting our understanding to how individuals from distinct cultures – "culture A" and "culture B" – communicate across their dominant languages, "language X" and "language Y." Lee critiques this framing for assuming communication merely bridges gaps between fixed linguistic and cultural boundaries, a simplification that obscures the fluid and contested nature of these boundaries themselves (Lee, 2022, p. 270). In this light, the author invites readers to adopt a "bird's-eye view" of language – not as a fixed, discrete system of codes, but as a dynamic semiotic practice shaped fundamentally by spatiality, movement, and interaction. He challenges traditional conceptions of language as bounded, countable entities and instead foregrounds translingualism as a fluid, everyday reality where communication flows across and beyond established linguistic borders. Language in this respect – manifested through signs and semiotic landscapes – becomes a vital site of inquiry, revealing how cultural identities are represented, negotiated, and at times reinvented.

Indeed, the consequences of this sort of understanding of the language were already highlighted by Haugen (1972, p. 25) many decades ago: "*The concept of language as a rigid, monolithic structure is false, even if it has proved to be a useful fiction in the development of linguistics. It is the kind of simplification that is necessary at a certain stage of a science, but which can now be replaced by more sophisticated models."*

These words from Haugen (1972) contribute to our understanding of the underlying ideas that have shaped the object of inquiry, whereby the existence of language is so deeply entrenched in the predominant paradigm of language studies that they are rarely questioned. When people are speaking "different" languages, the structuralist view encourages us to focus on the distinctiveness of those languages – as if each one exists independently of the others. But this raises an important question: how do we account for why one language, variety, or form is used in a particular context over another? Such questions challenge the assumption that language use can be fully explained by structural properties alone. Instead, the call for an ontological shift towards understanding language is socially embedded, relational, and dynamic – something that emerges through interaction, shaped by history, power, and identity (Gramling, 2016, 2021; Gurney & Demuro, 2023; Makoni & Pennycook, 2005; Matras, 2025; Pennycook, 2024). This call has been instrumental in revealing how the notion of language as a fixed and homogenous system is itself an invention that remains to be persistent by numerous ideological constructs and how effective communication can occur even when it challenges traditional norms that prioritise dominant perceptions of language boundaries.

In this book, I approach language not as a fixed object, bounded system, or innate biological possession, but as a living practice – something people *do*, not something they inherently *are* or *have*. Language, in this view, is shaped by use, by context, and always in motion rather than biologically predetermined or static. Language starts from the speaker, not from the code, grammar, or syntax. Seeing language this way helps us better understand how languages are constantly being shaped, reshaped, and negotiated through everyday interactions. This view rejects static definitions of language handed down through structuralist linguistics and instead focuses on showing language emerging through real-life social processes. The view – something people *do*, rather than something they inherently *have* – has been explored through a range of *"languaging"* perspectives: from *translanguaging* (Lee & Li Wei, 2025; Wong & García, 2025), *polylanguaging* (Arellano & Torres-Vásquez, 2025; Jørgensen et al., 2015), and *linguascaping* (Dovchin, 2018) to *translingual practice* (Canagarajah, 2012; Lee, 2017, 2022) and *metrolingual practice* (Pennycook & Otsuji, 2015). While each of these frameworks has distinct contextual and analytical roots, they share a common focus on the dynamic, fluid, and socially embodied nature

## 1.1 From Language/s to Languaging

of language use, challenging traditional views of language as a fixed and bounded system. While *polylanguaging* focuses on the languaging practices of urban youth in European social media contexts, *metrolingualism* examines everyday interactions among migrants in urban marketplaces and corner shops in Australia. *Linguascaping*, in contrast, broadly concerns the visual and spatial dimensions of language within linguistic landscapes. *Translanguaging* primarily relates to pedagogical contexts, where speakers strategically and fluidly draw upon their entire linguistic repertoires to facilitate learning, communication, and identity expression. In this book, however, it is not my aim to delineate all these conceptual distinctions. The notion of *languaging* already encompasses these various "-ing" dimensions of language use, representing a more integrated and holistic approach to understanding how people make meaning through language – an issue I have already addressed elsewhere in the book. Languaging, therefore, is understood as the active, embodied process of *doing* language. It is not something people are born with, but something they *do* – learned, shaped, and transformed through lived experiences and social interactions. Languaging is not an inherited trait, but an ongoing embodied experience and practice of meaning-making in the world. It is something people enact, perform, and reshape in response to the demands of their lived realities. Languaging is fluid and agentive – a practice rooted in *doing*, not in *having*.

Cowley's (2019, 2024, p. 1) vision on languaging takes on new life here. He argues that if we consider languages as structures, we might fail because "as structures, languages merely interact with other structures (in theories)."

> Descriptions of linguistic forms, functions, sentences, X bars, concepts, etc., do nothing at all. Living beings do not use mental proxies of symbols ("language"), but, rather, practices, bodies and brains.... Given how human subjects use languaging, agency is transformed by languages and practices. As we co-act, coordinative activity combines with the wording types that are also used in describing linguistic structure.

With the vision of languaging, Cowley (2019, 2024) turns to the notion that encompasses doing, thinking, talking, and understanding. When people communicate together – that is, when they co-act – they engage in more than just exchanging words. They participate in a coordinated social activity that involves gesture, tone, timing, shared understanding, and mutual responsiveness. In this process, the fluid and response nature of languaging (spontaneous meaning making in real time) interacts with more conventionalised, recognisable forms of language, such as vocabulary, grammar, and syntax – what Cowley (2024) refers to as *wording types*. These *wording types* are the same elements typically analysed in formal linguistics descriptions. In other words, human subjects are involved in languaging to *do* linguistic structures rather than *having* languages. Humans are "*made in languaging*" – not as a matter of *having* languages but as a way of actively enacting, shaping, and uttering linguistic structures. This integration of dynamic interaction shows that structure, in fact, emerges through coordinated social action. In other words, language structure is not just a pre-existing code we draw from – it is continually shaped and reshaped by how we use it in interaction.

I recall one example when I was visiting a remote school in Purnululu School, (Frog Hollow (see also Dovchin et al., 2026) in WA, I connected with a young Aboriginal boy who was eager to show me his drawings

Figure 1.1  David is drawing
(Photo by Sender Dovchin)

## 1.1 From Language/s to Languaging

(see Figure 1.1). I will discuss my encounters with the Aboriginal school in more detail in Chapter 2. He proudly held up one and began explaining it to me Dovchin et al. (2026). I asked him in Standard Australian English (SAE), "*Can you please explain to me what this picture is about?*" He responded in Kriol, "*Dasda berd flaiyen awei en dasda peeboorl gada rowep an dasda men wen ee draiben an ee traina sbeeya ad da krogedail*" *(that's a bird flying away that that's people with a rope and that's a man when he's driving and he's trying to spear at the crocodile)*. Although I did not fully understand everything he was saying, I could see how animated and enthusiastic he was. Wanting to keep the conversation going, I asked another question in SAE: "*Spearing the crocodile, wow, why is he spearing the crocodile?*" He replied again in Kriol: "*So ee, so ee, so ee jagem indoo det eemyoo*" *(so he, so he, so he chucked it (the spear) into that emu)* (see Figure 1.2) (Dovchin et al. 2026).

Here, our interaction was "*made in languaging,*" as Cowley (2019, 2024) would say, where doing, thinking, talking, and understanding converge in a moment of shared engagement between a child and me. Our conversation was not merely a mix of Kriol and SAE but an example of spontaneous meaning-making in real time. The Aboriginal boy's language practice did not align neatly with traditional models of language competence. He does not have English in the standardised monolingual sense, nor does he possess a singular, fully developed academic register in any one language. Yet, through languaging, he actively "*did language*" – navigating concepts, identities, and relationships across

Figure 1.2 David's artwork
(Photo by Sender Dovchin)

linguistic boundaries. Rather than drawing from separate, bounded languages, he engaged in a languaging, constituting meaning by drawing on the linguistic resources available to him in the moment. We were not having language but rather *doing language* within a shared social context. Although I was not able to fully grasp the linguistic content, the relational and affective cues – such as the child's excitement, tone, gesture, and engagement – guided our interaction. The boundaries of language systems (e.g., SAE, Kriol) were already blurred at this stage in favour of real-time meaning negotiation. Our interaction was not comforting to standard grammar, linguistic compatibility, or purity, but meaning emerged nonetheless through co-actions and responsiveness. This reflects the idea that humans are "*made in languaging*" – not defined by the possession of discrete languages but by their participation in socially situated, emergent acts of communication.

Languaging, therefore, invites us to focus on social action and interaction, rather than abstract systems. Through this lens, language becomes a dynamic, open-ended, and context-dependent activity. As Pennycook (2024, p. 4) reminds us, "if we are trying to deal with real-world contexts, it doesn't really make sense to draw on theories of language that haven't emerged from such contexts." Language is shaped by its speakers, situated in time and place, and deeply intertwined with the physical and social environments in which it occurs. Words, gestures, tone, bodily movements, and material objects all come together in the act of languaging – highlighting that language is not separate from the world but deeply *of* the world. By framing *language* as *languaging*, this book challenges conventional, objectified views of language that dominate much of applied linguistics. Instead, it centres a view of language as an emergent, lived, and embodied practice – one that resists tidy boundaries and demands that we pay attention to the messy, creative, and socially embedded nature of communication (Dovchin et al., 2026).

Languaging reminds us of Judith Butler's statement "*we do things with language*" (Butler, 2021, p. 8), in which she theorises that speech is not merely a vehicle for conveying information, but an act performed to produce effects that align with, or challenge, norms constituted by juridical and political systems (Butler, 2006). When Butler says "*we do things with language*," she invites us to see speaking as a form of action in itself – an act that can shape the world around us. Drawing on Austin's speech act theory, Butler emphasises that words do not simply describe reality; they enact it. For example, the phrase "I now *pronounce you married*" does not just state a fact but actively changes people's social and legal status. Every utterance carries the power to effect change. Butler extends this idea by showing that language is

## 1.2 Languaging or Code-switching?

deeply intertwined with power: each time we speak, we are either reinforcing or resisting existing social and political norms. Words have real, material effects – they can open doors to rights and opportunities or inflict harm and exclusion. Language is performative: it does not merely reflect the world; it actively shapes it. In Butler's view, language is not a static mirror but a dynamic tool through which society is continuously created and transformed. In this book, language understood in this way is *languaging*. Language is performative – it does not just repeat the world, it makes it. For this book, that active, world-shaping process is *languaging*.

### 1.2 LANGUAGING OR CODE-SWITCHING?

*"What is the difference between code-switching and languaging?"* This question resonates widely – not only within the specialised field of applied linguistics but also among undergraduate students, passionate language enthusiasts, educators, policymakers, and even seasoned linguists. It reflects a fundamental curiosity about how people navigate multiple languages and language varieties in real life (Balam, 2021; Goodman & Tastanbek, 2021; Treffers-Daller, 2024). When we talk about *languaging*, however, we must ask: are we simply referring to the act of switching back and forth between discrete linguistic codes, as implied by *code-switching,* or are we engaging with a more dynamic and holistic process of *languaging* – where speakers draw from an integrated, fluid linguistic repertoire that transcends conventional language boundaries? To answer this question, I follow Pennycook's (2024, p. 8) suggestion around *code-switching* versus *languaging*:

> people are talking about different things, some focusing on language as structure (How do we account for one language or another being used in a particular context?), others on language practices (What are people doing with different linguistic elements?).

This distinction is not merely semantic. Code-switching traditionally frames language use as alternating between separate, fixed systems – each with its own rules and boundaries. Indeed, when people are talking about *code-switching*, it is most often based on the understanding that the code-switchers function as two or three separate monolinguals. This means that each linguistic code used by code-switchers is expected to be produced "purely" and "fluently," as if it were independent and unaffected by the influence of the other languages (Ag & Jørgensen, 2013). For example, while *reminiscing* (having a conversation) with the

Mongolian nomadic herders, we began discussing the role of English in their lives, a topic I will explore in more detail in Chapter 3. In a playful tone, the herders described themselves as "multilinguals" shaped by today's globalisation. One of them said, "*Opa ni govoryu po Ruskii, and bas English. Buh heleer yarina shuudee.*" From the norms of the code-switching, this herder appears to be code-switching across Korean (*Opa ni* – your friend, your folk), Russian (*govoryu po Ruskii* – speak Russian) and Mongolian (*Buh heleer yarina shuudee* – We speak all languages). This highlights how code-switching is often compartmentalised into distinct language systems such as Mongolian, English, Korean, and Russian. Under this norm, when someone switches from the codes such as Mongolian to Russian or Korean, they are expected to speak each language "purely," as if functioning as two or three separate monolinguals – one speaking Mongolian, and another speaking Russian. This also means that people who can formulate more than one language will employ their multiple monolingual capacities in any given context appropriate to the relevant discussants' needs and language skills (Ag & Jørgensen, 2013; Jørgensen et al., 2015). The main norm of the code-switching, thus, is the principle of double or triple monolingualism – individuals who speak two or more languages are expected to use only one language at a time, and to use each language in a way that mirrors monolingual speakers. This norm assumes that languages exist as separate, bounded systems and promotes the belief that each should be used in a "pure" form – without blending elements from other languages. Within this framework, code-switching is accepted, but only as the alternate use of two or three distinct language systems. Even in translingual interactions, speakers are expected to switch clearly from one language to another, maintaining clear boundaries between them. This reinforces the idea that multilingual speakers must compartmentalise their languages and align their use with monolingual norms.

Related to this understanding of language, the epistemological knowledge of *languaging* challenges the norms of *code-switching*. The main critical questions are widely circulated: What if the language users do not necessarily orient to the distinction of separate language systems when they code-switch? What if they instead adapt to a communicative norm where they use all available resources to achieve their communicative aims? Then it is not suitable to categorise, for example, code-switching as bi/multilingual communication because it relies on the separability of pure linguistic categories. The norms of code-switching become much more complicated when the speakers are not necessarily fluent or pure in the languages they use. During my conversations with those Mongolian nomadic herders (see

## 1.2 Languaging or Code-switching?

Chapter 3), it became clear that code-switching in their context does not follow conventional boundaries. The herders are not fluent in either Korean, English, Russian or English – yet freely blend them with Mongolian in everyday speech. This mixing does not stem from clear distinctions between first and second languages but rather reflects how their conversation is *"made in languaging"* – shaped by former Soviet influence in Mongolia, English through media, and casual borrowings from Korean popular culture – has become a localised mode of communication. The herders' linguistic practice forms a kind of grassroots lingua franca, not defined by fluency but by flexibility, creativity, and their positioning in today's globalised world. This observation aligns with recent neuroscience, which tells us that human brain pools bring together elements and features from different semiotic resources while (re)coordinating, (un)selecting, and (de)activating specific parts of the linguistic repertoire for different purposes and in different contexts (Kroll & De Groot, 2009). The brains of multiple language users also command paralinguistic resources: from genres, gestures, styles, and modes to emotions, attentions, and memories when articulating language as part of everyday communication (Li, 2018). Multilinguals should not be thought of as multiple monolinguals coexisting in one mind. People rarely use language in a completely "pure" form. Instead, language users navigate intricate and layered criteria when selecting linguistic resources in specific contexts. Therefore, it is misleading to label code-switchers as "pure" language users, since their choices reflect complex linguistic indexicality and the fluid relationships between linguistic resources and conventional notions of distinct languages.

Languaging challenges the traditional view of parallel monolingualism by highlighting the importance of contact, accessibility, and availability (Goodman & Tastanbek, 2021; Otheguy et al., 2015). Rather than starting from fixed linguistic codes, grammar, or systems, communication begins with the speaker, who draws on all resources available to them – shaped by factors such as technology, digital media, popular culture, education, socio-economic status, ideologies, and migration – to create meaning (Jørgensen & Møller, 2014). In other words, as Jørgensen et al. (2015) note, individuals utilise whatever linguistic tools they have at hand to accomplish their communicative goals, regardless of their proficiency in particular languages. From this perspective, speakers' linguistic repertoires are continuously "dis-invented and reconstituted" (Makoni & Pennycook, 2005, p. 1) through ongoing acts of languaging and semiotic mobility. The focus is on language users' fluid and creative adaptation of diverse semiotic resources, shaped by their socio-historical experiences across multiple interactions in space and time (Hawkins & Mori, 2018). Languaging is seen as operating through complex, interwoven repertoires, composed of fluid and dynamic assemblages of semiotic resources, modes, emotions, styles, voices, genres, parodies, and signs (Pennycook, 2024). It frames language use as a holistic, creative process in which individuals skilfully combine multiple languages to construct meaning, shape identity, and communicate effectively across varied contexts (Wang, 2024). Recognising this perspective is crucial for appreciating the depth of contemporary multilingual communication and challenges conventional, rigid notions of language that fail to reflect speakers' lived experiences globally (Jørgensen & Møller, 2014). Consider Table 1.1, which presents two contrasting approaches to multilingual language use: *code-switching* and *languaging*.

This comparison highlights two contrasting theoretical orientations towards language use: one based on the norm of plural monolingualism, and the other informed by a languaging repertoire-based

Table 1.1 *Code-switching versus languaging*

| Aspects | Code-switching | Languaging |
|---|---|---|
| Theoretical basis | Based on the plural monolingualism norm – languages are seen as separate systems | Languages are one unified communicative repertoire |
| View of language | Languages are bounded, fixed, and distinct | Languages are fluid, dynamic, and interrelated |
| Speaker's role | Speaker is seen as switching between two separate language systems | Speaker is drawing from a single integrated linguistic register |
| Function in communication | Alternating languages for clarity, purity, correctness, and effect | Blending linguistic resources to make meaning and express identity |
| Assessment | Often assessed by how well the speaker adheres to pure linguistic norms, grammar, and standards | Recognised as a natural and legitimate linguistically fluid practice |

## 1.2 Languaging or Code-switching?

perspective. Under the plural monolingualism framework – code-switching – languages are viewed as bounded, fixed, and distinct systems, each existing in isolation from the other. The speaker's role within this model is seen as one of code-switching – shifting between two clearly defined language systems. Communication is shaped by a desire for clarity, correctness, and linguistic purity, and speakers are often assessed based on how closely they adhere to standard grammar and normative language use. In contrast, the repertoire-based languaging perspective sees language as fluid, dynamic, and interconnected. Rather than switching between discrete codes, speakers are seen as drawing from a single, integrated communicative repertoire, blending linguistic resources in creative and meaningful ways (Jørgensen & Møller, 2014). This approach values the speaker's agency in constructing identity and meaning, recognising such hybridity not as a deficiency but as a legitimate, natural way of using language (Wang, 2024). Assessment, accordingly, shifts away from rigid standards towards embracing linguistic fluidity as an authentic communicative practice. This contrast, therefore, reinforces the arguments that we need to shift from a separate (monoglossic) view of language to a holistic (heteroglossic) view (Goodman & Tastanbek, 2021).

### 1.2.1 Playfulness in Languaging: Linguistic Play and Playful Voices

In one of the workshops we ran at Mongol School, WA, we asked the children to create artworks related to Mongolia. Many of the students at this school were either born in Australia or moved here at a very young age. In most cases, their English is stronger than their Mongolian. This is why they attend weekend Mongolian language school – to learn the written Mongolian language, connect with their cultural heritage, and socialise with other Mongolian children. During one of these Mongolian art workshops, two children were painting their visions of "My Mongolia." As they worked, they began teasing each other and laughing, playfully languaging between English and Mongolian. Their interaction was full of lively languaging, drawing from both linguistic repertoires and playful voices as they painted (see Figure 1.3).

1. Tergel: *Look, bagshaa, minii art is the best!* (Look! Teacher! My art is the best!)
2. Nomin: *Best? Minii bodloor ... it looks like tolgoigui sheep! Haha* (In my opinion ... it looks like the headless sheep!)
3. Tergel: *Haha, yu? Thank you for the compliment!* (Haha, what? Thank you for the compliment!)

18    1 FROM LANGUAGES TO LANGUAGING

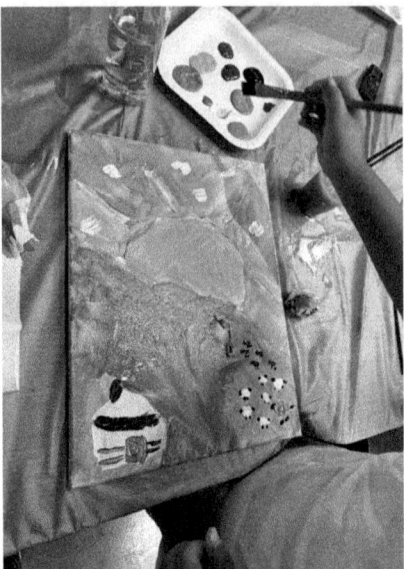

Figure 1.3 Headless sheep
(Photo by Sender Dovchin)

4. Nomin: *Tergel is the Queen of tolgoigui sheep, Nomin is the narnii Queen! Haha!* (Tergel is the Queen of headless sheep, Nomin is the sun Queen!)
5. Tergel: *Narnii Queen?* Your sun looks like a mustard sun!

They speak in a lively rhythm, their sentences tumbling effortlessly between English and Mongolian, while all laugh while playfully swapping brushes and adding silly doodles to each other's artworks (see Figure 1.4). "*Tergel is the Queen of headless sheep, Nomin is the narnii Queen! Haha!*" one says with mock seriousness, prompting the other to snort with laughter before firing back, "*Narnii Queen? Your Sun looks like a mustard sun!*" and both collapse into giggles. This is *languaging* at its most playful: fluid *linguistic play* between languages, whimsical invented titles, and voices pitched high or deep for comic effect. The boundaries between English and Mongolian blur into shared *playful voices* where humour, identity play, and friendship all mingle. Here, *languaging* is a canvas for both *linguistic play* and *playful voices* – the central theme of this section – where the *playfulness* is understood both from a linguistic perspective, as the fluid and creative mixing of English and Mongolian, and from an affective perspective, as

## 1.2 Languaging or Code-switching?

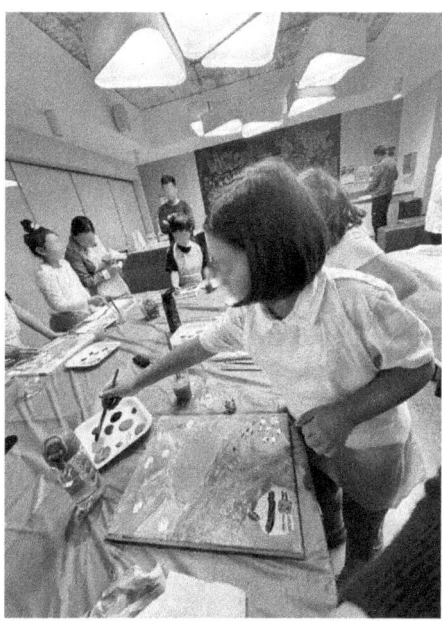

Figure 1.4 Mongol School
(Photo by Sender Dovchin)

a shared performance of humour, teasing, and identity play that strengthens peer bonds.

The concept of fluidity is central to much of the literature on *languaging*, and the notion of *play/playfulness* is closely linked to this very idea. Playfulness in *languaging* refers not only to the *linguistic play* – *imaginative, creative,* and *experimental* ways in which language users engage with their linguistic resources (Dovchin, 2024a; Jakonen et al., 2018), but also to the *playful voices* (Holflod, 2022; Parnell & Patsarika, 2014; Robson & LeVoguer, 2025; Waring 2013) – affective, embodied, and often joyful voices of communication that emerge when boundaries between named languages are blurred. Key linguistic features such as *creativity* (Nie & Yao, 2025), *innovation* (Ilonga, 2023), and *hybridity* (Guo et al., 2025) are foundational to the sense of *linguistic play* in languaging. *Creativity* refers to the ability of languagers to recombine linguistic and semiotic resources in novel, unexpected ways (Mu et al., 2025; Nie & Yao, 2025); *innovation* captures the emergence of new linguistic forms, meanings, and communicative strategies that challenge conventional language boundaries (Ilonga, 2023); and *hybridity* reflects the blending of diverse linguistic codes, styles, and registers that defy rigid categorisations of language (Guo et al., 2025). These elements collectively enable language users – especially those operating within linguistically diverse environments – to engage in imaginative, boundary-crossing interactions. This sense of *linguistic play* has been explored across a wide range of sociolinguistic contexts, highlighting the creative and agentive potential of languagers – particularly in linguistically diverse settings. For instance, studies have examined linguistic play in *language crossing* – the deliberate movement across socially or ethnically marked linguistic boundaries – as a means of identity negotiation and social positioning, particularly among youth in urban classroom settings (Rampton, 2017). Relatedly, *transglossic practices* – where speakers draw fluidly on their linguistic repertoires beyond the constraints of standardised language norms – exemplify the inherently playful, hybrid, and dialogic nature of language use in everyday life (Sultana, 2015). From a Bakhtinian perspective (1984, 1986, 1994), such practices reflect the operation of double voices, multivocalities, and heteroglossia, where multiple social and ideological perspectives coexist and interact within an utterance. Speakers navigate these overlapping voices creatively, producing meanings that are simultaneously personal, social, and intertextual, highlighting language as a dynamic site of negotiation, adaptation, and socio-cultural engagement (Sultana, 2015). In early childhood education settings, the merging of translanguaging with the imaginative possibilities of play-based learning has given rise to a powerful pedagogical space – *translanguaging playworld* (Oakley et al., 2025). Playworlds are co-constructed in imaginary scenarios where children and adults engage together in active play, using storytelling, games, toys, and symbolic activity to explore emotions, relationships, and learning. When translanguaging is integrated into this space, the playworld becomes not only imaginative but linguistically and culturally expansive (Oakley et al., 2025; Parini, 2025). de la Piedra & Johnson (2025) demonstrate how human learning is an embodied, affective, and contextually situated practice that emerges through interactions with both people and the material environment. In the music classroom, languaging is not just a linguistic act but is deeply intertwined with the body, musical instruments, and a range of semiotic resources, including multiple languages, musical notation, sounds, songs, gestures, and bodily movement. These interactions are further shaped by students' emotions, cultural references, and accumulated experiences within the community over time. Together, these elements create dynamic, multimodal assemblages that demonstrate how teaching and learning are collective, creative, and contextually grounded processes (de la Piedra & Johnson, 2025).

Beyond classroom settings, linguistic play is vividly present in performative music, popular music, and hip-hop culture, where linguistic innovation, stylisation, and remixing of codes become tools of resistance, identity-marking, and performative expression (Dryden & Izadi, 2023; Williams, 2017). For example, Dryden & Izadi (2023) investigate the social media activity of Aboriginal Australian hip-hop artist Danzal Baker, who goes by the stage name of Baker Boy, who is known for his hip-hop music that blends English and Yolngu Matha resources originating from Arnhem Land (Yolngu = person, matha = tongue/language). Baker Boy shows how he and his audience use linguistic and semiotic resources to create local–global connections in his hip-hop music and videos, recontextualising these resources for both local and international audiences. His followers, in turn, respond with their own linguistic, cultural, and identity expressions. In so doing, the study shows how these interactions are shaped by the histories of colonisation and the treatment of First Nations peoples' languages in both the Global North and South. Through these exchanges, Baker Boy celebrates his lived cultural and linguistic experiences, asserting their value and normality, while demonstrating how social media enables the fluid deployment of semiotic and linguistic resources across global and local contexts. Williams (2017) conceptualises "remixing multilingualism" as the creative linguistic play of combining, manipulating, and reimagining linguistic forms to produce new cultural expressions and identities, often through a process of bricolage. Drawing on ethnographic research in Cape Town's local hip-hop scene, it examines how highly multilingual artists, many from historically marginalised backgrounds, use performance to showcase their voices and identities in innovative ways. Through interviews, performance analysis, and interactional analysis, the study applies concepts such as stylisation, performativity, entextualisation, and enregisterment to explore how young speakers craft varied personae, styles, registers, and language varieties. In doing so, it offers fresh theoretical insights into multilingualism from a Global South perspective.

Digital communication spaces provide fertile ground for verbal and orthographic experimentation, as users engage in multimodal play – bending spelling norms, mixing scripts, and creating humorous, affectively charged expressions across platforms like social media and messaging apps (Liang, 2024). For example, Liang's (2024) study adopts a creative, translingual lens to explore online transcreation on social media, focusing on multilingual speakers who subtitle and translate video content using translingual English. It examines the interplay between translanguaging, translation, and transcreation, analysing figurative, phatic, and pragmatic expressions alongside manga visuals, anime actions, and comic-style multimodal performances in YouTube videos. Set within the context of transnational cultural flows such as Japanese pop culture and the Korean wave, the findings highlight how YouTubers employ playful transcreational strategies. The study advances theoretical and practical understandings of translingual transcreation in participatory social media discourse. Ilonga (2023) examines linguistic innovations in the digital advertisements of commercial banks in Tanzania, analysed through the lens of translanguaging theory. The research identifies linguistic plays such as the incorporation of foreign words, slang, idiomatic expressions, blending, truncation, vowel lengthening, and denominalisation – some even going beyond official advertising policies. The findings reveal significant linguistic shifts in Tanzanian advertising from the mid 2000s to early 2022, with the growth of digital advertising expected to continue as it aligns with global marketing trends and evolving language practices.

Overall, *linguistic play – the imaginative, creative, and experimental ways* in which individuals engage with their linguistic resources – extends far beyond surface-level ornamentation. Such playful practices embody deeper sociolinguistic processes, revealing speakers' capacity for creative agency and their determination to communicate on their own terms. In the fluid and dynamic spaces of contemporary languaging, these practices challenge conventional norms and open up possibilities for reimagining how meaning, identity, and social relations are negotiated. Such interactions are further infused with what Creese and Blackledge (2010, p. 111) term *"playful naughtiness"* – *playful voices* that subvert linguistic expectations and disrupt normative language ideologies, not in defiance but in joy (Robson & LeVoguer, 2025; Zhu et al., 2016). This spirit of play allows languagers to take pleasure in bending rules, pushing against fixed standards, and embracing ambiguity and contradiction. As Pennycook (2007a, pp. 41–42) argues, it is precisely in these moments that languagers experience the "pleasure of doing things differently" – a feeling of linguistic freedom that emerges when one is no longer confined by the demands of correctness, fluency, or monolingual norms. In English Medium Instruction (EMI) classrooms, researchers have documented that learners employ translanguaging not only as a tool for constructing meaning but also as a social and playful resource. Through *playful voices* such as joking,

## 1.2 Languaging or Code-switching?

teasing, and other forms of humorous interaction, students create moments of solidarity and camaraderie, while simultaneously challenging traditional hierarchies of language proficiency and authority (Tai & Li Wei, 2021). These practices reveal that translanguaging is not purely instrumental or cognitive; it is deeply embedded in the social life of the classroom, shaping relationships, identity, and participation in ways that extend beyond the formal curriculum (Tai & Li Wei, 2021). In such playful engagements, language users do more than simply communicate: they perform identities, thrive on ambiguity, spontaneity, and going with the flow, despite uncertainty, anxiety, and chaos that come with it (Zhu et al., 2016). They challenge linguistic hierarchies and assert ownership over the communicative process. The pressure to conform to a singular, target language is eased, enabling a space where languaging is not only accepted but celebrated. This leads to a sense of emotional safety, ease, and joy – a space where language becomes a tool for connection, rather than a gatekeeper of belonging. Consequently, languaging becomes intimately tied to *laughter* and *affect* – speakers tease, joke, mimic, and parody (Blackledge & Creese, 2009; Haugh, 2017), often engaging in humorous exchanges that build rapport and community. This humour is not incidental but central – it signals comfort, intimacy, and a refusal to take dominant linguistic norms too seriously. Through such *playful voices*, languagers carve out alternative and second lives, where their full repertoires are not only visible but actively celebrated and where the joy of expression transcends the confines of linguistic correctness (Holflod, 2022; Parnell & Patsarika, 2014; Robson & LeVoguer, 2025; Sultana, 2015; Zhu et al., 2016).

### 1.2.2 Languaging: Precarious Grounds and Precarious Voices

As the interaction unfolds at Mongol School, WA, continuing from the previous section, the children's conversation shifts towards learning and speaking Mongolian. The atmosphere begins in a light-hearted tone, with playful voices and linguistic play in full swing. However, what starts as playful languaging gradually turns into a moment of precarity when one child resists the use of Mongolian.

1. Bataa (frowning): *"Stop saying in Mongolian! I don't understand it!"*
2. Nomin (frustrated voice): *"Yu genee? You need to learn Mongolian!"* (What? *You need to learn Mongolian!*)
3. Bataa (angry, raised voice): *"You need to speak English!"*
4. Tergel (raised voice): *"Mongol helee suraa! Za yu?"* (You need to learn Mongolian! OK?)

5. Bataa (repeating Tergel and laughing): *"Mongol helee suraa! Za yu?"*
6. Tergel (laugh and raised voice): *"Shut up!"*

The exchange is a linguistic play where the children engage in teasing repetitions (line 5), sliding in and out of English and Mongolian (across all lines), playful voices such as humorous mimicry (line 5), and offensive phrases and laughter (line 6). Yet, beneath this surface of fun, there are precarious grounds where playfulness intersects with precarity. When Bataa voices feelings of exclusion for not being able to understand Mongolia (*"I don't understand it!"*) and reasserts English as the preferred medium (line 3), he not only expresses an immediate emotional vulnerability but also reveals a deeper *precarious ground* – the fragility of his ability to engage in his heritage language – Mongolian. This moment reflects more than just a breakdown in playful interaction; it signals the emotional strain of navigating identity in a context where heritage language competence is uneven among peers. On another level, this fragility is situated within the broader *structural precarious grounds* of heritage languages in English-dominant societies like Australia, where English is prioritised and heritage languages are often forgotten, devalued, or left to erode across generations (Dovchin, 2025b). In this sense, the child's anger and frustration are not isolated outbursts but are symptomatic of an overarching precarious structural attitude towards minority languages. From this perspective, the playful repetition of Mongolian (*"Mongol helee suraa! Za yu?"*) shifts from being a light-hearted game to a site of power struggle – a moment where language becomes a symbolic boundary between inclusion and exclusion. What began as friendly teasing is now charged with the weight of linguistic vulnerability and precarious voices such as *"Shut Up!"* This transformation highlights the inherently precarious nature of playfulness in languaging settings, its potential to both strengthen and strain peer relationships, depending on how language ideologies, comprehension, and structural forces shape the interaction. Block (2013), in this sense, cautions that any analysis of linguistic diversity must grapple with unequal social, economic, and political conditions that inform and constrain communicative practices. In languaging encounters, linguistic choices are rarely free – they are shaped by access to education, economic capital, racialisation, and linguistic ideologies. Sah and Li (2022) similarly argue that the celebration of fluidity can risk glossing over the structural constraints faced by many translanguagers. As Kubota (2015, p. 33) defiantly asks, "Can all English users regardless of their racial, gender, socio-economic, and other background equally

## 1.2 Languaging or Code-switching?

transgress linguistic boundaries and engage in hybrid and fluid linguistic practices?" These questions remind us that playfulness is not evenly distributed: they are privilege enabled by certain social positions and denied to others. Hence, while languaging offers a valuable reimagining of language, it must also be situated within broader critiques of precarity – inequality, power, and access. Only then we can fully appreciate both its potential and its limitations. In this section, I argue that playfulness in languaging must always be understood in tension with precarity, and the two concepts are inseparable and should not be treated as distinct.

While *playfulness* in *languaging turns* has emerged as a powerful framework in applied linguistics, offering innovative ways to conceptualise the ontological nature of language, a more complex and contradictory picture also begins to emerge – one that demands a deeper, more critical engagement with the assumptions underpinning playfulness. The recent shift in *languaging* urges us to understand that beneath its seemingly *playful* exterior lies *precarious* grounds (Dovchin, 2024a). In fact, the reason behind all of this playfulness is precisely the precarious positions of the creators of the playful (Dovchin et al., 2024). The recent evolution of languaging urges us to remain attentive to the socio-political and material conditions that shape who can play with language, when, and how. Beneath the surface of apparent linguistic playfulness exists a more precarious reality, particularly for language users operating within structures of inequality, marginalisation, or linguistic subordination (French et al., 2024; Jun & Mori, 2024). The reality of precarity is often obscured by discourses of *playfulness*, in which languaging practices are framed as celebrations of becoming, transformation, re-creation, and renewal (Dovchin et al., 2024). From this perspective, *languaging* must be understood not as an open-ended space of endless mobility, but as a process embedded in relations of power, access, and material reality (Dovchin, 2024a).

Hawkins & Tiwari's (2024) argument on translingual precarity is relevant here. Translanguaging and transmodal communication are inherently precarious, as they carry risks of unequal positioning and reinforce status hierarchies. Using the example of Ugandan and Indian youth exchanging videos, they show how creative acts intended to display innovation and resourcefulness were reinterpreted through outsider lenses as signs of poverty, inspiring pity towards "the other" while reinforcing positive self-perceptions. Both groups, however, expressed pride in their lives and sought to share lessons of ingenuity – Ugandan youth showcasing local creativity, and Indian youth producing a video on *jugaad* (improvisation) to demonstrate their own resourcefulness. These exchanges illustrate how participants continuously reposition themselves and others within broader historical, cultural, and ideological flows, often reinscribing precarious grounds. Hawkins & Tiwari (2024) argue for the importance of a transmodal analytic approach that attends to semiotic complexity, relational positioning, and power – precarity in communication across diversity. Such attention is essential for fostering critical cosmopolitanism and moving towards more equitable global relations. As Hawkins & Tiwari (2024, p. 105) note,

> translanguaging, and all communications, are semiotic functions – they are leveraged in meaning-making between people – and are always and everywhere embedded in, shaped by and constitutive of power relations. Therefore, precarity and playfulness are not either/or constructs; communications are always precarious, always embedded in sociocultural and sociopolitical contexts, always risking inequitable positioning and relations, whether or not they involve a degree of playfulness.

Within the field of languaging, the notion of *precarity* has been integral, even if it has not always been explicitly labelled as such. Here, precarity refers to the linguistic and communicative practices shaped by the lived experiences of marginalised communities navigating unstable conditions – what Tsing (2015, p. 2) describes as "life without the promise of stability" – conditions that undermine both material security and emotional well-being (Dovchin, 2022). Languaging itself emerged as a bottom-up framework, connected to concepts like "globalisation from below" and "language from below" (Pennycook & Otsuji, 2015), offering a lens to examine how marginalised speakers in precarious contexts resist sociolinguistic conventions, disrupt dominant ideologies, and transgress linguistic boundaries in order to contest the status quo (Li Wei & Zhu, 2020). Otsuji & Pennycook (2024) have developed an understanding of *precarious assemblages* – a relational understanding of languaging and precarity. Precarity is not limited to economic insecurity or marginalisation but also includes fragile social networks, cultural and religious practices, gender norms, and language policies. For them, it is important to avoid equating precarious language use with precarious lives, as language is only one element within broader precarious assemblages shaped by political economy, material conditions, and social relations. A key risk lies in imposing Northern assumptions that view unstable work or non-normative language practices as inherently

## 1.2 Languaging or Code-switching?

precarious. While some theories treat precarity as a shared condition enabling collective action, its relational and isolating nature complicates such possibilities. An assemblage approach, however, offers a more productive lens. It moves beyond deterministic views that tie linguistic marginality to economic exclusion, instead recognising how diverse factors such as economic, social, material, and linguistic factors intersect to both produce and unsettle precarity. Overall, while instability often refers to fluctuating or uncertain conditions, it does not necessarily equate to *precarity*, which I understand as the *embodied and affective experience* of living within such unstable conditions. In other words, instability describes the structural or material dimension (e.g., insecure employment, migration status, or linguistic marginalisation), whereas *precarity* captures the *lived consequences* – the sense of vulnerability, dispossession, or lack of agency that individuals experience as a result of those unstable conditions. Thus, their approach positions precarity not simply as the presence of instability but as the *socially mediated experience* of that instability, shaped by intersecting factors such as language, identity, and belonging. This distinction allows for a more complex understanding of how linguistic and social inequalities are felt and negotiated in everyday life.

In line with these ideas on precarity, recent scholarship emphasises that the lives of languagers are deeply shaped by precarity (Dovchin et al., 2024) – a state of persistent instability (Bourdieu, 1962/1994) intertwined with uncertain social, economic, and political conditions (Standing, 2011), compounded by intersecting forms of marginalisation (Chang & Canagarajah, 2024; Schierup & Jørgensen, 2016), and laden with emotional strain and vulnerability (Butler, 2004; Canagarajah, 2022). This perspective aligns with emerging critical frameworks such as *raciolinguistics* (Rosa & Flores, 2017), *linguistic racism* (Wang & Dovchin, 2023), *unequal Englishes* (Tupas, 2015), *unequal languaging* (Sah & Li, 2022), *linguicism* (Uekusa, 2019), *translingual discrimination* (Dovchin, 2022), *accentism* (Lippi-Green, 2012), and *linguistic citizenship* (Williams et al., 2022). Across these literatures, the cumulative forms of precarity experienced by languagers – ranging from homesickness, unemployment (Chang & Canagarajah, 2024), academic setbacks, and pressures to use "pure" English (Hopkyns & Sultana, 2024; Horner, 2024), to racism, sexism, and classism (Dovchin, 2025b), family separation, grief, and loss (Ladegaard, 2014, 2015, 2018) – are well documented. The compounding of these stressors significantly impacts languagers' emotional resilience, physical health, and mental well-being, often eroding their sense of belonging. The long-term consequences can be severe, including linguistic inferiority complexes

(Tankosić et al., 2021), depression and anxiety (Piller, 2016), trauma and shock (Busch & McNamara, 2020; Canagarajah, 2022), self-harm, eating disorders, substance abuse, and even suicidal ideation (Dovchin, 2020).

Connected to these *precarious grounds* are also what may be termed *precarious voices* – expressive forms that manifest through a range of paralinguistic and embodied modalities, such as crying, weeping, yelling, or, in Bakhtinian terms (1984, 1986, 1994), *grotesque voices* that include swearing, cursing, or other disruptive utterances (Dovchin, 2024a; Dryden et al., 2021; Ladegaard, 2014, 2015, 2018). In online contexts, these precarious voices can extend to hate speech, verbal aggression, and hostile and offensive exchanges (Dovchin et al., 2026; Guo & Jiang, 2025; Schmid, 2025). Such voices often emerge from, and respond to, experiences of precarious grounds such as exclusion, marginalisation, or linguistic injustice. Yet, despite their significance in revealing the emotional and socio-political dimensions of languaging, these forms of expression have been largely sidelined in existing literature, which tends to (spotlight) *playfulness* as the dominant interpretive frame. Consequently, the affective, resistant, and sometimes volatile dimensions of precarious voices remain under-represented in scholarly accounts, leaving an incomplete picture of the complex ways people use language to navigate precarious conditions. This book, therefore, aims to broaden the concept of precarity in relation to languaging by focusing on *precarious voices* – those of millions of language users who express vulnerability, uncertainty, or marginality in their communication, yet whose experiences are frequently under-represented in scholarly discussions.

### 1.2.3 Languaging: Playful Voices and Precarious Grounds

When I was visiting an Aboriginal boarding school in WA, I sat down for a yarn with a group of boys during a lunch break. I casually asked if any of them could tell me something in their traditional language. Without hesitation, Jarrah – whose mob is from Miriwoong, Kununurra, WA, and whose ancestral language is Miriwoong – responded by singing "*Gooloo-gooloob Yarroondayan*" (We are all happy!). His voice was bright and animated, his body language expressive. Almost immediately, the other boys around him erupted into laughter. Intrigued, I asked them, "*Why are you all laughing?*" They replied with cheeky smiles, "*He is just singing the songs. He doesn't even know how to speak it!*" "*Shame job!*" "*Big shame!*" The laughter grew louder, mixing with playful teasing and mockery.

## 1.2 Languaging or Code-switching?

On the surface, this moment was light-hearted – full of playful voices – joking, parody, singing, energy, and joy. But it also revealed much more. What I witnessed was a powerful instance of *languaging* – a fluid, dynamic sliding, and negotiation between the combination of various linguistic repertoires – Miriwoong ("*Gooloo-gooloob Yarroondayan*" (We are all happy!)), Aboriginal English expressions ("Shame job!" (Embarrassing behaviour!) "Big shame!" and my own use of English, which is also Mongolian-accented. The *languaging* was formed by *linguistic play*. The entire mood was filled with *playful voices*. But within that playfulness was a poignant tension. Jarrah's attempt to sing in Miriwoong was met with laughter that hinted at more than just amusement. It hinted at shame, discomfort, embarrassment, and even a sense of cultural disconnection. The entire interaction was marked by joy, play, and laughter. Yet this lightness coexisted with something darker. Beneath the surface of this playfulness lies a sense of precarity – the lingering effects of colonisation, linguistic racism, and language loss. The boys' laughter, while warm and spontaneous, also reflects the fractured relationships many Aboriginal people have with their traditional languages – languages that were once silenced and punished by the colonisers (Wigglesworth & Oliver, 2024). In this moment, the languaging is both a form of play and a site of precarity (see also Dovchin, 2025b).

At the heart of this interaction lies precarity. The boys are growing up in a society where speaking their traditional languages is not always supported, celebrated, or even possible. Many are only partially fluent in their traditional languages – they may know a few words or phrases, often learned through family members, but not enough to feel confident using them (Dovchin, 2025b). So, when Jarrah sings in Miriwoong and the others laugh, their reaction is layered: it is both play and precarity, pride and shame. The laugher becomes a façade – a way of dealing with the gap between who they are, who they want to be, and structural conditions that have made that gap so difficult to bridge. In this way, their laughter becomes a reflection of a colonial interruption and of the disrupted intergenerational transmission of Aboriginal languages. This moment reminds us that even the most playful expressions of language can carry the weight of historical violence and language loss. But it also shows that through playfulness and shared language practices, these boys are actively negotiating their identities, reclaiming space and keeping their language and culture alive – even if imperfectly and even through laughter. While the languaging often challenges rigid linguistic boundaries experimentation, it simultaneously reveals the conditions of instability and constraint under which such play becomes meaningful. Languagers often rely on linguistic resources that are only accessible – or only gain social legitimacy – when actively mobilised in context. This suggests a paradoxical precarity within playfulness: a constrained playfulness that challenges the idea of languaging as wholly unrestricted or universally empowering. This reminds us of Wigglesworth & Oliver's (2024) argument on how translanguaging in Aboriginal classrooms embodies both playfulness and precarity, creating a productive yet fragile tension. On the playful side, Aboriginal children's enthusiasm for exploring differences across languages can spark curiosity, creativity, and engagement. Activities such as discussing phonological or discourse-level variation or reflecting on their role as custodians of Indigenous languages open space for joyful exploration, pride, and imaginative use of linguistic resources. This linguistic play supports their learning, fosters collaboration, and validates their multilingual repertoires. At the same time, there is a precarious dimension of translanguaging. Aboriginal students' willingness to draw on their full linguistic range depends heavily on teacher attitudes. A supportive teacher enables playful experimentation, but a negative reaction risks shaming students, delegitimising their backgrounds, and reinforcing the deficit view that Aboriginal children have "no" appropriate language. Such precarious positioning underscores the vulnerability of students negotiating between languages and ideologies in unequal power relations. Wigglesworth & Oliver (2024) suggest that translanguaging offers a way to transform precarity into possibility. By validating all linguistic resources and resisting rigid binaries of "home" versus "school" languages, teachers can shift classroom dynamics from marginalisation towards inclusion. Yet, the very act of translanguaging remains precarious, always vulnerable to misrecognition or rejection. Thus, translanguaging is never purely playful or purely precarious; rather, its power lies in the ongoing negotiation between these forces, where playfulness can mitigate precarity but cannot erase it.

This tension of playfulness and precarity can also be interpreted as *semiotic precarity* by Lee (2022), who draws our attention to the instability and uncertainty of certain cultural and linguistic signs, symbols, and semiotic markers when they are encountered outside their "native" context. Just as playful languaging unfolds on precarious social and material grounds, sites of semiotic precarity render cultural features visible precisely because their meaning is unstable or contestable. It does not claim that culture exists only in its representations; rather, it highlights moments in which cultural features become visible, negotiable, or open to reinterpretation because their meaning

## 1.2 Languaging or Code-switching?

is not fully secure. For Lee (2022), both linguistic play and cultural representation are, therefore, never neutral but emerge within structures of power, inequality, and uncertainty, revealing how creativity and precarity are inseparable in language practice. Pennycook & Otsuji (2015) introduced *metrolingualism* as a framework which points out that languages are not pre-given but emergent, context-dependent practices. Here, the spatial, temporal, and mobile aspects of urban communication are important. However, we also need to recognise at fixity – such as invoking named languages – can have symbolic, ideological, and strategic value. Crucially, fluidity and fixity are not opposites in this model, they coexist and co-constitute meaning, identity, and social relations (cf. Prinsloo, 2023). Ultimately, metrolingualism offers a powerful alternative to conventional framings of language, revealing how mobility, hybridity, and essentialism are intricately entangled in the lived realities of language users navigating complex global and local contexts. As they urged us not to "construe fixity and fluidity as dichotomous, or even as opposite ends of a spectrum, but rather to view them as symbiotically (re)constituting each other" (Otsuji & Pennycook, 2010, p. 244). In other words, *semiotic precarity* may differ from other forms of precarity discussed earlier. While earlier discussions focus on *material* and *structural* forms of precarity, such as economic insecurity, unstable employment, or precarious migration status, *semiotic precarity* here refers to the symbolic and communicative dimension of precariousness. It highlights how individuals experience vulnerability and marginalisation through language, discourse, and other semiotic resources that index social hierarchies and power relations. In other words, *semiotic precarity* does not stem solely from material instability but from the *unequal value and legitimacy* assigned to certain linguistic and semiotic practices.

In this book, I call on applied linguists to reflect more deeply on the ways playfulness is entangled with precarity. I argue that playfulness should not be seen merely as light-hearted, but as a force that highlights our capacity for transformative and even subversive action. At the same time, we must remain attentive to the tensions between playfulness and precarity. Critical questions arise: How can what is fundamentally "precarious" be framed as "playful"? Could playfulness itself be another expression of precariousness? And why has languaging, inherently precarious in nature, so often depended on the idea of playfulness to gain legitimacy? To move forward, mainstream understandings of languaging must shift towards a sharper examination of precarity – its socio-ontological dimensions, its unequal distribution, and the structural conditions that render some groups more vulnerable than others. This book therefore seeks to highlight the unstable realities shaped by a history of precarity (Bourdieu, (1962/1994) and to explore how these realities intersect with the playful dimensions of languaging.

### 1.2.4 Structure of the Book

I will further expand on the intricate connections between *First Knowledging* and *First Languaging* in Chapter 2, particularly as they intersect with the tension of playfulness and precarity. Drawing on my ethnographic visits to Australian Aboriginal schools across Western Australia, I explore how these two interwoven practices are lived, performed, and negotiated by Aboriginal children and educators. First Knowledging, rooted in ancestral wisdom, cultural practices, and land-based ontologies, is not transmitted through rigid forms but through dynamic, living languages – what I term First Languaging. These languages embody a fluid interplay of orality, gesture, and spirit, often expressed in classroom settings through storytelling, yarning, art, and song (Dovchin, 2025b). Yet, this vibrant linguistic expression exists in precarious tension with institutional constraints, standardised curricula, and settler–colonial educational systems that often suppress or marginalise these ways of knowing and being. Within this complexity, I focus on the role of playfulness – not merely as a form of child's play, but as a radical act of resistance, creativity, and resilience within a framework of uncertainty and survival. By centring the lived realities of Aboriginal learners, this chapter reveals how First Knowledging and First Languaging offer not only pedagogical alternatives but also cultural continuities that defy dominant narratives.

In Chapter 3, I introduce the concepts *nomadic knowledging* and *nomadic languaging* through ethnographic encounters with Mongolian nomadic herdsmen (Dovchin, 2025a). Centred on the practice of the *nomadic reminiscing circle*, it explores how nomadic communities integrate additional languages such as English within their land-based epistemologies, while safeguarding cultural and linguistic boundaries. These practices embody both fluidity and rootedness, playfulness and precarity, reflecting the adaptability and resilience of nomadic life. By examining how English is accepted only when mediated by humility and respect, the chapter highlights the relational ethics underlying nomadic engagements with language. It argues that applied linguistics must learn from nomadic perspectives, which emphasise mobility, contextual responsiveness, and land-connected ways of knowing,

## 1.2 Languaging or Code-switching? 33

thereby offering new pathways for rethinking language in global and local contexts.

Chapter 4 examines the notion of *racialised languaging*, which emphasises that languaging practices are never assessed independently of the bodies, identities, and social positions of their speakers. It demonstrates how language is evaluated not only in terms of what is said but also through the racialised perceptions of who is speaking and how society chooses to listen. The chapter argues that accents, dialects, and speech patterns associated with racialised communities are often constructed as inferior, humorous, deficient, or even criminal, while similar features in White speakers are normalised or excused. By centring languaging as a site of racial meaning-making, the chapter exposes the ways in which communication is entangled with race, racism, and embodied identities. Racialised languaging is further situated within the broader colonial matrix of power, where Western linguistic norms and White racial identities are privileged over non-Western languages and non-White speakers. Drawing on critical scholarship and empirical examples, this chapter illuminates how colonial legacies continue to shape contemporary postcolonial Anglophone contexts, perpetuating inequalities that advantage White, monolingual English speakers while marginalising those who speak from racialised positions.

Chapter 5 explores the interplay of playfulness and precarity in *AI-mediated languaging*. Drawing on examples from social media users experimenting with generative AI, the chapter illustrates how AI reshapes communication, linguistic practices, and social interaction. These playful engagements demonstrate AI's capacity to expand linguistic creativity and produce novel forms of meaning, while simultaneously revealing its fragility and the ethical tensions inherent in its use. By exposing the cultural assumptions, power relations, and value judgements embedded in AI systems, such moments highlight the non-neutral and unpredictable nature of AI technologies. The chapter argues that while AI opens up new possibilities for expression, it also demands critical reflection on issues of power, identity, and social norms. Ultimately, these examples highlight the (dis)engagement with AI's potential while recognising and addressing the risks it poses to language and society.

Chapter 6 brings the book to a close by advancing an understanding of languaging as a relational, embodied, and political practice. Rather than treating language as a neutral vehicle for transmitting information, the chapter emphasises how languaging is deeply entwined with questions of identity, belonging, and power. It is shown to be simultaneously playful and precarious, resistant and creative, continually challenging static and purified notions of language. This concluding discussion foregrounds the lived realities of linguistic diversity, realities shaped by colonial histories, racial hierarchies, global mobilities, and technological mediations, yet also sustained through everyday acts of creativity, solidarity, and care.

The chapter further develops the notion of *pedagogical languaging* as a way of reframing education in response to the radical cultural and communicative reconfigurations of the twenty-first century. Pedagogy, it argues, must move beyond the delivery of standardised curricula to become the intentional design of spaces where learners mobilise their full semiotic repertoires, such as linguistic, embodied, cultural, and digital, in dynamic, relational, and multimodal meaning-making. Such a reframing requires abandoning deficit perspectives on learners' non-dominant practices and instead recognising these as epistemic resources that expand possibilities for knowledge, creativity, and critical insight. In doing so, pedagogical languaging positions education not as the policing of correctness, but as the co-construction of interactional spaces where diversity is affirmed and all learners' contributions are made central to the work of learning.

# 2 First Languaging, First Knowledging

## 2.1 HUMANS AND REINDEER

I embarked on a three-week horseback journey to *taiga* – the deep forest of remote far northern Mongolia – to meet the Tsaatan people (Reindeer people) – an Indigenous tribe and one of the last reindeer-herding nomads in the world. Originating from Russian Siberia and Mongolia's northern region of Hovsgol, the Tsaatan people are considered as one of the world's earliest domesticators of reindeer (Windle et al., 2025). Written records by a travelling Chinese monk in AD 499 show that the Tsaatan people maintain a profound relationship with their reindeer from ancient times (Vitebsky, 2006). Today, around 300 *Tsaatan* people live in the Mongolian *taiga*, as they move regularly from one site to another, seeking pasture for their reindeer. The livelihood of the Tsaatan people and reindeer is interdependent because this relationship allows them to survive the harsh subarctic environment of the far north of Mongolia (Kurowski, 2025). As an Elder Tsaatan herder, Tsamjid, explains: *"Our reindeers are our life. Without them, we perish"* (Interview, 30 June 2025). Reindeers are their most valuable of all possessions and are the central aspect of their survival, from milking to producing dairy products, from transportation to creating artefacts (Keay, 2006). In principle, the Tsaatan people's identity and origin are deeply connected with that of reindeer (Windle et al., 2025). Children are expected to learn stories, songs, and legends about reindeer. Adults express their gratitude and appreciation for reindeer as one protected reindeer per family is identified as a "sacred one" by a shaman and allowed to wander freely just like a member of the family. There is an unspoken total commitment to the reindeer, as mistreating reindeer is considered as a cultural taboo. In fact, the community's ancient tradition of shamanism largely precludes the slaughter of reindeer by placing sacred value on the animals (Keay, 2006; Kurowski, 2025; Windle et al., 2025; Vitebsky, 2006) (see Figure 2.1).

36  2 FIRST LANGUAGING, FIRST KNOWLEDGING

Figure 2.1  Reindeer and Urts (teepees) (Credit: Tsaatan Reindeer)

Much of the existing research on human–animal interactions has centred on conflict, focusing on protecting humans, their livelihoods, and property from wildlife, as well as safeguarding wildlife from human harm (Jolly & Stronza, 2025). This conflict-oriented framing reinforces human–nature dualisms and positions people and wild animals as adversaries. Yet, interactions are not always negative; they can also be neutral, adaptive, and mutually beneficial, illustrating long-standing patterns of coexistence (Jolly & Stronza, 2025). For millennia, humans have depended on animals for resources necessary for survival. Through domestication, man has sought to ensure these resources by creating systems that bring humans and animals together into arrangements of coexistence. Together, humans and animals are arranged into a harmonious coexistence (Dovchin & Dovchin, 2024; Dovchin et al., 2024; Jolly & Stronza, 2025). Such possibilities have often been overlooked or simplified in conservation, with coexistence treated as a distant ideal rather than an everyday reality. In fact, Tsaatan people have for generations coexisted and coadapted with animals within multispecies landscapes. The Tsaatan people are one of the few surviving societies in the modern world who have still managed to sustain the knowledge system of subsistence-based human–animal relationship in the face of industrialisation, modernity, and capitalisation. They have deep ecological wisdom, which remains to maintain balance in

## 2.1 Humans and Reindeer

human-animal systems (Keay, 2006; Kurowski, 2025; Windle et al., 2025). Their knowledge system illustrates reciprocity and reverence uncommon to most human-animal systems in today's industrialised world. This perspective emphasises that the lives of humans and other beings are deeply intertwined, and that coexistence – inclusive of occasional conflict – should be seen as a norm rather than an exception (Keay, 2006; Kurowski, 2025; Windle et al., 2025; Vitebsky, 2006). The Tsaatan people remind us how humans can still utilise animals for resources while still maintaining balance, respect, and sustainability in the face of an ever-changing world (Dovchin & Dovchin, 2024). Perhaps the Tsaatan people can teach us a lesson to reconsider our modern systems of domestication as opportunities to foster ecological sustainability, reciprocity, and humanness simultaneously (Dovchin & Dovchin, 2024).

The Tsaatan people have developed the profound ability to predict weather patterns based on the behaviours of their reindeer. Reindeer, according to the Tsaatan people, often respond to subtle environmental changes that humans might not immediately detect, making them valuable indicators of impending weather conditions (Dovchin et al., 2024). As Tsamjid, a reindeer herder, explains, *"We learn and predict about our surroundings from our reindeer. They subtly and explicitly tell us about our motherland"* (Interview, 30 June 2025). Reindeer herders rely on their animals' movements and eating habits to forecast harsh weather, known locally as *zud*, which refers to extreme cold conditions with snow blizzards that threaten livestock survival. Reindeer may refuse to graze in specific areas if a snowstorm is approaching, and reindeer may dig deeper into the snow in anticipation of food shortages. Reindeer people also believe that milk yields from reindeer fluctuate with changes in atmospheric pressure and humidity. This unique relationship with their land, sky, environment, and reindeer is apparent in their daily life and is chronicled in multiple oral stories, folk tales, and even folk songs. This profound Indigenous knowledge system, which is rooted in a spiritual connection to their animals and ancestral lands, is essential to their physical and cultural survival, and embodies their reciprocal relationships with land, human and non-human beings, and the natural world (Whyte, 2017). It is inconceivable to disconnect humankind from the natural world, and just like many other Indigenous tribes around the world, the Tsaatan people do not adhere to the foundational Western science and philosophy, according to which humans are separate from, superior to, and entitled to exploit the land and the natural world (O'Faircheallaigh, 2023). The knowledge system of the Tsaatan people reminds us of the core ideas embedded within *First Knowledging* – the practice of the *First Knowledge* system that has ever existed on our planet (Neale, 2021; Pennycook, 2024). It reflects First Nations peoples' knowledge systems: ancient, land-based wisdom carried, sustained, and practised by Indigenous communities across generations (Neale, 2021; Pennycook, 2024). This knowledge is relational and land-based, transmitted through oral traditions, cultural practices, and community. The Tsaatan people's fundamental knowledge system, in this sense, is based on their broader environmental understanding, honed over generations through careful observation, respect, honour, and interaction with nature, animals, and land. As an Elder shaman from the Tsaatan community explains,

> Everything in nature has its own spirit. We cannot see them with our eyes, but they exist. The owner of the water is Los, Savdag owns the sun, and Batakshan is the owner of the land. Sometimes I have seen them, but they are invisible to most people. The spirit of Batakshan (owner of the land) spreads good energy to nature. Sometimes he plays with the reindeer. He paints their bodies with nature colors. Sometimes he makes their antlers circular or curly. (Kurowski, 2025, p. 9)

In his words, as in other Indigenous communities around the world, he reveals the Tsaatan people's relational and spiritual kinship with all of nature (Cumpston et al., 2022; Langton & Corn, 2023; Neale & Kelly, 2020; Noon & De Napoli, 2022; Pennycook, 2024). The shaman further adds, "For many centuries, we have been living in nature and preserving its wildness. We have been preserving nature through our own traditions [...]" (Kurowski, 2025, p. 45). This profound connection to the land has given rise to a body of knowledge that is, in itself, a form of science. First Nations knowledge systems have always been more than "culture" alone; they embody ways of knowing that are empirical, adaptive, and deeply attuned to ecological balance (see Figure 2.2). Framing this knowledge as both "science" and "culture" challenges narrow Western distinctions and highlights the holistic wisdom that has sustained communities and ecosystems for generations (Cumpston et al., 2022; Langton & Corn, 2023; Neale & Kelly, 2020; Noon & De Napoli, 2022; Pennycook, 2024). As Pennycook (2024) notes, following Neale (2021, p. 14), it is important to eliminate the myths that Indigenous people had no knowledge system and that Indigenous people had no scientists and doctors, or that Indigenous people were incapable of innovation. Because if Indigenous people were able to survive and maintain cultural and linguistic practices

## 2.1 Humans and Reindeer

Figure 2.2 Reindeer and Uvugdorj, a Tsaatan elder from the Eastern Taiga, moving to his spring camp. Uvugdorj was renowned for his intellect and wisdom (Credit: Tsaatan Reindeer)

stretching back tens of thousands of years, and if they had developed *"first"* understandings of nature, land, water, sky, seasons, astronomy, star configurations, and navigation, then, while they may not have the modern technological instruments, they nevertheless have remarkable knowledge systems about the land, sky, animals, and ecology (Pennycook, 2024, pp. 111–112).

Being engaged in the essence of *First Knowledging* also brings forth an awareness of the practice of *First Languaging*, where *First Languages* on our planet have been a living and evolving expressions since the beginning of human existence (Song & Lin, 2025). Humans have always been *languaging* – it is simply that the First Nations peoples have maintained this clarity and connection to it because First Nations people have not simply used *First Languages* – they have interwoven them with spiritual expression, storytelling traditions, and embodied systems of *First Knowledges*. *First Languaging*, in this sense, is not simply about acquiring a "First Language" in the traditional psycholinguistic sense: rather, it profoundly reflects the place-based dimensions of how language is lived (Neale, 2021; Pennycook, 2024). Through *"First Languaging,"* First Nations people have developed and transmitted a *"First Knowledge"* system about us, our Earth, and our ecological system to survive and maintain culture, stretching back tens of thousands of years (Cumpston et al., 2022; Langton & Corn, 2023; Neale & Kelly, 2020; Noon & De Napoli, 2022; Pennycook, 2024). *First Languaging*, in this sense, refers to the dynamic ways in which First Nations peoples weave together *First Languages* through their systems of *First Knowledges*, including their social, cultural, spiritual, linguistic, oral, traditional, identity practices, along with semiotic resources, and relationships with both human and non-human beings.

The Tsaatan people, in this sense, fully embody *First Languaging* as they engage in fluid linguistic play through blending multiple linguistic, paralinguistic, semiotic, and spiritual repertoires – drawing from the past, present, and future in every interaction. The fundamental Tsaatan knowledge system, as the shaman has noted, "*spiritual play with reindeer*" (Kurowski, 2025, p. 9), is also reflected in their ways of languaging. As the shaman earlier described, "The spirit of Batakshan (owner of the land) spreads good energy to nature. Sometimes he plays with the reindeer. He paints their bodies with nature colors. Sometimes he makes their antlers circular or curly" (Kurowski, 2025, p. 9). This cosmology reflects a worldview in which humans, spirits, animals, and landscapes are entangled through play, creativity, and reciprocity. In this context, language is not merely descriptive but performative, animating the land and its beings with agency. The playful acts attributed to Batakshan – *owner of the land* – exemplify the Tsaatan people's relational cosmology, in which spiritual forces are expressed through reindeer, and the animals themselves become living canvases of the land's vitality. In this cosmology of *play*, Dukhan is the traditional language of the Tsaatan people – a nearly extinct Turkic language and dialect variety of the Tuvan language. While the Dukhan language is still their First Language, their contact with the mainstream Mongolian society has led to integrating the registers of the Mongolian language, especially since the rule of the Mongol Empire and later the Qing Dynasty. Because the Tsaatan people originally migrated from regions of present-day Tuva (Russia) to Mongolia, their linguistic repertoires are also blended with Russian linguistic repertoires. In addition, English is also present as the number of Western tourists has dramatically increased in the last few years to visit the Tsaatan people. English is also familiarised by its popularity through media channels such as popular culture resources, the Internet, and mobile technologies. Dukhan, Mongolian, English, and Russian – each language register, alongside the occasional dialects and varieties, coexisted in a rich orchestra for the Tsaatan people, woven together with shaman ceremonial chants, storytelling, laughter, vocalisation, body postures, hand

## 2.1 Humans and Reindeer

gestures, and touch with their reindeer, songs, and dances. In particular, their First Language – Dukhan – is deeply tied to the "*sacred power of language*" as the Tsaatans embody a spiritual connection to ancestors, land, and the cosmos through their shamanistic chants (Keay, 2006; Kurowski, 2025; Windle et al., 2025). Each chant is more than just words – it is the linguistic play of traditional languages, sounds, and phrases meant to invoke specific energies or entities. *First Languaging*, in this sense, becomes a way to keep their sacred traditions alive while adapting them to contemporary contexts, blending old and new expressions. *First Languaging* is interwoven with bodies, spiritual sense, and land, and is very much alive.

Nevertheless, for the Tsaatan people, *First Languaging* is not simply fluid expressions – they are deeply entangled with the precarious grounds of survival, linguistic and cultural continuity. While often characterised by hybridity, linguistic play, and adaptability, the languaging practices of the Tsaatan people emerge from and respond to the weight of existential threats (Keay, 2006; Kurowski, 2025; Windle et al., 2025). In a world where few societies have preserved the integrity of land-based human–animal relationships, the Tsaatan people – through their enduring bond with the reindeer – stand as a powerful exception. They have managed to uphold their traditions despite the overwhelming pressures of modernisation, industrialisation, and westernisation, all of which have gradually eroded the foundations of their cultural and economic life. This persistent transformation pushes the Tsaatan way of life towards the edge of cultural and linguistic extinction, leaving their language and customs suspended by a fragile thread (Keay, 2006; Kurowski, 2025; Windle et al., 2025). Their socio-economic conditions remain acutely precarious including their language and culture – they are often excluded from the benefits of mainstream society and pushed to its margins by global systems that prioritise uniformity. As an elderly Tsaatan herder, Tsamjid, describes, "Our language hangs on like the last snow in spring – melting, but still here. The young ones go far for school, for work and when they return, they are different. The world outside does not see us, does not hear us. But we still speak, still remember. If we stop, even for a little while, our language could slip away." Yet, it is precisely in this space of marginality that the Tsaatan people express extraordinary resilience. Their commitment to reindeer herding, to their rhythms of ancestral lands, and to a lifeworld beyond modernity metrics is an active refusal of disappearance. Here, every act of *First Languaging* becomes a negotiation between precarity and playfulness – a vital and creative force grounded in precarity. Their linguistic and cultural engagements are shaped not in spite of precarity, but through it. Playfulness, in this context, is not a detachment from hardship but a reimagining of existence – it is a form of cultural and linguistic work that resists erasure through creative, fluid, and resilient persistence. As Tsamjid, an elderly Tsaatan herder, adds, "Our life is never steady. Sometimes the life gives. Sometimes it takes. But still, we tell our stories. That's how we stay strong. Even when things fall apart, we laugh away. It reminds us who we are, and who we might become" (Interview, 5 October 2024). For the Tsaatan people, their traditional practices and worldviews are not static relics but living, breathing modalities of resistance. They offer a vision of life that is both profoundly rooted in ancestral knowledge and imaginatively open to uncertain futures. This playfulness within precarity, then, is not frivolous – it is a subtle yet profound act of survival and self-determination (see Figure 2.3).

In this chapter, I will further expand the intricate connections between *First Knowledging* and *First Languaging*, particularly as they intersect with the tension of playfulness and precarity. *First Knowledging*, rooted in ancestral wisdom, cultural practices, and land-based ontologies, is not transmitted through rigid forms but through dynamic living language – what I term *First Languaging*. It embodies a fluid interplay of orality, storytelling, yarning, and First Languages. Yet, this vibrant linguistic expression exists in precarious tension within institutional constraints that often suppress these ways of knowing, being, and speaking. Within this complexity, I focus on

Figure 2.3 Humans and reindeer: The Eastern Taiga, the fourth-generation shaman from Soyon tribe, D. Yesun Erdene, in his autumn camp (Credit: Tsaatan Reindeer)

the role of playfulness – not merely as a form of linguistic play but as a radical resistance, creativity, and resilience within a framework of precarity, uncertainty, and survival. For now, drawing on my ethnographic visits to Australian Aboriginal schools across Western Australia, I explore how these two interwoven practices are lived, performed, and negotiated by Australian Aboriginal young people.

## 2.2 COUNTRY AND DREAMING: AUSTRALIAN ABORIGINAL YOUNG PEOPLE

The First Knowledge system of Australian Aboriginal people is deeply connected to Country. For Australian First Nation's people, according to Neale (2021, p. 13),

> Country is a worldview that encompasses our relationship to the physical, ancestral and spiritual dimensions': Country does not belong to people: They belong to Country.

Aboriginal people have always been on Country because they were on Country in the time before time began. Country is not just land nor just a physical place for Aboriginal people – it is a living entity that includes people, animals, waterways, skies, plants, and spirits (Jackson-Barrett & Lee-Hammond, 2018). Country is cared for, and in turn, it cares for people. Humans, therefore, are custodians of the continuity of Country, its diverse species and natural abundance. Country is alive – all beings on Country are interconnected and relational (Kingsley et al., 2013). Country, therefore, holds stories and laws which are respected as the physical and spiritual anchor that informs the Aboriginal way of thinking and being (Taylor-Bragge et al., 2021).

Central to Country is a Dreaming story which describes how Country, its people, and animals came into being, passed down through generations (Jackson-Barrett & Lee-Hammond, 2018). As Worimi Professor John Maynard (cited in Taylor-Bragge et al., 2021, p. 429) notes,

> [...] we came directly out of the Dreamtime of the Creative Ancestors and our people lived and kept the earth as it was on the very first day.

This statement indicates that the Country carries stories of the Dreaming – a concept of creation – and being on Country allows for existence and identity for Aboriginal people (Taylor-Bragge et al., 2021). The Dreaming is the Aboriginal way of thinking – the ancestral time of creation, when spirit beings shaped the world – its landscape, laws, and life. The Dreaming is not a story about past events but an ongoing reality. Elders share the Dreaming stories that embed cultural laws, moral codes, and environmental knowledge tied to Country. The Dreaming, thus, reflects what Country teaches. It also underpins how Country speaks to us, how we listen, and how we speak to Country. Put simply, Country is the place, and the Dreaming is the meaning and origin. Together, they sustain Aboriginal ways of knowing, being, and doing (Cantley, 2025; Ober et al., 2025).

The First Knowledge system of Australian Aboriginal people, deeply rooted in Country and the Dreaming stories, is most vividly expressed through *First Languaging*. First Nations peoples are often described as "*natural languagers*," possessing a profound instinct for languaging that stems from their sociolinguistic and cultural histories, which encompass multiple linguistic and semiotic repertoires (Tankosić et al., 2024; Vaughan, 2019). They move fluidly across these diverse resources – languages, dialects, and semiotic repertoires – to yarn, share stories, express views and emotions, and perform their identities (Cantley, 2025; Ober et al., 2025). Such languaging practices not only preserve linguistic diversity but also enable Aboriginal peoples to navigate contemporary contexts (Tankosić et al., 2024). Through *First Languaging*, they share the Dreaming stories that reflect what Country teaches. It also underpins the sharing of Dreaming stories, reflecting how Country speaks to us, how we listen, and how we speak to Country. *First Languaging* is a process, Country is the place, and the Dreaming is the meaning and origin. Together, they sustain Aboriginal ways of knowing, being, and doing (Cantley, 2025; Ober et al., 2025).

While working with my colleagues at Kutja School – an Australian Aboriginal boarding school (the pseudonym *Kutja* means "*learning language*" – a name given by the school's Elder), I witnessed how *First Languaging* facilitated our immersion in *First Knowledging* (Dovchin 2025b). Most of the Aboriginal students come from remote communities across Western Australia to Kutja school. This school, originally established in the 1940s as a mission, was created with the goal of preparing young Aboriginal men for careers in agriculture, aiming to enhance their employment opportunities. Initially focused on boys, it later transitioned into a co-educational boarding school. In the 1990s, it became recognised as an independent institution. Today, the school is more than just an educational institution – it serves as a safe space for Aboriginal students to build strong relationships not only among students but also between students and staff, creating a community based on mutual respect, friendship, and bonding. The students come

## 2.2 Country and Dreaming

from diverse linguistic backgrounds, but the experience of living and boarding together strengthens their bonds, forming lasting connections that contribute to their personal and academic growth (Tankosić et al., 2025).

When I first set foot in the classroom, I was deeply aware of how intellectually, emotionally, linguistically, and culturally challenging and politically strenuous real-world Aboriginal research could actually be (McLennan & Woods, 2018), given the high rate of transgenerational childhood trauma Aboriginal and Torres Strait Islander children and youth have been exposed to (Atkinson et al., 2014). The experiences and transfer of trauma-related behaviours and attitudes are most prevalent due to the combined effects of colonialism and government policies and practices. As a result, young Aboriginal people have developed a low sense of safety and trust in others. Furthermore, many Aboriginal students who were exposed to transgenerational trauma have difficulties with attention and focus, memory, language, and literacy development, as well as behavioural and emotional problems (Atkinson et al., 2014).

Due to my lack of experience in interacting and communicating with Aboriginal people, I was anxious, fearful, and uncomfortable. I introduced myself, where I was from, and who I was, because for Australian Aboriginal people, the question of *"Where are you from? Who is your mob?"* is an important question (Ober et al., 2024). I explained to the students that my Mongolian heritage is not classified as *"Indigenous"* in the way the term is used in international frameworks such as the United Nations Declaration on the Rights of Indigenous Peoples. That said, Mongolia has rich *First Knowledge* traditions, particularly in shamanism, pastoralism, and land stewardship, which resonate with Indigenous knowledge systems worldwide. I was wearing my traditional Mongolian dress called, *"deel,"* with a few PowerPoint images, showing some of the traditional characteristics of Mongolia. I could see that the students were mesmerised by my story, as I felt a silent appreciation of hospitality, warmth, curiosity, and sincerity from these Aboriginal students (Tankosić et al., 2025). I found myself emotionally present with these young Aboriginal people in a way that developed a playful and positive connection. During the various classroom activities, when we created artworks, wrote postcards and letters, and created posters together, the students were constantly engaged with creative, fun, and positive interactions. Playful voices – through teasing, giggling, and joking, filled with laughter and warmth – allowed them to share personal interpretations of their stories, building deeper connections within the group, with us, and with the teachers (Tankosić et al., 2025).

At Kutja school, I found myself actively participating in *First Knowledging* – honouring and engaging with Indigenous ways of knowing, being, and doing with the generosity of these Aboriginal young people, which was often profoundly connected with a strong sense of Country and being "*on Country.*" See Table 2.1, where in a seemingly ordinary exchange around artworks, something profoundly epistemologically rich is unfolding in terms of the interrelationship between *First Languaging* and *First Knowledging*.

The interaction between Sender and the two girls, Marilyn and Marie, becomes a microcosm of *First Knowledging* – a holistic and embodied process in which *First Languaging* is central. The Aboriginal students are not simply communicating: they are transmitting knowledge about Country, seasons, and food systems, drawing on their lived relationships with Country, language, and culture. When Marilyn responds to Sender's initial question of what she is drawing, her confident response "*Miriwoong Dawang!*" (Miriwoong Country) in her traditional language – Miriwoong – is positioning her art piece as an act of *First Knowledging*, as she tells a story about her Country (line 2). For Marilyn, *Miriwoong Dawang* is not just a geographical location. As Taylor-Bragge et al. (2021) have noted, Country is a living entity for Marilyn. Country is sentient. It holds law, spirit, identity, and kinship. By naming her art piece as "*Miriwoong Dawang,*" Marilyn is inviting Sender into a different epistemic world – one where land, language, and knowledge are inseparable. This is the

Table 2.1 *Miriwoong Dawang*

| Line | Speaker and dialogue |
| --- | --- |
| 1. | Sender: What are you drawing, girls? |
| 2. | Marilyn: *Miriwoong Dawang* (Miriwoong language meaning Miriwoong Country). |
| 3. | Sender: What does it mean? |
| 4. | Marilyn: *Miriwoong* Country. |
| 5. | Sender: Fantastic! What is the yellow? |
| 6. | Marilyn: *Yelowan* (Miriwoong Kriol meaning "yellow") Sun. |
| 7. | Sender: Beautiful. How about the blue? |
| 8. | Marilyn: *Riba* (river in Kriol) hole. |
| 9. | Sender: What does it mean? |
| 10. | Marilyn: It means *Boornbeng* (hot season in Miriwoong). Hot season. We have a lot of food around in hot season. Plants and animals come out. Foods for Miriwoong people. *Riba* holes are dotted around the Country. Water holes have lots of food! |
| 11. | Sender: *Wow.* Interesting. Thank you for describing that! |

## 2.2 Country and Dreaming

practice of *First Knowledging* in motion: the transmission of knowledge through language, image, memory, and dialogue interwoven with land. As the dialogue continues, the linguistic play becomes visible in Marilyn's *First Languaging* practice: slipping and sliding across Miriwoong – *"Boornbeng"* (hot season); Kriol – *"Yelowan"* (yellow) for sun; *"Riba"* (river) hole; and Aboriginal English for *"deadly"* (meaning excellent and cool). Here, Marilyn's *First Languaging* expresses more than semantic content – it encodes ecological, cultural, and relational knowledge. Marilyn explains how during *boornbeng*, food becomes abundant, animals emerge, and the land offers nourishment (line 10). Marilyn teaches Sender about seasonal cycles, food systems, and interdependence with Country. Notably, it is a reversal of traditional teacher–student roles: the student becomes the teacher, and the teacher becomes the learner. Sender's role is not to evaluate or control, but to ask with curiosity: *"What does it mean?" "What is the yellow?" "What about the blue?"* and so on. These questions invite Marilyn to lead the First Knowledge sharing.

Overall, this moment exemplifies how *First Languaging* is a conduit for *First Knowledging*, especially when the students engage in knowledge sharing about Country, its seasons, landforms, and ecology in their own communicative repertoires. They are transmitting the First Knowledge system through artful storytelling, while engaging playfully and reciprocally across linguistic and cultural boundaries (Dovchin et al., 2026). *First Knowledging* here is not fragmented, not through textbooks or abstract definitions: it is embodied and storied through *First Languaging*, through shared inquiry, curiosity, and laughter with Aboriginal young people who live and know Country. Language here does not merely describe reality – it creates it, connects it, and teaches it (Biddle & Swee, 2012). It is through languaging that the girls teach me not just the meanings of words but how we understand Country: as alive, as generous, and as the heart of Miriwoong existence (see Figure 2.4).

As the conversation moves forward, the tone shifts subtly into playful voices. In Table 2.2, Marie whispers to Marilyn, and they giggle together (line 1). Sender notices and leans in with playful response, *"What are you girls giggling about?"* (line 2). The space has transformed from inquiry to intimacy, from explanation to co-created playful moments. Marilyn and Marie have opened their linguistic and cultural knowledge; they now ask for a reciprocal gesture, *"Can you tell us something in your language? It was deadly!"* (line 3). Sender playfully responds in Mongolian, *"Chi yu zurj baina?"* (What are you drawing?) (line 4), echoing her original English question, now rendered in Mongolian, loops the interaction back to the beginning, but with

Table 2.2 *Tell us something in your language!*

| Line | Speaker and dialogue |
|---|---|
| 1. | Marilyn: (She whispers something to Marie's ear and together giggles.) |
| 2. | Sender: What are you girls giggling about? |
| 3. | Marie: Can you tell us something in your language? It was deadly. |
| 4. | Sender: Sure. *Chi yu zurj baina?* (Mongolian language, meaning "What are you drawing?") |
| 5. | Marilyn and Marie: Deadly! (Everyone laughs together). |
| 6. | Sender: Do you girls can say something in Miriwoong too? |
| 7. | Marilyn: Can't do that. We only have a few Elders left. |
| 8. | Sender: Do you want to learn? |
| 9. | Marilyn: Yes, but no shame. |

Figure 2.4 Creating Aboriginal artworks
(Photo by Sender Dovchin)

renewed energy and mutual playfulness. The girls respond with delighted admiration – *"Deadly!"* (Awesome! Cool!) (line 5) – a powerful Aboriginal English phrase, showing how linguistic registers, play, respect, and reciprocity are woven into *First Languaging* practices. In this moment, languaging becomes a site of shared play, not just the content of knowledge that matters but shared with joy and laughter (see Figure 2.5).

As the interaction continues, it reveals the *precarious grounds* surrounding Aboriginal languages such as *Miriwoong*. When Marilyn

## 2.2 Country and Dreaming

Figure 2.5 The girls
(Photo by Sender Dovchin)

notes, "*can't do that. Only a few Elders left*" (line 7), she is pointing to the precarious state of intergenerational transmission of traditional Aboriginal languages, where the language's survival depends on a dwindling group of knowledge holders. This highlights the precarity of *Miriwoong* as it faces the risk of further decline or extinction. My question "*Do you want to learn?*" (line 8) highlights the tension between the desire for language revitalisation and the social and emotional challenges that often accompany it. Marilyn's reply, "*Yes, but no shame*," (line 9) is especially significant, suggesting that shame is a central barrier to Aboriginal language use and learning, particularly among younger generations. While in Standard Australian English, shame is typically associated with guilt or embarrassment, in Australian Aboriginal English (AAE), it conveys a broader, shared experience rooted in colonising racial hierarchies (Hamilton et al., 2016; McKnight et al., 2020).

Since the late eighteenth century, following the British invasion and colonisation, First Nations peoples have endured systemic racialisation across every aspect of life: dispossession of land, suppression of language and culture, and the forced removal of children from families. Colonial regimes treated Aboriginal languages as markers of racial inferiority, enacting assimilationist policies that denied communities their linguistic human rights. These violent structures entrenched White supremacy and severed Aboriginal peoples from their cultural, spiritual, linguistic, and epistemological foundations. Before colonisation, more than 250 distinct Aboriginal languages were spoken across the continent; today, only about 12 are still being actively learned as First Languages. For many Aboriginal people, the loss of traditional languages has meant the erosion of identity, cultural knowledge, and ancestral connections, disrupting the intergenerational transmission of Indigenous heritage (Biddle & Swee, 2012). Within this context, shame can be understood as a racialised emotional experience, historically tied to the loss of ancestral languages and sustained through ongoing linguistic marginalisation (Oliver & Exell, 2020).

Even when there is a willingness to learn, such emotional precarity – manifested as shame – can constrain the process of language reclamation and practice. This interaction illustrates that precarity is not only about the material decline of languages but also about the affective and social vulnerabilities shaping their use. Aboriginal people continually navigate these precarious grounds, balancing pride in First Knowledge with the internalised stigma that has historically devalued their languages (Dovchin, 2025b).

## *2.3 WRITING IN FIRST LANGUAGE*

We introduced a new task for the students: writing a letter to their friends. The purpose of this activity was not only to strengthen their writing skills but also to provide them with an opportunity to express themselves more personally. Through the letters, students were encouraged to share who they are, what they do in their daily lives, and to exchange knowledge about their culture and knowledge. In this way, the task fostered both language development and Aboriginal ways of understanding, doing, and being. Darren, an eighteen-year-old young Aboriginal man from Marble Bar, Warralong, a small Aboriginal community in the Pilbara region of Western Australia, writes a thank you letter to his peers at another Christian school they had visited the previous year. In this letter, Darren teaches us First Knowledge systems deeply rooted in his Country, with his reference to hunting and fishing for survival, where land and water are both sustenance and spiritual entities. As Darren writes, "Below are some of the things I like hunting: Kangaroo, bush turkey, emu and goanna." His words reveal a powerful connection to what can be described as a First Knowledge system. These traditional foods are part of the oldest known food practices on earth, often referred to as

## 2.3 Writing in First Language 51

"bush tucker" or bush foods – plants and animals native to Australia and historically eaten by Indigenous Australians. For tens of thousands of years, Aboriginal peoples have sustained themselves through hunting, fishing, and foraging, maintaining a deep respect for and stewardship of their environment (Knorr & Augustin, 2025). With an unbroken cultural history extending beyond 50,000 years, Aboriginal communities have not only survived but also adapted to the complexity and constant changes of the Australian landscape. Darren's letter, therefore, is more than a personal reflection on his interests; it embodies an enduring First Nation's peoples' cultural practices of living in balance with the land and drawing sustenance from it in a sustainable and culturally meaningful way (Newton, 2016). Darren demonstrates his knowledge of native foods, presenting the importance of Aboriginal ecological knowledge. The ability to hunt and fish independently reflects self-sufficiency and respect for the land, highlighting the intergenerational transmission of survival skills within Aboriginal communities (Knorr & Augustin, 2025; Newton, 2016).

Darren also expresses his enjoyment in the activities he was involved in during his school visit, where he participated in woodworking and listened to music – both of which align with Aboriginal knowledge systems that values learning through doing, storytelling, and oral traditions. Darren's appreciation of hospitality is also evident as his acknowledgment of the warmth received during his visit reflects the reciprocal nature of hospitality in Aboriginal culture – a fundamental aspect of Indigenous relationships, where visiting and being welcomed onto another's land is met with deep respect and gratitude (Ross & Nursey-Bray, 2020). Darren's voice in the letter is playful – with a smiling face, conveying his warmth, friendliness, and positivity. It suggests a light-hearted tone, making his letter feel more personal and cheerful (see Figure 2.6).

One thing I have noticed in the letter was the consistency of using Standard Australian English (SAE), despite being encouraged to use their traditional languages, including Kriol or any other language of their choice. Nevertheless, as seen in these letters, the Aboriginal students use their official classroom language – SAE, absent from *First Languaging* practices they were dominantly using in the verbal interactions. The pressure of using SAE in the classroom setting was evident across all students (Ober et al., 2025). I ask Darren why he has not used any traditional languages in his letter (see Table 2.3).

Darren's response, "*Because I have to write it in English because I'm at school, Miss*" (line 2), captures a subtle but profound tension between personal linguistic identity and the institutional demands of

Table 2.3 *Darren*

| Line | Speaker and dialogue |
|---|---|
| 1. | Sender: Why don't I see much of your traditional language here? |
| 2. | Darren: Because I have to write it in English because I'm at school, Miss. I will be in trouble if I don't write it correctly (subtle laughter). |
| 3. | Sender: But you can write your traditional language here. It's OK for this task. |
| 4. | Darren: Not sure! Miss! |
| 5. | Sender: Do you want to learn how to write it? |
| 6. | Darren: Of course. I wish they taught here at school. |

Figure 2.6 Writing a letter
(Photo by Sender Dovchin)

schooling. While delivered plainly, it reflects the precarity of a long history of linguistic suppression and colonialingualism (Meighan, 2023): English is not merely a medium of instruction but a gatekeeper of authority, recognition, and legitimacy within the educational system. The phrasing "*I have to*" and "*I will be in trouble*" (line 2) signals the internalisation of unspoken rules that Aboriginal students quickly learn – that the languages tied to their Country, kin, and culture hold no formal place in the school system.

Oliver et al.'s (2024) study illuminates similar dynamics, showing that monolingual, English-centric schooling structures reproduce systemic

## 2.3 Writing in First Language

inequalities for First Nations students. In alignment with Darren's experience, Oliver et al. (2024) highlight how national assessments such as the National Assessment Program - Literacy and Numeracy (NAPLAN) reinforce the dominance of SAE and marginalise other linguistic practices. What is assessed dictates what is taught; thus, written SAE literacy becomes the central teaching priority, even when curricula explicitly acknowledge the role of oral language and First Language/dialect acquisition. Darren's comment exemplifies the consequences Oliver et al. (2024) identify in their study: Aboriginal students navigate an educational landscape where their oral traditions and multilingual repertoires are rendered invisible or undervalued. The focus on written SAE literacy not only overlooks the linguistic strengths of First Nations students but also reproduces historical patterns of linguistic suppression. Here, Oliver et al.'s (2024) observation reinforces that without systemic change - where assessments and pedagogy account for the full linguistic repertoire of students - the educational system continues to perpetuate cultural and linguistic inequities, leaving learners like Darren constrained by the imperative to conform linguistically rather than to flourish authentically.

Even when I gently offer an alternative - *"But you can write your traditional language here. It's OK for this task"* (line 3) - Darren hesitates, not because of unwillingness but because the damage has already been done. *"Not sure, Miss!"* (line 4), Darren says quietly, and with admission comes a far greater than individual uncertainty. What Darren voices is a generational rupture, revealing the dwindling chain of transmission that once sustained vibrant oral traditions, complex linguistic systems, and an entire First Knowledge worldview embedded in language. These are not just forgotten words - they are stolen connections, the consequence of assimilation policies and the colonial education system that erased, criminalised, and silenced Aboriginal communities for generations for speaking their traditional languages (Bednarek & Meek, 2025). Darren's relationship with his traditional language is not one of rejection but of precarious rootedness in colonial legacy.

Darren's phrasing - *"I wish they taught here"* (line 6) - reveals a deep emotional and cultural attachment that is in tension with his limited literacy access to his traditional language or confidence in that language. His sentiment evokes a strong connection to his Aboriginal belonging, yet the transition to written expression, particularly in institutional or school settings, seems blocked by a lack of instruction and the perceived illegitimacy of Aboriginal languages in formal writing. Darren's choice, therefore, is not merely linguistic but existential (Bednarek & Meek, 2025). It reflects a form of precarity in *First*

*Languaging*, where the desire to maintain one's linguistic and cultural roots is overridden by the necessity to perform in the dominant language for survival. His experience draws attention to how broader systems of education and society continue to marginalise Indigenous languages – not through overt prohibition but by making SAE the only viable pathway to legitimacy and success.

Yet, in the midst of this loss, a spark remains. When asked if he wants to learn, he says yes – his voice carrying a mixture of hope and resignation – but it is difficult. And it is. It is difficult not just because of language reclamation resources, time, and intergenerational teaching but also because it means confronting deep historical trauma. For a young Aboriginal person like Darryn, learning his traditional language is not simply about vocabulary or grammar, it is about reclaiming something that was forcibly taken. The difficulty is emotional, cultural, and institutional. Schools rarely make space – real, consistent, resources space – for this kind of learning (Verdon & McLeod, 2015). Even where symbolic gestures are made, such as allowing a student to use traditional language in an assignment, the system still operates on the assumption that SAE is the only real measure of academic success (Oliver et al., 2024; 2025).

Overall, these exchanges between us speak volumes. They tell the story of young Aboriginal people negotiating the invisible but deeply felt borders of language and legitimacy. It is a story of *First Languaging in precarity* – where language is not merely a tool for communication, but a contested site shaped by ongoing colonial legacies, systemic racism, and institutional neglect. These young Aboriginal people's hesitance is not a failure of motivation or cultural pride – it is the predictable outcome of a system that has never truly valued or protected their ancestral linguistic heritage. The issue for these young Aboriginal students is not their supposed inadequacy in their traditional languages or SAE but the conditions of vulnerability they face, including language loss, cultural marginalisation, and systemic racism. As Chinnery (2015) notes, we can see that precarity is not merely a condition of vulnerability but also a call to pedagogical responsibility in today's increasingly diverse classrooms. Instead of blaming children, responsibility lies with educators, policymakers, and institutions to create supportive conditions for learning and revitalising their traditional language. Until schools shift from permission to transformation – embedding First Languages not as tokenistic add-ons but as foundational living parts of the curriculum – students like Marylin, Marie, and Darren will remain at the margins of their own traditional languages. And yet, in their quiet desire to learn their traditional languages, we also hear resilience, the desire to reconnect, to learn, to belong not just in school but in story, in language, and in land.

## 2.4 KAARDA FRIEND!

Noongar is the language of the Noongar people, the traditional custodians of the land on which Boorloo (Perth, Western Australia) is situated, and Noongar is the language traditionally spoken in this region. Due to colonisation, the use of the Noongar language declined significantly across the twentieth century. Today, fluent speakers of Noongar are limited, but there is a growing movement to revitalise and reclaim their language. The desire to learn and reconnect with the Noongar language is strong among Noongar families and communities in and around Boorloo. For many Aboriginal communities, including the Noongar people, languages such as Noongar serve as both ancestral languages and additional languages – particularly for younger generations who may be in the process of language reclamation due to histories of colonial linguistic suppression (Shiosaki, 2025; Steele et al., 2025).

Tamara is a Noongar Yamatji woman and Noongar language teacher dedicated to preserving and revitalising her ancestral language. She began her teaching journey in 2021, driven by a passion for culture, community, and the power of language to connect generations. Her work focuses on making the Noongar language accessible, meaningful, and alive for the next generation, ensuring that it continues to thrive for years to come. Every Tuesday morning since February 2025 until December 2025, Tamara has been teaching Noongar to an Aboriginal playgroup, and I have been observing these play-based sessions.

During my observations, I have learned not only about the First Knowledge system of Noongar culture but also about how *First Languaging* may function as a scaffold, enabling children to express themselves, learn their languages, and develop critical awareness. At the beginning, the children had little or no knowledge of Noongar. Yet over time, they began confidently naming native animals, identifying family members, and even singing in Noongar. Their growing enthusiasm reflected an emerging sense of linguistic agency. This progress illustrated how *First Knowledging* – the embodied, relational, and culturally situated ways in which children come to understand the Noongar culture – and *First Languaging* – the use of emergent linguistic repertoires to express and explore these knowledges – work hand in hand to enable these children as active language learners and knowledge holders.

One play example stands out: Tamara introduces Australian native animals including *emu*, *kangaroo*, and *goanna puppets* to the children (see Figure 2.7). The play-based nature of the session allows children to engage physically, socially, and linguistically with the concept, demonstrating how playful interactions facilitate language learning while embedding cultural knowledge. The playful voices of children fill the playgroup as they all imitate running like emus or act like those animals. Tamara says, "*Look! It's a 'yongka' (Kangaroo!) What does 'yongka' do?*" Children start jumping like kangaroos, while repeating Tamara's "*Yongka!*" Tamara continues, "Here is our *kaarda* (goanna) friend," prompting the children to repeat enthusiastically, "*Kaarda friend!*" "*Goanna, Kaarda!*" the children chant. Linguistic play embedded within *First Languaging* is fluidly mixed across Noongar, Aboriginal English (AE), and SAE, reflecting the full use of linguistic resources and legitimising all languages available in the playgroup. SAE and AE are employed as a scaffold to teach Noongar, but they never diminish the value of Noongar itself. Introducing new Noongar words seamlessly within English utterances allows children to anchor unfamiliar

Figure 2.7 Kaarda friend!
(Photo by Sender Dovchin)

## 2.4 Kaarda Friend!

terms within a familiar linguistic framework, making learning both accessible and engaging.

Storytelling and embodied play are central to the session. When Tamara focuses on the *goanna*, she situates the animal within Aboriginal Dreaming stories, highlighting its role as a creator spirit and totemic figure. Goannas are featured in parables that teach Aboriginal ways of living and hunting (Campbell-McLeod, 2013). The *First Languaging*, meanwhile, scaffolds children's agency, allowing them to participate actively in First Knowledge making. As one child stands up, she excitedly grabs a flashcard and runs to her father, asking to see a photo of him holding a goanna he had caught. When the photo appeared, she pointed proudly and exclaimed, *"Look! Kaarda! Kaarda!"* In this moment, the child extended the learning space beyond the playgroup, connecting what she had learned in Noongar language sessions with her family's lived practices of hunting and *bush tucker* – any bush food native to Australia and historically eaten by Indigenous Australians and Torres Strait Islander peoples. The goanna (*kaarda*) is not simply a vocabulary item – it is part of a broader cultural ecology, representing a source of food, a totemic being, and a figure in Aboriginal Dreaming stories. By linking the word *kaarda* to her father's hunting photo, the child demonstrates how *First Knowledging* – the embodied, relational, and ecological knowledge of Aboriginal life – intersects with First Languaging. Her use of digital technology to share the image reveals a multimodal process of meaning-making, where visual, linguistic, and cultural resources are woven together. This act exemplifies how Indigenous ways of living, such as goanna hunting as bush tucker, become central to learning. It also highlights the child's agency in asserting that Indigenous lived experience is a legitimate and authoritative source of knowledge, not peripheral to education (Oakley et al., 2025). In Aboriginal traditions, hunting goanna is more than a subsistence practice: it is a family and community activity that embodies ecological expertise, intergenerational teaching, and cultural responsibility (Kickett-Tucker et al., 2025). Men, women, and children all participate in tracking, catching, and preparing goanna, sharing both the labour and the knowledge. By naming *kaarda* in the classroom and then grounding it in her family's experience of hunting, the child brings these traditions directly into the learning space.

Tamara's response – *"Beautiful! That's 'Kaarda!' The big 'Kaarda!' You're teaching us too!"* – exemplifies deep listening and a non-hierarchical learning environment. By encouraging the child as a knowledge holder, she enacts reciprocal learning and co-construction of knowledge. Moving fluidly between Noongar and English, Tamara shifts power towards the children, acknowledging that learning is a shared, relational, and playful process. When I joined the exchange, I also checked the photo and expressed excitement: *"Wow! That's a real 'kaarda!' Your dad caught it? Deadly! Kaarda!"* I sought to validate the child's experience and position Noongar knowledge at the centre of the interaction. My enthusiastic engagement exemplifies languaging in practice, as English, Noongar (*"Kaarda!"*), and Aboriginal English (*"Deadly!"*) are intertwined, while multimodal resources – verbal, visual, and cultural – are used collaboratively to make meaning. This encounter highlights how First Knowledging and First Languaging thrive in play-based learning spaces, where children's agency, language, and lived experiences are simultaneously celebrated and nurtured. This playful, spontaneous act transforms language learning into a process of cultural assertion, where First Knowledging and First Languaging work together to scaffold identity, belonging, and critical awareness. This hands-on cultural knowledge, transmitted through playful games and interactions, embeds embodied and relational learning, showing children how language, play, and lived experience are intertwined. The playgroup becomes a space where linguistic, cultural, and ecological knowledges are simultaneously enacted and explored (Oakley et al., 2025).

Yet this moment also illuminates the *precarious grounds* upon which First Languaging takes place in contexts of language loss. Butler (2004) reminds us that precarity is a politically induced condition, one that renders certain lives and practices more vulnerable to erasure than others. For Aboriginal peoples, the precarity of language is a direct outcome of colonial violence, including assimilation policies, the forced removal of children during the Stolen Generations, and the systematic delegitimisation of Indigenous languages (Beaufils et al., 2025). The fact that most of the children in this Noongar play-based language program began with little or no knowledge of their ancestral language is a stark reminder of this history. First Languaging, in this context, does not emerge in abundance but in scarcity, where even the utterance of a single Noongar word carries immense weight as an act of survival and continuity. Parents' strong desire for their children to learn Noongar also highlights the intergenerational wounds of linguistic dispossession. While many parents are themselves speakers of SAE and/or Aboriginal English, their deep longing to hear their children speak Noongar testifies to their resistance against linguistic erasure. This aligns with Hinton's (2013) and Leonard's (2019) works on language reclamation, which emphasise the crucial role of families and communities in ensuring the survival of endangered languages. In

## 2.4 Kaarda Friend!

this case, parents' commitment to Noongar learning is not simply pedagogical but deeply political, embedding *First Languaging* within a struggle for cultural sovereignty and justice. For Tamara, the Noongar teacher leading the sessions, the precarity of First Languaging is both a professional and personal reality. Her teaching is filled with concern about the ongoing loss of Noongar, yet sustained by her determination to revitalise and transmit the language. Each session – whether naming animals, singing songs, or sharing Dreaming stories – is not only instructional but a radical act of reclamation. As scholars such as Meighan (2025a,b) and Lane (2025) note, (trans)languaging pedagogy, fluidly drawing on multiple linguistic repertoires, enables learners to access, practise, and expand endangered languages without devaluing their existing linguistic resources. Tamara's teaching reflects this principle, as she integrates SAE and AE alongside Noongar, creating a languaging space where all linguistic practices are legitimised. In doing so, she not only resists the historical erasure of Aboriginal languages but also positions children's diverse linguistic repertoires as assets, rather than deficits. The classroom thus becomes a site of both cultural continuity and epistemic justice, where language learning is inseparable from healing, identity assertion, and the reassertion of Noongar sovereignty.

This is where the paradox of *First Languaging* becomes most evident. On one hand, play-based Noongar learning empowers children to act as First Knowledge holders: their enthusiasm, playful voices, laughter, and multimodal meaning-making embody the generative, relational spirit of First Languaging. On the other hand, this occurs within the precarious context of language loss, where deep intergenerational transmission has been fractured. The scene is marked by precarity – the knowledge that the children are growing up in a society where their ancestral tongue has been historically silenced, where English dominance continues to marginalise Indigenous voices, and where the intergenerational transmission of Noongar is at risk of rupture. Morcom (2025) argues that Indigenous language revitalisation is marked by inherent tensions; while it can serve as an emancipatory act, it may also be accompanied by pain and silence. Colonisation has created epistemological voids that can be understood as forms of silence, and recognising how these silences emerge and persist is crucial for addressing the challenges faced in reclamation efforts. Attending to silence and the emotional dimension of revitalisation is therefore essential. Teachers like Tamara, thus, must shoulder the immense burden of revitalisation, often with minimal structural support or recognition. The children's playful utterances of Noongar expressions thus operate on multiple levels. It is an act of joy and play, asserting the integration of linguistic and ecological knowledge. It is an act of resistance, defying the colonial erasure of Noongar. And it is an act of precarity, revealing how fragile and contingent the continuation of First Languaging remains. Yet within this precarious ground lies profound generativity: each word spoken, each song sung, each embodied act of storytelling and play becomes a moment where *First Knowledging* and *First Languaging* converge to resist erasure and to assert cultural continuity. Following Chinnery (2015), precarity here is not reducible to mere vulnerability or deficit. Rather, it can be understood as a condition that calls for the *precarity* and *pedagogical responsibility* – an ethical demand placed upon educators, policymakers, and communities to recognise that precarity is inseparable from social justice. The sustainability of such efforts depends not only on the dedication of individual teachers and parents but also on broader institutional and societal commitments to language revitalisation – curricular integration, government support, and long-term funding.

Precarity, in this sense, invites us to see the playgroup not simply as a site of risk but as a living pedagogy of hope, where the very instability of language transmission sharpens the urgency of care, creativity, and commitment. The work of Tamara, the parents, and the children demonstrates how *First Languaging* is both intimate and insurgent. Their insistence that the Noongar language must not only survive but thrive reframes language revitalisation as a collective act of resistance against colonial erasure. Each playful act of First Languaging insists that Aboriginal children deserve to inherit their linguistic birthright, and that society bears responsibility to ensure its flourishing. In this way, the Noongar playgroup illuminates how the precarious grounds of *First Languaging* do not signal weakness, but rather become the very ground from which resilience, renewal, and justice are enacted. The sustainability of such efforts depends not only on the dedication of individual teachers and parents but also on broader institutional and societal commitments to language revitalisation – curricular integration, government support, and long-term funding.

## 2.5 TOWARDS PEDAGOGICAL FIRST LANGUAGING AND FIRST KNOWLEDGING

In this chapter, I have explored the dynamic interplay between the playfulness and precarity of *First Languaging* and its relationship with

## 2.5 Towards Pedagogical *First Languaging* & *First Knowledging*

*First Knowledging* (Song & Lin, 2025). The deep, reciprocal connections to Country, animals, and land – central to Indigenous epistemologies – stand in contrast to Western ways of knowing, which often impose a material and spiritual separation from the environment. However, the holistic, interconnected worldview inherent in *First Knowledging* offers a transformative lens through which we can rethink language, its role, and its relationship with the world. In this sense, to engage with *First Knowledging* is to engage with *First Languag*ing, as the two are fundamentally inseparable, woven together through story, experience, and the lived realities of First Nations peoples.

From this perspective, integrating *First Knowledging* and *First Languaging* epistemology into language classrooms may offer a transformative approach to promoting meaningful and transformative change for both Indigenous and non-Indigenous students. By recognising how *First Languaging* corresponds to Indigenous ways of knowing, being, and relating to the world, educators can create more inclusive and culturally responsive learning environments that honour linguistic diversity and Indigenous knowledge systems. In standard language classrooms, it is common to separate language systems to be acquired from their real-life contexts. This kind of linguistic pedagogical separability could assist in teaching certain aspects of linguistic systems but may have very little applicability in contexts where language, learning, and land are part of a whole (Leonard, 2017, 2019). As Leonard (2017, 2019) highlights, mainstream understandings of "language" often default to global, standardised models rather than Indigenous perspectives that see language as relational and inseparable from people and culture. Language reclamation, therefore, is not only about teaching the language but also about restoring cultural knowledge, practices, and identities, while challenging the power structures that produced erasure. It is a community-driven process that affirms continuity, resists colonial categorisation, and embeds languages back into the fabric of everyday life, pedagogy, teaching, and learning. The pedagogy of *First Knowledging* and *First Languaging*, thus, could create a linguistically and culturally safe space where the student can express their playfulness and precarity without the constraints of Western-oriented classroom settings.

As Wang (2024) highlights, the need for applied linguistics to deepen its engagement with Indigenous epistemologies to enhance active student learning has become a central focus. This involves not only valuing local knowledge systems but also incorporating *languaging* strategies – such as *translanguaging* – as decolonial pedagogical tools. These practices can help First Knowledge systems into educational settings in ways that are meaningful to all learners, not just those from Indigenous backgrounds. In line with Song and Lin's (2025) argument, translanguaging must extend beyond a minority-specific framework and be positioned as a universal pedagogical strategy. In contexts like Aotearoa/New Zealand, promoting social justice through education involves not only safeguarding Indigenous languages and ways of knowing within Indigenous communities but also inviting all students – regardless of background – into the national project of cultural recognition. Wang's (2024) study shows that students are open to assessment approaches that reflect diverse cultural and linguistic identities. Students' positive attitude towards translanguaging may stem from a growing awareness of the significance of the Māori language and knowledge in shaping local schooling experiences. Students' digital and multimodal compositions further demonstrate their capacity to use translanguaging in authentic and purposeful ways. These findings emphasise the potential for translanguaging to be embedded into curriculum design, particularly assessment that honours cultural diversity and promotes critical and inclusive learning.

Steele et al. (2022) critically examine the potential of translanguaging to support more equitable educational outcomes for students from Australian Aboriginal backgrounds. They identify persistent social, cultural, and linguistic biases embedded in current assessment frameworks and argue that these practices often fail to recognise the full linguistic capabilities of Aboriginal students. By calling for fairer and more culturally responsive approaches, the authors advocate for assessments that allow students to engage through their entire linguistic repertoire. They assert the need to reframe assessment practices to move away from deficit-based models and echo the call to "*stop measuring Black kids with a white stick,*" urging educators to adopt inclusive, strength-based assessment strategies that empower Aboriginal learners. Moving towards pedagogical *First Languaging* highlights the urgent need to reimagine language education through decolonial, culturally sustaining, and linguistically inclusive frameworks. It is time for educators and institutions to move beyond tokenistic gestures and instead advocate transformative classrooms, assessment practices, and curriculums where First Knowledges, First Languages, and First Nations peoples are genuinely recognised, respected, and centred as integral to the teaching and learning process.

# 3 Nomadic Languaging and Nomadic Knowledging

## 3.1 NOMADIC REMINISCING CIRCLE [ХУУЧ ХӨӨРӨХ]

The Mongolian phrase - [Хууч Хөөрөх] [Khuuchi Khuurukh] - commonly translates into English "storytelling" or "reminiscing" to explain participating in deep conversations, recalling memories, sharing narrative and stories in a communal gathering with Elders, family, and friends, sitting in a circle in the Mongolian *ger* - a traditional portable dwelling used by nomadic herders in Mongolia. In its simplest form, "*reminiscing*" means "having a deep conversation" - but in Mongolian *malchid*'s (nomadic herders') contexts, it is beyond that. It is a Mongolian nomadic way of storytelling, sharing knowledge, and constructing meaning which has been practised by nomadic herders for thousands of years (Dovchin, (2025a)).

In a similar vein to "*yarning*" - an Australian Indigenous way of talking and deep listening for developing Aboriginal understanding and passing on knowledge to the next generation (Cantley, 2025; Robertson et al., 2005) - "*nomadic reminiscing*" is seldom an individual practice as it embodies joint dialogues for all involved in the process. Just as "*yarns*" are a culturally shared oral construct of the lived experiences of the Australian Aboriginal people on Country, "*nomadic reminiscing*" is about passing down a nomadic knowledge system orally from generation to generation on *Nutag* (Land) (Dovchin, (2025a)).

When Aboriginal people gather in a *yarning circle* - a circle where everyone sits in a culturally safe space and shares their stories (Cantley 2025; Cumming-Potvin et al., 2022), they reflect what the Country teaches us, how the Country speaks, how we listen, and how we speak to Country. Similarly, when Mongolian nomadic herders gather in a "*nomadic reminiscing circle*," they teach us what their *Nutag* (Land) tells us - an ongoing, alive, and interwoven knowledge-sharing system with the past, present, and future. It lives through stories, land, language, and relationships, continuing to guide the everyday lives of nomadic herders (Gardelle & Zhao, 2019). In so doing, they build relationships and trust, reciprocal dialogue, deep listening, and shared storytelling (see Figure 3.1).

During or afterwards, the nomadic herders invite their guests to join them for horse riding and a traditional Mongolian dinner. This is a must and an extension to nomadic hospitality. I became a part of this *"nomadic reminiscing circle,"* where I sat with a group of nomadic herders in the Mongolian *ger* (see Figure 3.1) in Tuv aimag (province) (Date: 29 September 2024). We specifically shared our knowledge about the role of English and other additional languages in their daily lives. Drawing on this *"nomadic reminiscing circle,"* I will seek to introduce the intertwined land-based epistemologies of *"nomadic knowledging"* and *"nomadic languaging"* based on a philosophy where life, nature, time, language, and identity are understood as inherently fluid but attuned to the cycles of the land. This nomadic fluidity exists in tension with the *contextual rootedness* – the need for linguistic boundaries to protect nomadic knowledge systems (Dovchin, (2025a)). English is, for example, accepted into the Mongolian nomadic epistemology only when it enters with humility, respect, and care. *"Nomadic knowledging"* and *"nomadic languaging"* also exist at the interplay of playfulness

Figure 3.1  Nomadic reminiscing circle
(Photo by Sender Dovchin)

## 3.2 Mongolian Nomadic Herders – Malchid

and precarity, where creative and playful acts of linguistic practices open up spaces of joy even as they are shaped by conditions of precarity, uncertainty, and the fragility of everyday survival. This tension highlights that the *languaging turn* in applied linguistics must attend not only to fluidity but also to rootedness, to playfulness but also precarity. Just as nomads adapt to ever-changing environments, applied linguistics must remain responsive to shifting identities, evolving language practices, and contextualised local practices (De Korne et al., 2025; Weenie, 2025). This chapter, therefore, seeks to present how Mongolian nomadic herders envision the role of English and other additional languages through ideas such as *"nomadic knowledging"* and *"nomadic languaging,"* which could offer a more inclusive perspective on land-connected and relational ways of understanding language.

### 3.2 MONGOLIAN NOMADIC HERDERS – MALCHID

Mongolia is a landlocked country in Central Asia, bordered by Russia to the north and China to the south. Known for its vast, rugged steppe and sparse population, it is one of the most sparsely populated countries in the world, with a population of around 3.4 million. Most of the population belongs to the Khalkha Mongol ethnic group, which speaks the Mongolian language and makes up over 80 per cent of the population. It is also home to ethnic minorities such as the Kazakh people and the Indigenous Tsaatan (reindeer) people, each with their own languages and customs. Traditionally, shamanism served as the primary spiritual belief system among Mongolian nomads. In the sixteenth century, Tibetan Buddhism became the dominant religion, blending with existing shamanistic practices (Bawden, 2013; Rossabi, 2005).

Historically, Mongolia has been inhabited since the Stone Age. Nomadic tribes roamed the steppes, forming tribal confederations until the end of the twelfth century, when Chinggis Khan united the Mongol tribes in 1206 under the Great Mongol Empire. In the seventeenth century, the Mongol Empire fell under the rule of the Qing Dynasty, which lasted until its collapse in 1911. While Mongolia declared its independence, it also faced occupation by Chinese and Russian forces. By 1921, with Soviet support, Mongolia expelled Chinese troops and established a communist government. In 1924, the Mongolian People's Republic was declared under the heavy communist rule of the Soviet Union. During the Soviet era, Russian was taught as a compulsory subject from secondary to higher education.

The traditional Mongolian script, Uyghur, was replaced by Russian Cyrillic, which was officially adopted in 1946. The current standard Mongolian orthographic system still remains Cyrillic (Bawden, 2013; Rossabi, 2005).

In 1990, peaceful democratic protests led to the end of communist rule, marking Mongolia's transition to a democratic system and a free market economy. A new constitution was adopted in 1992, ensuring freedom of speech and the right to vote. Mongolia rapidly embraced economic liberalisation, opening its borders to global trade and people's movement (Bawden, 2013; Dovchin, 2018; Rossabi, 2005). Western languages, including English, have begun to play a significant role in Mongolia's educational system, as reflected in key policies such as the Nationwide Programme on English Language Education (2009–2020). Since 1996, English has been taught as a required foreign language, beginning in the fourth grade. In 2015, the Ministry of Education, Culture and Science introduced a new national Core Curriculum for English Language Education in public schools, introducing new textbooks. Despite these government efforts, the effectiveness of the new curriculum remains limited. Key issues include teachers' unfamiliarity with the new curriculum, socio-economic inequalities in resources and learning conditions, and misalignment between textbooks and real-life contexts (Marav et al., 2022).

Mongolia possesses the world's largest remaining contiguous common grazing area, covering over 80 per cent of its 156 million hectares. While pastures are formally state-owned, they are effectively managed as common property. Many Mongolians continue to live as nomadic herders, moving with the seasons to find pasture for their livestock, known as the "*tavan hoshuu mal*" ("five jewels" or "five kinds of livestock") – horses, sheep, goats, yaks/cows, and camels – the five domesticated animals that form the foundation of Mongolian nomadic herding culture (Upton, 2010). Certain nomadic herding families may hold more exclusive rights to critical seasonal pastures, particularly in winter, demonstrating how exclusive and inclusive management principles may coexist within Mongolian pastoralism (Upton, 2010). They live in traditional *gers* (portable round dwellings), adapt with flexibility to environmental conditions, and maintain a close-knit relationship with family and kinship. Mongolian nomadic tradition is deeply rooted in traditional ecological knowledge, self-sufficiency, strong ties to nature and land, communications with ancestors and spirits, and respect for horses, other animals, sacred landscapes, mountains, water, and steppe (Batdelger et al., 2025; Myadar, 2020).

Regrettably, since the democratic revolution, Mongolian nomadic herders have become one of the most marginalised populations in Mongolia, particularly regarding their children's access to public education, including English language education. They face a displacement crisis through multiple external factors such as *zud* (severe winter disasters) and frequent seasonal movements, which disrupt consistent school attendance as they move to find suitable pastures for their livestock (Soma, 2025). Many remote areas lack nearby schools, forcing nomadic children to travel long distances or live in under-resourced dormitories or boarding schools (Kurowski, 2025). Economic pressures also play a role, as children are needed to assist with herding tasks, especially during peak seasons. In recent years, the expansion of multinational mining operations has intensified this challenge, as many nomadic herders have been displaced from their lands, further disrupting their way of life and their children's access to stable education (Batsaikhan, 2025; Dovchin & Dovchin, 2024; Morgan & Sengedorj, 2022). Despite these challenges, Mongolian nomadic herders are determined for their children to learn English and other additional languages, recognising its importance while also holding their own unique visions on the role of languages.

## 3.3 EXPANDING DECOLONIAL TURN

The recent decolonial turn has sharply critiqued applied linguistics for privileging Anglocentric and monolingual norms, which are often legitimised through decontextualised, standardised ideologies disconnected from the linguistic and cultural realities of learners. Such orientations frequently erase the plurality of lived language practices that actually sustain communication in multilingual societies. In many contexts, applied linguistics continues to operate within capitalist and neoliberal frameworks, aligning language learning with market logics and instrumentalist agendas. This predicament not only reinforces Western epistemologies but also contributes to the marginalisation of Indigenous, minority, and local knowledges, which are often positioned as secondary or even irrelevant (Baker et al., 2025; Galante et al., 2024; López-Gopar & Nava, 2025; Meighan, 2025b; Pennycook, 2007b; Pentón Herrera & McNair, 2021; Sah & Li, 2024).

Moreover, these colonially rooted practices are sustained by elite decision-makers – international agencies, publishing industries, and policymakers – who, for example, frame English Language Teaching (ELT) as a one-size-fits-all solution to educational and economic advancement. In doing so, ELT is placed firmly within the commodification of English, where language is packaged, marketed, and sold as a passport to modernity, global citizenship, and individual success. English thus becomes a form of symbolic capital, constructed as a necessity for survival in a competitive global economy, while alternative linguistic resources are rendered invisible or devalued. This logic turns English into a transactional currency, where its acquisition is tied to employability, upward mobility, and participation in global markets, thereby reproducing hierarchies of privilege that privilege English speakers and disadvantage those outside these linguistic economies. From a decolonial perspective, such dynamics call for a fundamental rethinking of applied linguistics, not simply adding local languages to existing frameworks, but disrupting the epistemic dominance of English and recognising linguistic diversity as a site of knowledge production, cultural continuity, and epistemic justice (Baker et al., 2025; Galante et al., 2024; López-Gopar & Nava, 2025; Meighan, 2025b; Pennycook, 2007b; Pentón Herrera & McNair, 2021; Sah & Li, 2024).

Such Western approaches are fundamentally incompatible with Indigenous knowledge systems, which are grounded in relationality and reciprocity that value collective and intergenerational ways of knowledge sharing that are deeply connected to the land. When English, for example, is imposed without regard for Indigenous ways of being, it can displace local languages, diminish cultural continuity, and contribute to the erosion of linguistic diversity. This decolonial turn, therefore, urges that we must move beyond surface-level inclusion to actively centre Indigenous voices that honour spiritual, environmental, and social relationality central to Indigenous knowledge (Kovats Sánchez et al., 2022; Ober, 2025a; Venegas & Leonard, 2023).

Building on this idea, the decolonial trend has begun to urge us to actively centre Indigenous voices within this broader *languaging turn*. In this context, the idea of *First Languaging* and *First Knowledging*, which I have discussed in Chapter 2, is rightly being centred in the current discussion. However, there is less recognition of *nomadic knowledging* and *nomadic languaging*, such as those practised by Mongolian nomadic herders (Dovchin, (2025a)). *Nomadic knowledging* and *nomadic languaging* profoundly reflect a relational worldview that aligns closely with *First Knowledging* and *First Languaging*, which deserve recognition alongside other Indigenous and land-based knowledge traditions. *Nomadic knowledging* and *nomadic languaging* reflect insightful ecological and land awareness, mobility-based learning, and relational worldviews that align closely with Indigenous knowledge. While Mongolia is not

## 3.3 Expanding Decolonial Turn

officially recognised as Indigenous by the United Nations (UN), recent genetic studies show that modern Mongolian people are genetically close to the original lineage leading to Native Americans (Brissenden et al., 2015; Dulik et al., 2012). It is considered that ancestors of Native Americans migrated from Siberia and Mongolia across the Bering Land Bridge (Beringia) into the Americas around 15,000–30,000 years ago, most likely during the Last Glacial Maximum (LGM) (Hoffecker et al., 2020). Mongolian heritage, language, and culture share, thus, many similarities with Indigenous cultures, not only in Native America but also with Indigenous communities worldwide. Both Mongolian and some Native American tribes, especially the Plains tribes, historically lived as nomadic horse riders, relying on archery, hunting, herding, and spiritual traditions tied to nature. Mongolian Tengrism (worship of the eternal blue sky, Tengri) has parallels with Native American animistic and shamanistic spiritual traditions (Balogh, 2010).

However, because Mongolian nomadic people are not formally recognised as Indigenous under dominant global frameworks, their knowledge systems are often overlooked or excluded from international conversations on decolonisation and Indigenisation. This lack of recognition reflects the politics of categorisation, where definitions of "Indigeneity" are frequently shaped by Western-centric institutions such as the United Nations or state governments, and do not adequately capture the complex histories and lived realities of nomadic peoples (Canessa, 2014; De la Cadena, 2010; Dovchin et al., 2024). As a result, Mongolian nomadic epistemologies – rooted in spiritual, ecological, and intergenerational practices – are frequently marginalised or dismissed as merely cultural heritage rather than as legitimate and living systems of knowledge. This exclusion is particularly striking given that Mongolian nomadic culture represents one of the last surviving large-scale nomadic traditions in the world, with a lineage that stretches back thousands of years (Mignolo, 2007; Tuck & Yang, 2012). These traditions encompass sophisticated understandings of land stewardship, animal husbandry, ecological balance, and cosmology, all of which challenge dominant models of human–environment relations (Myadar, 2020; Soma, 2025; Tugjamba, 2025). By ignoring such contributions, global discourses risk reproducing a narrow vision of decolonisation that privileges certain Indigenous experiences while silencing others, thereby reinforcing epistemic hierarchies (Mignolo, 2007). Recognising Mongolian nomadic communities within decolonial and Indigenisation debates would not only expand the scope of these conversations but also affirm the diversity of Indigenous and traditional knowledges that continue to shape alternative futures (Tuck & Yang, 2012).

## 3.4 NOMADIC KNOWLEDGING AND NOMADIC LANGUAGING

Just as Indigenous peoples' knowledge system is deeply connected to their Country, Mongolian nomadic herders share an enduring relationship with their ᠨ ("*Nutag*" – Land) they have been inhabiting for thousands of years. The central nomadic knowledge system is: the land does not belong to humans, but rather humans belong to the land (Dovchin & Dovchin, 2024; Myadar, 2020). This is embodied in the Mongolian proverb "*humans, land and the natural world are connected through an umbilical cord*" (Dovchin, 2025a; Dovchin & Dovchin, 2024). I refer to this system as *nomadic knowledging* – a form of relational intelligence that is practised through an ongoing negotiation between humans and land, based on adaptation, survival, resilience, and the continuity of knowledge across generations (Dovchin, 2025a). Through *nomadic knowledging*, the *Malchid* (nomadic herders) have survived and thrived for over a thousand years, maintaining a deep, reciprocal relationship with the vast ecosystem of the Mongolian steppe. Their ways of life are inseparable from the rhythms of the land, where every aspect – nature, time, identity, and the human life cycle – is interconnected and interdependent. In this worldview, nothing is fixed, and permanence is understood as an illusion; the steppe itself is constantly shifting, demanding attentiveness and responsiveness from those who inhabit it. Survival and well-being are not achieved through resisting change but through the cultivation of flexibility, adaptability, and a respectful responsiveness to the environment (Myadar, 2020; Terbish, 2025). The Malchid navigate the challenges of their environment by moving in harmony with ecological and seasonal cycles, reading subtle signs in the land, and making decisions that sustain both human and non-human life (Terbish, 2025; Zhao, 2025). To live well, one must attune oneself to the "*Nutag*" – the homeland – understanding its rhythms, respecting its limits, and aligning human activity with its flows rather than imposing rigid control (Dovchin & Dovchin, 2024; Myadar, 2020). This approach to existence embodies a relational epistemology, where knowledge is not abstract or static but emerges through ongoing practice, observation, and interaction with the land. It is a knowledge system that privileges movement, sensitivity, and reciprocity, revealing how nomadic lifeways offer profound insights

## 3.4 Nomadic Knowledging and Nomadic Languaging

into sustainable living, ecological stewardship, and adaptive resilience (Terbish, 2025; Zhao, 2025). This relational approach to knowledge is closely aligned with *First Knowledging*, which I have discussed in Chapter 2, as it centres lived, place-based, and embodied ways of knowing. Just as *First Knowledging* emphasises direct engagement with the environment, intergenerational transmission of knowledge, and the ethical responsibility of humans to other-than-human beings, so too does *nomadic knowledging* cultivate an intimate, reciprocal relationship with the land. It guides human action through attentiveness, adaptability, and respect for ecological and social rhythms. Through this profound connection to the land, Mongolian nomadic herders have developed extensive knowledge of weather patterns, climate, animal behaviours, land navigation, native medicinal herbs, and ecological cycles – demonstrating that they are scientists in their own right (see also Chapter 2 for Mongolian nomadic reindeer people). Their knowledge systems are empirical, adaptive, and deeply attuned to ecological balance, reflecting a holistic understanding of the environment that is both practical and ethical (Myadar, 2020; Terbish, 2025; Zhao, 2025). Just as First Nations peoples have cultivated profound knowledge to survive, maintain cultural and linguistic practices over tens of thousands of years, and develop early understandings of land, water, sky, seasons, astronomy, and ecological interactions (Neale, 2021; Neale & Kelly 2020), so too have Mongolian nomadic herders developed sophisticated systems of knowledge about the land, sky, animals, and ecosystems, demonstrating a remarkable, living science embedded in their nomadic lifeways.

This principle of mobility that defines nomadic life is vividly reflected in their language use. Just as *nomadic knowledging* moves with the body across the land, so does language – it shifts, stretches, and transforms fluidly in response to changing social and environmental contexts. For Mongolian nomadic people, languaging is not a sporadic act but a fundamental dimension of communication – a relational, adaptive, and resilient form of expression deeply embedded in their nomadic lifeways and land-based epistemologies. This *nomadic languaging* involves sophisticated *linguistic play*, combining new sounds, meanings, and structures drawn from multiple written resources (Bao et al., 2025) such as the world's only vertical script, calligraphy, religious texts, early literary works, and oral traditions, including epic poetry, folk songs, riddles, and proverbs that preserve their knowledge (Sun & Sornyai, 2025). Expressions often convey respect for Elders, animals, and sacred places, while oral repertoires employ metaphorical play, rhythmic variations, chants, and throat singing (Sun & Sornyai, 2025). Across centuries of mobility, trade, and cultural contact – including historical colonisation pressures from China, Sovietisation, and later globalisation – Mongolian nomadic herders have blended diverse linguistic repertoires, including multiple Mongolian varieties (e.g., Khalkha, Buryat, Oirat), Kazakh, Russian, and other dialects (Gerelt-Od, 2025; Gu et al., 2025). Nomadism has thus generated remarkable linguistic sophistication. Despite any external pressures, Mongolian nomadic herders have resisted linguistic assimilation, creatively blending global and local languages while asserting both linguistic and cultural sovereignty (Dovchin, 2025a).

*Nomadic languaging*, in this sense, reflects the flexible, adaptive, and relational nature of communication. Just as *First Languaging* in Chapter 2 emphasises lived, Country-based, and embodied ways of learning and communicating, so too does *nomadic languaging* emerge dynamically through embodied practices, complex oral and written traditions, and responsiveness to land-based contexts. Language, therefore, is not a fixed object but a living, moving practice – embedded in place, shaped by the land, and carried across generations. This fluidity is not merely recited; it is continually reimagined, reinterpreted, and adapted to new circumstances, enabling nomadic knowledge to be simultaneously preserved and transformed. In this way, language functions as a performative, generative act – a fluid, lived practice that is inseparable from the broader nomadic knowledge system. In the following sections, I will explore how *nomadic knowledging* and *nomadic languaging* are intertwined at the intersection of *playfulness* and *precarity*, drawing on examples of *nomadic reminiscing* and linguistic engagement that sustain both cultural knowledge and linguistic resilience.

## 3.5 THE STORY OF A WEEPING CAMEL

The horse is not only an animal of utility but also a living symbol of Mongolian identity and survival. Historically, Chinggis Khan's empire was literally built on horseback – the speed, mobility, and endurance of Mongolian horses made possible the vast conquests of the thirteenth century. In Mongolian nomadic culture, horses are regarded as sacred beings, often associated with the sky, the wind, and the spirit of the steppe. To this day, they occupy a central place in rituals, festivals, folk stories, and oral traditions (Erdenechuluun, 2025;

## 3.5 The Story of a Weeping Camel

Rossabi, 1994; Yazdzik, 2011). Horses are also central to *nomadic knowledging*: learning how to ride, care for, and communicate with horses is a deeply embodied practice, passed down through intergenerational teaching. Through their relationship with horses, nomads acquire resilience, adaptability to the harsh environment, and a profound interconnection with *Nutag* (Land). This is a profound nomadic knowledge not written in books but lived in daily practice. It is often noted that Mongolia is home to nearly 5 million horses – more than the country's human population. From an early age, children are initiated into this knowledge system: it is said that some children begin riding horses before they can properly walk, often as young as two or three years old. In this sense, the horse is both a companion and a teacher, shaping the physical, emotional, and spiritual life of Mongolian nomads (Rossabi, 1994; Yazdzik, 2011).

In the Mongolian ger, I found myself actively participating in *nomadic knowledging* – engaging with the ways of knowing, being, and doing practised by nomadic horsemen, which were often deeply connected to a strong sense of *Nutag* (Land) and the experience of being "*on Nutag*." In what appears to be an ordinary exchange about Mongolian horses, something epistemologically rich is unfolding, revealing the intricate interrelationship between *nomadic languaging* and *nomadic knowledging*. The discussion involves a group of Mongolian nomadic herders, all of whom are horsemen, primarily responsible for the care and training of their horses. Dorj, for example, is a state-recognised, award-winning horseman who manages over 500 horses, many of which have won prizes at national horse races and festivals. In the interaction in Table 3.1, Giingoo, they are discussing one of the nomadic oral traditions – "*giingoo*" – long-drawn chants sung to inspire and honour horses (Yoon, 2019). The atmosphere of the conversation is playful and positive, illustrating how learning, storytelling, and knowledge transmission in nomadic contexts are simultaneously social, embodied, and deeply connected to land and livelihood.

Naadam (*Наадам*) is Mongolia's biggest annual national festival, sometimes called the "Three Manly Games Festival" – wrestling, archery, and horse racing, traced back centuries to ancient Mongolia. It is celebrated every year in July (11–13) and is also linked to Mongolia's national Independence Day. The traditional Mongolian horse race is one of the most iconic and exciting events of the *Naadam Festival* (Zhao, 2025). Unlike typical short-distance races, Mongolian horse races are endurance-based, often covering distances between 15 and 30 kilometres, testing not just speed but the stamina and resilience of both horse and rider. The young horse riders are as young as five or six, ride bareback, showcasing

74  3 NOMADIC LANGUAGING AND NOMADIC KNOWLEDGING

Table 3.1 *Giingoo*

| Line | Speaker and dialogue |
|---|---|
| 1. | Dorj: *Chi giingoo gej medne biz dee? Manai uvug deedsiin ardiin urlagaas garaltai. Delhiin haana ch baihgui dee!* <br> (You know what *giingoo* is, right? It comes from our ancestors' folk art. You won't find it anywhere else in the world.) |
| 2. | Sender: *Medelgui yahav.* <br> (Of course, I know!) |
| 3. | Dorj: *Za ter chini l manai malchidiin hel yaria soyoliin tomoohon heseg shuudee. Giingoo! Giingoo! geel huuhduud ehleheer setgel sergeel yavna shuudee!* <br> (Well, that's a big part of our herders' language, speech, and culture. When kids start chanting *Giingoo, Giingoo* (he starts singing *Giingoo* in a loud voice), it really lifts your spirit.) |
| 4. | Group: (Group laughter.) *Manai hun yanziin goy giingooloon shuudee!* <br> (Our guy here – he does such a beautiful *giingoo*!) |
| 5. | Dorj: (Laughs loudly.) *Tegelgui yadiin. Giingooddoggui aduuchin gej yu baih vee.* <br> (Of course! What kind of horseman doesn't know how to *giingoo*?) |

remarkable horsemanship passed down through generations. The races are vibrant community events, fostering cultural and social bonds, honouring the strength and spirit of Mongolian horses, which are revered as national symbols. In essence, the Naadam horse race is much more than a sport – it is a living tradition that connects Mongolians to their history, land, and deep bond between humans and horses in the vast Mongolian steppes. *Giingoo*, in this sense, is a Mongolian horse rider chant performed during horse races to encourage and communicate with horses. Sung in a melodic and uplifting tone, the chant typically includes the word *giingoo*, uttered with great cheer (Yoon, 2019). Rooted in Mongolia's oral singing traditions, *giingoo* functions not only to motivate the racing horse but also to energise the rider, the crowd, and even the surrounding landscape such as the spirits of the mountains and the steppe. It shares melodic features with the Mongolian *urtiin duu* (long songs) and its performance reflects a deep cultural, emotional, and sonic connection between humans and horses (see Figure 3.2).

The reminiscing between nomadic herdsmen centres around *giingoo* – it is invoked as a living, playful, and relational mode of *nomadic languaging*. Dorj's statements such as "*You know what giingoo, is right? It comes from our ancestors' folk artistry. You won't find it anywhere else in the world*" (line 1) assert that rituals like *giingoo* are not merely cultural performances but integral to nomadic ways of knowing, being, and languaging. Rather

## 3.5 The Story of a Weeping Camel

Figure 3.2 Before the horse race
(Photo by Sender Dovchin)

than being confined to only words, *giingoo* is an uplifting ritual co-created between humans and horses through sound, words, touch, singing, and beats. As Dorj declares, *"When kids start chanting giingoo, giingoo, it really lifts your spirit"* (line 3). It signals how *giingoo* functions as a participatory and multispecies experience – children ride horses, elders cheer from afar, and horses respond not to just instruction but to the vibrational and joyous cadence of the chant. The rhythmic exuberance of *giingoo* channels excitement, anticipation, and joy, weaving the playfulness of languaging that includes not only people but also animals and land itself.

When Dorj breaks into a *giingoo* chant mid-conversation, it brings to mind Shaila et al.'s (2013) work on *musical transglossic practices*, where language users weave song lyrics and melodies into their talk not only to play and have fun, but also to blur linguistic boundaries and create shared moments of connection (cf. Dovchin et al., 2017). The playful voices fill the ger – the laughter and teasing thrive (line 3). Here, languaging becomes a shared playful space for connecting a collective bond. Such laughter signals familiarity and comfort – crucial markers of nomadic herders' bonding. These playful voices are not a diversion from serious discourse – they are a part of the discourse – the *nomadic languaging*. Dorj's emphatic declaration "*What kind of horseman doesn't know how to giingoo?*" (line 5) shows what it means to be a nomadic horseman through playful provocation. It frames *giingoo* as a rite of passage, where nomadic cultural legitimacy and horsemanship are playfully – but meaningfully – linked to one's legitimacy to participate in the reminiscing circle.

This vocal play is typical of nomadic traditions, where imitation of natural sounds like those used to calm or communicate with animals is both functional and expressive. Playfulness is not a trivial add-on here: it is central to how Mongolian nomadic horsemen communicate. *Giingoo* functions here as a trans-species languaging – a communicative modality that defies linguistic boundaries, exemplifying what might be called acoustic languaging, where communication is emergent, embodied, and situated within the nomadic horsemen and their relationships with their horses (Yoon, 2019). *Giingoo* invites us to reimagine language as mobile, playful, and vivid. In this sense, *giingoo* is both the *subject* of the reminiscing and the *medium* through which the conversation enlivens itself. *Nomadic languaging*, in this sense, becomes the multi-voiced playful voices – a chorus of laughter, brief enactments of the *giingoo*, overlapping laughter and speech – polyphonic and multisensory. Language here is not simply verbal and grammatical performance by the Mongolian nomadic herders but embodied, acoustic, performative, tuneful, and playful languaging practices – a form of living language passed not only through words but is heard, felt, and enacted across human and horse relationships. This represents a form of epistemological knowledge recently emerging under the framework of posthumanist applied linguistics, where humans and non-human entities engage in dynamic, dialogic relationships, co-creating meaning and knowledge together. Rather than positioning humans as the sole producers of language and knowledge, this approach emphasises the entangled interactions between people, animals, technologies, and the environment, highlighting how linguistic practices are shaped through these multispecies and material relationships. It challenges anthropocentric assumptions in traditional applied linguistics, proposing a more distributed and relational understanding of communication, learning, and meaning-making (Pennycook, 2017; Shah & Shah, 2025; Siffrinn & Coda, 2024). In sum, this interaction illustrates how playfulness is not peripheral but constitutive of *nomadic languaging*. *Giingoo* is not merely spoken about – it is evoked, embodied, and relived through laughter, performance, and communal bonding. It invites a broader rethinking of language as mobile and fluid but rooted in a nomadic way of life (see Table 3.2). The group continues teasing each other:

## 3.5 The Story of a Weeping Camel

Table 3.2 *Teasing*

| Line | Speaker and dialogue |
|---|---|
| 1. | Group: (Laughter together and some brief acts of *Giingoo* from the group.) *Manai Baatar Giingoolono ch. Angliaaar ch alna shuu dee bas!* (Our Baatar does *Giingoo* and nail in English too!) |
| 2. | Dorj: *Kamsamidaa geed l.* (Like Kamsamidaa (in Korean).) |
| 3. | Group: *Naadah chini Angli yum uu?* (Is that English?) |
| 4. | Dorj: *Bish yum uu?* (Is that not?) |
| 5. | Group: (Laughter). |

The group's laughter and the joke – "Our Baatar *does Giingoo* and nail in English too!" (line 1) – highlight *nomadic languaging* as a source of playfulness and humour. By juxtaposing culturally rooted vocal practices such as *giingoo* with *English*, the herdsmen playfully collapse boundaries between nomadic vocal expressions and globalised language repertoires. When Dorj says "*Kamsamidaa*" – a Korean phrase meaning "thank you" (line 2), he displays a mock English or Korean, where the imagination of these languages is playfully mistaken and conflated – not out of ignorance but as a deliberate, humorous act that reflects the group's comfort with linguistic fluidity. The use of "*Kamsamidaa*" is not random – it reflects the growing influence of Korean culture in Mongolia, which has seen a major influx of Korean restaurants, K-dramas, and K-pop, even for remote nomadic communities in post-socialist Mongolia (Shinjee & Dovchin, 2023a, b). The presence of Korean suggests that even *nomadic languaging* is being reshaped by transnational cultural flow, making space for new linguistic exposures to be absorbed and recontextualised in multiple ways. The group's response "*Is that English?*" and Dorj's playful reply "*Is that not?*" trigger another burst of laughter, showing how linguistic boundaries are blurred for comic effect. Dorj's response serves as a clever twist that satirises the hegemony of English, suggesting that perhaps any foreign-sounding word could be mistaken for English in today's globalised world. The laughter that follows is not merely about the language mistake but about the shared recognition of linguistic diversity. Dorj's answer functions as Bakhtin's (1981) *double-voiced discourse*: on the surface, it responds playfully to the question, but on a deeper level, it satirises the assumption that foreign-sounding speech is always English. This irony illustrates Bakhtin's (1981) idea that utterances often carry more than one intention or evaluative stance. Overall, Dorj's use of Korean and the group's feigned confusion between Korean and English reflect a playful mixing of global languages, not through formal proficiency but through playful interactions. It shows how even global languages such as Korean and English are absorbed into *nomadic languaging* – not with rigidity but with creativity and humour. Overall, this exchange highlights how playfulness in *nomadic languaging* extends beyond local verbal repertoires (*giingoo*) into the global linguistic repertoire (Korean and English). It reveals a culturally grounded yet globally aware linguistic play that blends humour, mimicry, mockery, and critical commentary – all in a few lines of dialogue (see Figure 3.3).

At the centre of this interaction lies a critical tension between playfulness and precarity. While *nomadic languaging* invites a sense of playfulness, fluidity, and creativity, Mongolian nomadic herdsmen also assert their cultural and linguistic boundaries – boundaries shaped by the historical and ongoing precarity they navigate. Their openness to accept external linguistic and cultural resources, such as Korean and English, is not without condition: these influences are welcome only

Figure 3.3 Mongolian nomadic herders
(Photo by Sender Dovchin)

## 3.5 The Story of a Weeping Camel

when approached with respect for existing nomadic knowledge systems. In this way, nomadic herdsmen's playful voices are not merely spontaneous – they are also acts of cultural stewardship (Dovchin, (2025a)). Through such everyday interactions, they safeguard their intangible heritage, resisting the erosion of their knowledge systems and protecting their nomadic culture from future precarity (see Table 3.3).

There is a well-known documentary, *The Story of the Weeping Camel*, which was nominated for an Oscar (St Ours, 2011). The film portrays the ancient nomadic ritual of *khoos* – a practice where herders use music to make a mother camel "weep" and accept her rejected calf. Nomadic herdsmen begin talking about this ritual, and the playful mood gradually shifts into a softer, more sombre tone as the conversation slows, marked by heavy pauses. Khongor begins to explain what *nomadic languaging* truly means to him, describing how their

Table 3.3 *Khoos*

| Line | Speaker and dialogue |
|---|---|
| 1. | Khongor: *Er ni bol mania nuudelchin Mongolchuud tavan hoshuu maltaigaa l amidarlaa shuud holboj irsen. Giingoo mori gehed inge hoosloh temeend geed l. Inge hooslohiin jishee ni bid maltaigaa gants ug yaria heleer bish duu, huur, hugjimeer hurdeg. Ene chini l nuudelchin Mongolchuudiin hel shuu dee.* (Generally, we nomadic Mongolians have always connected our lives closely with our five jewels referring to five types of livestock. Whether it's *Giingoo* for horses or *Khoos* for camels – it's not just words that connect us with our animals, but also through songs, melodies, and tunes. That's the true language of nomadic Mongolians.) |
| 2. | Dorj: *Tiim shuu. Gobi yavbal inge hooslohiig harah heregtei shuu. Ene saihan ulamjilalaa bid hadgalah heregtei.* (That's right. If you go to the Gobi, you must see how they do the *Khoos*. But we must protect and document it because it is an oral tradition.) |
| 3. | Sender: *Hoosolhod duuldag bil uu?* (Do they sing during the *Khoos*?) |
| 4. | Dorj: *Hoos Hoos* (mimicking hoos) *geel duulna tiin.* (Yes, they sing like "*khoos khoos*" (mimicking the sound).) |
| 5. | Khongor: *Ih uruvdmuur shuu dee. Botgoo golood tegeed morin huur sonsood nulims unagaagaad tegeed botgoo amluuldag* (deep sigh). (It is very heartbreaking to watch. Rejecting the baby camel and then listen to *morin khuur* and then weep and then accept the baby camel.) |
| 6. | Dorj: *Aaan yarihgui. Khooslono gedeg chini zuvhun Mongold shuudee. Temee mash uruvch amitan gej baigaa.* (Yeah, tell me about it. *Khoos* is only in Mongolia. Nowhere else. Camels are extremely smart animals with warm heart (mood shifts to sombre tone).) |

language has always been intertwined with their livestock, referencing *giingoo* and *khoos* as examples (line 1). Here, Khongor describes how, after painful labour, a mother camel can become traumatised and may reject its newborn calf – refusing to nurse or bond with it. The calf, helpless and confused, cries out while the mother remains unresponsive. In such cases, nomadic herders often turn to a traditional *khoos* ritual – an ancient ceremonial practice that involves music and spiritual care. A local musician is invited to perform the *morin khuur* (horse-headed fiddle) – a traditional Mongolian musical instrument central to nomadic life. As the melodic sounds of the *morin khuur* play in the air, a female camel herder performs a special singing ritual called *khoos*. The purpose of this ritual is to move the mother camel emotionally, evoking compassion and recognition of her calf. Remarkably, the mother often begins to weep real tears and eventually accepts and nurses her baby (St Ours, 2011). The *Khoos* ritual – also known as *khoos*, *khooslokh*, or *inge khooslokh* – is now inscribed on the UNESCO Intangible Cultural Heritage List, recognising its cultural and spiritual significance. When Khongor recalls this ritual, he draws a powerful connection to *nomadic languaging* – a linguistic practice that extends beyond words. It is a play of sound, emotion, healing affect, melody, and relational attunement. In this context, language is not only spoken – it is sung, felt, and lived. The *Khoos* ritual reflects a deeply respectful relationship between humans, animals, and the land. It highlights how Mongolian nomadic knowledge systems are embodied and multisensory, relying on music, harmony, tune, and affect as essential communication tools. When I clarify if they sing during the *khoos* ritual (line 3), Dorj's response is – "*Yes, they sing like 'khoos khoos*'," mimicking the sound of "*khoos*" in a performative and embodied way, which creates a playful moment of shared amusement (line 4) (see Figure 3.4).

Meanwhile, while the interaction appears playful and performative on the surface, it also carries deep precarity, both sociolinguistic and existential. When Dorj (line 2) mentions that "*we must protect and document it because it is an oral tradition*" in reference to *khoos*, he refers to the precarious condition that *khoos* exists within an environment that is constantly under threat, not only in terms of use but also survival. *Khoos*, and by extension other nomadic oral rituals, is a fragile verbal and linguistic form – often passed down orally, not institutionalised, and rarely documented. With urban migration and displacement, the knowledge and context needed to perform *khoos* are at risk of fading. This verbal nomadic tradition is, thus, precarious in its transmission, existing only in lived and embodied practice. The singing of *khoos* is

## 3.5 The Story of a Weeping Camel

Figure 3.4 Ингэ хөөслөх (Demonstrating *khoos-ing the camels*) (Photo by Sender Dovchin)

usually performed by female camel herders and is ephemeral – it lives in the moment, in voice, gesture, and atmosphere. This means it cannot be easily archived or commodified, as its survival depends on ongoing practice, making it precariously poised between continuity and erasure. *Khoos*, or any other nomadic oral rituals, while appearing playful and simple, is layered with precarity rooted in ecological, cultural, gendered, and communicative fragility. Its beauty lies in its embeddedness in nomadic life, but that same embeddedness also exposes it to its disappearance amid shifting social, economic, and climatic landscapes. Recognising this precious side deepens our understanding of *nomadic knowledging* and *nomadic languaging* not just as language but as a site of care and survival.

As the conversation unfolds, the ground of their dialogue becomes precarious. What begins in a casual tone gradually shifts into a heavier, sombre mood. The herders are not only talking about camels – but they are also indirectly reflecting on the fragility of their cultural heritage. The ritual of *khoos* itself embellishes precariousness: a calf's life hangs in the balance, just as the nomadic way of life and its practices hang under the pressures of displacement, modernisation, and social change. By situating the practice in this way, their talk moves into a space where cultural survival becomes as vulnerable as the rejected calf. Dorj's response highlights this tension.

By insisting that "Khoos *is only in Mongolia*" and praising camels as "*extremely smart animals with warm hearts*," he raises a *precarious voice* that both defends and affirms cultural uniqueness. His voice carries a protective quality, asserting identity in the face of potential loss.

Khongor's voice is fragile and affect-laden, saturated with sighs and sombre tones that carry grief, exhaustion, and cultural vulnerability. Rather than the polished, coherent voice often privileged in multilingual research, his expression resonates with what Butler (2004) terms the "conditions of precarity," where voice itself becomes a register of exposure. These fragile vocalisations recall Bakhtin's (1984, 1986) reminder that voices are not merely rational but can be disruptive, affective, and resistant. Though Khongor does not employ the grotesque in the form of cursing or swearing, his sighs destabilise expectations of authoritative voice, embodying instead what Phipps (2019) describes as the ethical entanglements of precarious communication. At the same time, Khongor's fragile tones are dialogic, resonating with others in a shared soundscape of precariousness. As Dovchin (2024a) argues, precarious voices often emerge relationally, articulating grief, pride, and resilience all at once. His sighs thus exceed the personal, rendering audible the socio-political conditions of exclusion and linguistic injustice (Dryden et al., 2021). Attending to such fragile voices shifts focus away from the dominance of playfulness in studies of translingual practices and towards the affective, resistant, and embodied dimensions of languaging. Khongor's voice, then, not only communicates but enacts – insisting that sighs, tones, and silences must also be recognised as vital expressions of life lived under precarious conditions. Together, nomadic voices articulate a shared precariousness – expressing grief, pride, and cultural vulnerability all at once.

Overall, we see how nomadic herders' *nomadic languaging* – the blending of words, gestures, and embodied affect – makes sense of their world. In Khongor's narration of the ritual of *khoos*, his utterance is punctuated by a "deep sigh," a form of languaging that goes beyond words. The sigh carries the weight of heartbreak, signalling empathy not only for the calf but also for the fragile bond between human, animal, and tradition. Through this affective performance, language becomes a way of reliving the ritual, not merely describing it. We witness how *nomadic languaging* is used not only to describe but to *embody* emotion, how conversations take place on precarious cultural grounds, and how voices emerge that are simultaneously fragile and resistant. In mourning for a camel and celebrating a ritual, Khongor, and Dorj reveal how deeply entangled language, culture, and precarity are in the lived realities of nomadic herders.

## 3.5 The Story of a Weeping Camel

### 3.5.1 English in Nomadic Languaging: An Intruder or an Ally?

During the nomadic reminiscing, one of our main themes was the role of English and its impact on nomadic people and their children. The key idea was that nomadic people welcome English, as they have always been open to different cultures and languages, though with certain boundaries. This ambivalent stance – at once welcoming and guarded – speaks directly to the question posed in the title, *English in Nomadic Languaging: An Intruder or an Ally?* For nomadic communities, English is not simply imposed as an intruder, nor is it uncritically embraced as an ally; rather, it is positioned within a relational framework where its value depends on the respect it shows for nomadic knowledge systems. In this sense, English becomes both a potential resource and a potential threat, its role negotiated within the ethical and cultural boundaries that nomadic people themselves establish (see Table 3.4).

Ulaanaa's statement (line 1) – "*Of course, where else would we find such joy as just being here like this?*" – reflects his deep satisfaction with life as a nomadic herder. His joy comes from the simplicity and presence of daily life on the steppe, highlighting a close connection to his land and his livestock. The ease and playfulness in his words suggest that contentment in nomadic life arises not from material wealth, but from harmony with the land, community, and the practices that define his identity. The speaker's voice carries an immediacy and playfulness, emphasising delight in simple presence with laughter when he states, "*Er khunii jargal ezgui khee*" ("A real man's happiness is in the empty steppe") – quoting a traditional Mongolian proverb. The laughter signals humour and lightness, softening the assertion while emphasising joy in simplicity and solitude. The laughter also highlights the performative aspect of *nomadic languaging*, where humour and self-awareness coexist with serious cultural values, reinforcing identity while acknowledging life's challenges. Meanwhile, in the Mongolian cultural context, a "real man" (эр хүн) embodies resilience, courage, and self-reliance (Ahearn, 2018; Billé, 2014). The steppe, vast, and empty, symbolises freedom, autonomy, and a space where one can enact these masculine ideals without societal constraints. The proverb conveys that fulfillment for men is inseparable from the challenges and openness of nomadic life. Mongolian nomadic masculinity also refers to the culturally idealised traits of a "real man" shaped by the nomadic lifestyle and the legacy of the Mongol Empire (Ahearn, 2018; Billé, 2014). Rooted in the practices and values of Chinggis

## 84  3 NOMADIC LANGUAGING AND NOMADIC KNOWLEDGING

Table 3.4 *English is nomadic*

| Line | Speaker and dialogue |
| --- | --- |
| 1. | Ulaanaa: *Medeej bid nar endee ingeel baij baih shig jargal haana baihav. Er khunii jargal ezgui kheer* (laughs). *Gehdee huduunii bidnii amidral hetsuu shuu dee! Zud gej neg daisan baina. Za tegeed suuliin ued uul uurhai gej neg yum garch ireed bidniigee suiruuleed baina.* <br> (Of course, where else would we find such joy as just being here like this? The joy of a real man is in the empty steppe. But life in the steppe is tough for us. Zud (dzud) is one enemy. And now lately, this thing called mining has emerged and is destroying us. This means that our lifestyle, tradition, culture, and even language can be harmed.) |
| 2. | Khongor: *Huduunii malchid bid nar gehdee yamar ch berhsheeltei uchirsan davan tuuldag uchirtai. Manai uvug deedes deer ued Oros, Hyataduud geel darluulj irsen. Manai nuudelchidiin amidral heveeree l baigaa shuu. Chinggis Khaanii ued bol buur huchirheg guren gej yavj baisan. Mash olon hel soyol shashiniig manai khaan neg dor evtei nairtai udirdaj baisan shuu dee. Bid Chinggis Khaanii uv, surgaalig dagan murdukh uchirtai.* <br> (But we, the nomadic people of the steppe, are used to overcoming any hardship. Our ancestors lived under Russian and Chinese domination in the past. Yet the life of us nomads remain unchanged. During the time of Chinggis Khan, it was an extremely powerful empire. Our Khan ruled over many languages, cultures, and religions together in harmony. And, we should be following his legacy.) |
| 3. | Ulaanaa: *Odoo America geel. Manai zaluuchuud Angliaar Mongol helneesee iluu yaridag boljee.* <br> (Now it's America, they say. Our young people seem to speak English better than Mongolian these days.) |
| 4. | Khongor: *Manai huuhduud Angli hel surah heregtei. Gehdee Angli hel manai nutagt guadaj bish guij orj ireh yostoi shuu. Bidnii amidrald tus bolno uu gehees bid nar yu gej Angli helend guyaduulah ve, tiimee?* <br> (Our children need to learn English. But English should come here begging us, not whipping us with a stick. English should uplift our nomadic lifestyle. We should not be whipped by English, right?) |

Khan's era, it emphasises courage, resilience, and strategic skill in warfare and leadership, alongside independence, self-reliance, and mastery of the steppe environment. It also includes responsibility towards family, community, and the preservation of cultural traditions, playfulness, humour, and loyalty, reflecting the social and relational aspects of nomadic life (Gardelle & Zhao, 2019). This form of masculinity embodies both the physical and moral qualities

## 3.5 The Story of a Weeping Camel

celebrated in Mongol culture and the historic empire (Ahearn, 2018; Billé, 2014).

Yet, this playfulness is immediately unsettled by precarity. The tone shifts: "But life in the steppe is tough for us. *Zud* is one enemy. And now lately, this thing called mining has emerged and is destroying us" (line 1). Here, Ulaana names the threats, such as climate disasters and extractive industries, which destabilise not only the nomadic survival but also culture, tradition, and even language itself. Ulaanaa's statement captures environmental precarity, in which he mentions *zud* – a harsh climatic phenomenon that devastates livestock, which has long been a threat embedded in nomadic herders' life (Soma, 2025). On the other hand, the emergence of mining as a new "enemy" signals a shift from climate precarity to anthropogenic precarity, brought about by global capitalism. This extractive industry not only disrupts the physical landscape but erodes nomadic ways of being, living, and speaking, threatening the very ecology within which nomadic knowledge practices have evolved (Dovchin & Dovchin, 2024).

What emerges is a striking tension: joy in presence on one hand, vulnerability on the other. This interplay of playfulness and precarity captures the lived reality of nomadic life, where words themselves carry the weight of survival. Ulaanaa shows an act of resilience, holding together the tension between delight and danger, between continuity and the risk of loss. He also implicitly values independence and the capacity to thrive in precarity, reflecting how Mongolian nomadic culture celebrates both endurance in the face of environmental hardships (e.g., *Zud* and extractive industry) and the ability to find joy and identity through engagement with the land.

*Nomadic languaging*, which depends on situated and embodied practices, is also displaced and endangered. Khongor (line 2), in this sense, asserts the precarity of foreign colonisations through his historical reference to Russian and Chinese control of Mongolia. However, Khongor's statement also reflects a deep awareness of the fluid but adaptive resilience of the Mongolian nomadic culture, highlighting how the flexibility of *nomadic knowledging* has allowed it to survive major historical shifts such as Soviet rule and Chinese colonisation and continues to shape its response to current global transformations, such as the spread of English and the United States. Baatar acknowledges that during this precarious era, their ancestors managed to preserve essential aspects of nomadic knowledge and language while also engaging with the imposed colonial systems.

Khongor (line 2) further shifts towards a mythic past, where Chinggis Khan and his empire served as the ultimate model of strength and harmony. His rule is remembered not for conquest alone but for the capacity to unite diverse languages, cultures, and religions under a single vision, offering an image of inclusivity, law, and order (Falus, 2025). This heirloom transforms into a moral imperative: the present generation is urged to follow the Khan's legacy, positioning his leadership as both a historical truth and a guiding principle for contemporary life. The mention casts Mongolian identity as both timeless and aspirational, where survival is not just remembered but demanded of those who inherit the nomadic tradition (Falus, 2025). This historical adaptability is now being mirrored in the current era, where English is viewed as an ally that must be incorporated into the nomadic way of life. Rather than rejecting change, they accept it with the understanding that survival depends on balancing cultural preservation with openness to transformation, and English is positioned as an ally just like historical reforms in the past, and must be gradually localised to ensure the nomadic knowledge system continues to thrive in a globalised world.

However, from the nomadic herders' perspectives, they also invite English with clear boundaries, ensuring that external influences do not override or erase their traditional knowledge systems and language. As Sanduijav (2021) argues, Mongolian people find richness and satisfaction in a grounded existence, remaining calm and peaceful so long as their cattle and horses are near their dwellings. This statement aligns with Khongor's assertion (line 4), "Our children need to learn English. But English should come here begging, not whipping us with a stick. English should uplift our nomadic lifestyle. We should not be whipped by English!" He uses a Mongolian proverb, "*guyadaj bish guih*" (not whipping but begging), which often refers to the idea that persuasion and humility achieve more than force, highlighting the nomadic value placed on respectful request over coercion. There are many traditional nomadic proverbs, phrases, terms, and understandings in Mongolian that are derived from cattle and animal husbandry, deeply shaping the feelings and mentality of nomadic herders (Sanduijav, 2021). The proverb "*guyadaj bish guih*" is part of this linguistic ecology: it draws metaphorical force from the everyday practices of tending to animals, especially horses, where control through violence is seen as less effective than a gentle approach. Just as a herder coaxes

## 3.5 The Story of a Weeping Camel

a horse with patience and care rather than constant whipping, so too does this proverb emphasise persuasion, humility, and respectful communication over coercion (Dovchin, 2025a). In this way, the proverb not only encodes nomadic knowledge but also reveals how Mongolian nomadic herders map the ethics of human–animal relations onto broader social interactions (Sanduijav, 2021).

In a similar vein, another Mongolian nomadic herder, Perliijantsan, explains that they do not resist English but rather welcome it, especially for their children, for its fluidity to transmit and elevate nomadic knowledge. As Perliijantsan, a nomadic sheep herder, explains,

> We want our children to learn English. But English should flow with our stories, oral traditions and ways of telling stories. We don't believe English is a language from outside. It becomes part of how we share our stories, our wisdom, and how we live and travel. Just like our folk tales, proverbs, and oral stories which carry our history, English can help us to continue our voice without changing who we are.

Perliijantsan accepts English to expand their nomadic way of life. He desires English to be intertwined with the *nomadic knowledging system* that is inseparable from the nomadic resilience. Just as storytelling and other nomadic traditions serve as vital tools for a complex web of *nomadic languaging*, rather than being an externally imposed intruder, English is welcomed as a complementary resource that enhances *nomadic languaging*, thereby enhancing their children's capacity to adapt, communicate, and assert their identity (Dovchin, (2025a)). In this context, while *nomadic languaging* is fluid, resilient, and playful, it also becomes a form of cautious negotiation, not free-flowing hybridity. This is a *contextual rootedness* – an insistence on protecting core elements of their language and identity – a direct response to the precarity they live with daily (Dovchin, (2025a)). English is positioned as subordinate, requiring humility to their "land," by extension to their culture and language. This dynamic highlights a critical tension: emphasis on fluidity confronts the nomads' intentional preservation of boundaries. Such a stance resonates with critiques of deconstructivist models of languaging (MacSwan & Rolstad, 2024), which often overlook the protective role of linguistic borders in sustaining minoritised and land-rooted languages. Importantly, these boundaries should not be mistaken for linguistic purism or standardisation; rather, they are vital expressions of cultural sovereignty and land-based epistemology. *Nomadic languaging*, therefore, is best understood not as unrestricted mobility but as a situated practice that combines fluidity with rootedness. It represents a mode of linguistic movement that remains accountable to land, where boundaries safeguard knowledge and serve a protective, rather than exclusionary, function. *Nomadic languaging* is understood not as wholly open-ended mobility or unrestricted *languaging*. From this view, *nomadic languaging* is not simply a celebration of linguistic fluidity or playfulness. It is a strategic and sometimes defensive practice shaped by a deep awareness of what is at stake: the risk of cultural and linguistic erasure and the decline of ancestral knowledge (Dovchin, 2025a).

Overall, for Mongolian nomadic herdsmen, English is neither simply an intruder nor an unquestioned ally; rather, it is positioned within a relational framework where its value depends on the humility it shows towards *nomadic knowledging* systems. This perspective aligns with the notion of *linguistic hospitality* (Ricoeur, 2007), where the welcome of another language is contingent on reciprocity and respect, rather than domination. In the context of Mongolian pastoral life, such relationality is deeply rooted in the ethics of herding, where human–animal relations are based not on force but on careful negotiation, patience, and mutual attunement (Fernández-Giménez, 2000; Humphrey & Sneath, 1999). Within this framework, English is not rejected outright, nor embraced without question, but is subjected to what Canagarajah (2013) calls the *negotiated practice* of linguistic diversity – adapted, localised, and re-embedded into cultural life. For nomadic communities, this means English can only thrive if it enters respectfully, without erasing the authority of the Mongolian language and pastoral knowledge. As Phipps (2019) reminds us, decolonising multilingualism requires sensitivity to the ethical boundaries communities themselves set, rather than imposing external hierarchies of value. In this light, the role of English is precarious: it becomes meaningful only when it acknowledges and coexists with the epistemic traditions of the steppe. Thus, English is not cast as an enemy of nomadic life, nor idealised as its saviour. It is instead continuously negotiated within the ethical and cultural boundaries that nomadic people establish, much like a new horse in the herd, accepted only once it learns to move in rhythm with the others. This positioning underscores that the survival of nomadic knowledge systems in a globalised world depends not on resisting English, but on ensuring that English itself learns humility in the face of nomadic wisdom.

## 3.6 IMPLICATIONS FOR APPLIED LINGUISTICS

Scholars in current debates on decolonising higher education research and teaching have started highlighting the fact that decolonisation requires engaging with knowledge systems articulated through multiple languages and shaped by diverse worldviews. They advocate for the repositioning frameworks such as *translanguaging* towards *transknowledging* – the movement between different epistemological systems (Andrews et al., 2023; Song & Lin, 2025). In line with this argument, we need to ask ourselves: What would applied linguistics look like if it practically integrated *nomadic knowledging* and *nomadic languaging* into its frameworks for curriculum design, assessment, research practices, and teacher education? To operationalise these ideas within the field requires not just incremental change but a paradigm shift – one that moves away from decontextualised, standardised, and universalist models towards relational, fluid, and culturally rooted approaches. *Nomadic knowledging*, rooted in nomadic traditions, land-based practices, and interspecies relationships, offers rich epistemological resources that are often overlooked in mainstream applied linguistics. Similarly, *nomadic languaging*, with its emphasis on fluid and performative communication, challenges narrow definitions of linguistic purity and proficiency. Rather than treating language as neutral code or a disembodied system to be mastered, *nomadic languaging* views language as situated and embedded in local ecologies and ways of nomadic life. In practice, this means that curricula shaped by such perspectives would centre local cultural practices and knowledge systems – not as supplementary or exotic context, but as foundational sites of meaning making. Nomadic reminiscing, storytelling, traditional vocal practices such as *giingoo* and *khoos*, seasonal migration narratives, and ecological knowledge could serve not only as context but content for linguistic inquiry and language development. *Nomadic languaging* practices would be validated as legitimate modes of communication, rather than dismissed as interference.

Assessment frameworks would likewise need to be reimagined. Standardised metrics and universal benchmarks often marginalise learners and speakers who engage in non-normative but deeply meaningful linguistic practices (Castillo-Montoya & Madriaga, 2025; Steele et al., 2022). Alternatives such as narrative performance, storytelling, community-based evaluation, and land-based literacies would offer more culturally responsive and ethically rooted ways to assess linguistic competence, while also honouring cultural sovereignty and diversity. As Ochir, a nomadic horseman, notes, "Our nomadic tradition has oral traditions which cannot be replaced or translated by any other language [...]. That's why it is essential for our children to teach English, which can explain our nomadic traditions, such as 'айраг бүлэх, гэр барих, дээл оёх'. We could never replace these nomadic traditions in English." For Ochir, teaching English and assessing English learners is not about replacing nomadic traditions but about better reflecting the nomadic children's lived experience and cultural sovereignty. Assessment should recognise how English can serve as a complementary tool that helps children express these practices within their cultural contexts. This approach acknowledges that meaning is inseparable from land, relationships, and culture and that linguistic assessment must honour these connections to truly capture nomadic children's competencies. English is thus reimagined not as a universal standard but as a flexible resource that supports nomadic knowledge without displacing it.

Applied linguistics must also inform teacher education and professional development with a strong foundation in critical language awareness, cultural humility, and land-based perspectives (Back et al., 2025). Teachers and researchers alike should be equipped to co-design language learning experiences with communities, drawing on local knowledges, oral traditions, and folk genres. This entails resisting deficit models that portray nonstandard varieties or rural and remote learners as lacking and instead adopting strength-based approaches that recognise the linguistic and cultural richness these learners bring (Chen & Buckingham, 2025). Furthermore, research in applied linguistics must reckon with its own role in reproducing epistemic hierarchies (Andrews et al., 2023; Song & Lin, 2025). Embracing *nomadic languaging* requires epistemic reflectivity and a commitment to collaborative, participatory, and community-led methodologies. Language is not merely an object of study but a living, relational practice shaped by land, history, and identity. As such, research must be embedded within and accountable to the communities it engages, contributing to their resilience and cultural continuity rather than extracting knowledge from them (Andrews et al., 2023; Song & Lin, 2025).

Ultimately, welcoming *nomadic knowledging* and *nomadic languaging* into applied linguistics is not about romanticising tradition or rejecting dominant languages (Song & Lin, 2025). It is about reimaging applied linguistics as a space of respect, responsiveness, and relationality. Dominant languages like English must be positioned not as default mediums of power but as allies – accepted only when they

## 3.6 Implications for Applied Linguistics

enter with humility and in accordance with ethical terms set by local communities. This vision offers a transformative approach to applied linguistics – one that supports linguistic justice, affirms cultural identity, and promotes more equitable and inclusive ways of teaching, learning, and researching language in a rapidly changing world.

# 4  Racialised Languaging

## 4.1  SOFIA VERGARA AND THE ELLEN SHOW

Sofia Vergara is a Colombian–American actress best known for her role as Gloria in the ABC sitcom *Modern Family*. Her Colombian Spanish accent, when speaking English, is often portrayed as a source of playfulness, humour, sensuality, or comic relief (Casillas et al., 2018; Ruiz, 2025). In *Modern Family*, her character's accent is exaggerated to highlight her "foreignness" and is frequently tied to stereotypes of being fiery, emotional, loud, and overly passionate. A notable example of this portrayal appears on *The Ellen DeGeneres Show* (TheEllenShow, 2023), where her co-star Julie Bowen mockingly imitates Vergara's accent. Ellen adds to the mockery by joking that Vergara's accent has *"gotten worse and worse over the years,"* followed by, "*I can barely understand you.*" The audience erupts into laughter, reinforcing the humour at Vergara's expense and highlighting how her act is used as a joke and mockery (TheEllenShow, 2023).

At first glance, these moments may seem like harmless, playful banter. Vergara speaks in her authentic voice, while her co-star performs a parodied version of her speech, accompanied by Ellen's joking remarks about her accent – all of which are met with audience laughter. This is a classic example of *playful languaging*, where language is used creatively and humorously to entertain or build rapport, often through exaggerated and caricatured speech styles and parodies to highlight difference for humourous effect (Ghajarieh et al., 2024; Theodoropoulou, 2021). Yet, there is a darker and more precarious side to this. Many YouTube commentors for this interaction between Ellen and Sofia expressed their discomfort and frustration, highlighting the racism embedded in such humour. When influential White figures like Ellen – backed by predominantly White audiences – mock the accents of racialised individuals on globally viewed media platforms, it reinforces harmful stereotypes about people of colour whose

## 4.1 Sofía Vergara and the Ellen Show

first language is not English (Casillas et al., 2018; Ruiz, 2025). As Casillas et al. (2018, p. 65) describe:

> For white, English-speaking audiences of ABC, the sound of Vergara's accented English and her lack of command of American idioms ("mixing pot" in lieu of "melting pot") works to vocally distance Gloria from SAE (referring to Standard American English) and notions of whiteness. In the process, Gloria's vocal body – accented English, Spanish outbursts, language errors, and "screaming" – crafts her as foreign, as an immigrant, and ultimately as Latina and funny. Gloria's linguistic stumbles with words and phrases often prompt audience laughter directed, at times, solely at her. Both social psychologists and sociolinguists remind us that "laughing with" serves as a form of agreement, whereas "laughing at" signals hostility [...].

Vergara herself has publicly spoken about how her accent limits her career opportunities. In one interview, she remarks, "I'm always looking for characters because there is not much that I can play with this stupid accent. I can't play a scientist or be in *Schindler's List*" (Garvey, 2024). While said with a touch of humour, her words reflect a harsh precarity; despite her English fluency and fame, Vergara is repeatedly cast in roles that reinforce narrow Latinx stereotypes – the maid, the migrant wife, the comic relief – rather than the doctor or lawyer. This stereotypical depiction of Latina women or Latinidad has been pervasive throughout Hollywood films and television, shaping societal judgements, prejudices, and misrepresentations of Latinas (Cortés, 2025; Gallegos, 2012). Latinidad refers to the shared cultural, social, and political identity of Latin American people or those of Latin American descent, encompassing diverse nationalities, traditions, and experiences (Gallegos, 2012). Terms such as "fiery," "spicy," and "lustful" have become closely associated with Latinidad, leading to Latina actresses – like Sofía Vergara – being frequently typecast as characters who are promiscuous, manipulative, or driven by deceitful motives (Cortés, 2025; Gallegos, 2012). Despite her fluency in English, Vergara is frequently portrayed – implicitly or explicitly – as linguistically deficient. Her pronunciation, use of idioms, and grammar are often mocked, including by her co-stars and in public TV interviews.

From this perspective, in Vergara's case, the portrayal reinforces long-standing racialised stereotypes of the "*hot Latina*," where her accent becomes a central symbol of an exoticised and hypersexualised persona. Her accent is not treated as a neutral linguistic trait: rather, it is interpreted as a racialised marker – a mechanism through which her identity is stereotyped, exoticised, and commodified in the mainstream media (Dumlao & Willoughby, 2024). This depiction perpetuates the idea that people of colour remain perpetual outsiders, regardless of how successful, talented, and accomplished they may be (Casillas et al., 2018; Ruiz, 2025). For Vergara, global celebrity status does not shield her from being reduced to an accent which functions as a metonym for her race, ethnicity, and presumed foreignness. This exemplifies the core of *racialised languaging* – the understanding that it is not only *what* is said, but *who* is saying it and *how* they are racially perceived that shapes how their language is heard, interpreted, and judged. This exemplifies the core of *racialised languaging* – the understanding that it is not only *what* is said, but *who* is saying it and *how* they are racially perceived that shapes how their language is heard, interpreted, and judged. In this sense, *racialised languaging* is not simply about the language practices of racialised individuals, but about the broader social processes through which language becomes entangled with race and power. It is an interactional phenomenon that occurs when listeners and institutions impose racial meanings onto speech, accents, or linguistic behaviours. Thus, while racialised individuals may be positioned as the ones "doing" the languaging, the racialisation itself emerges through societal perceptions, hierarchies, and listening practices that construct some speakers as deficient or foreign and others as normative (Anya, 2016; Dovchin, 2025c; Flores & Rosa 2015; Grammon, 2025; May, 2023; Rosa & Flores 2017; Smith, 2025; Wang & Dovchin, 2023). Racialised individuals are consistently constructed as linguistically deficient, irrespective of their actual language proficiency. Central to this is *native speakerism*, an ideology that grants linguistic authority to White English speakers and idealises their Standard English varieties (Jenks & Lee, 2020). Conversely, English varieties spoken by people of colour are often racialised and pathologised. In this context, the implicit question "What colour is your English?" captures how language becomes a site of racial judgement (Creese & Kambere, 2003). This reflects a White gaze, where White listeners interpret the speech of non-White speakers as deviant, while White speakers' linguistic practices are normalised and valorised, reinforcing racial hierarchies through language (Flores & Rosa, 2015).

This chapter focuses on *racialised languaging* – a concept that highlights how linguistic practices are never evaluated in isolation from the bodies, identities, and social contexts of language users. As mentioned earlier, it is not only *what* is said but *who* is speaking and *how* they are racialised and *how* society listens that determines whether their language is valued or devalued. *Racialised languaging* refers to the process by which certain ways of speaking, writing, interacting, or

## 4.1 Sofia Vergara and the Ellen Show

signing are interpreted through racially embodied lenses and used to marginalise, stereotype, or exclude particular individuals or communities. It reveals how language becomes a site of racial meaning-making – where the accents, dialects, or speech patterns of racialised speakers are constructed as inferior, humorous, deficient, or even criminal, while similar features in White speakers may be normalised, celebrated, or excused (Anya, 2016; Dovchin, 2025c; Flores & Rosa, 2015; Grammon, 2025; May, 2023; Rosa & Flores, 2017; Smith, 2025; Wang & Dovchin, 2023). In this sense, *racialised languaging* does not contradict the earlier, emancipatory notion of *languaging* as a creative, fluid, and agentive act of meaning-making. Rather, it extends it by exposing the unequal social conditions under which languaging occurs. While *languaging* emphasises the agency of speakers to make meaning across linguistic boundaries, *racialised languaging* foregrounds how those same practices are differently valued and policed depending on the speaker's racial positioning. Thus, the concept highlights the tension between the liberatory potential of languaging and the racialised hierarchies that constrain whose languaging is legitimised, understood, or heard.

*Racialised languaging* highlights how linguistic practices are embedded within a colonial matrix of power, where Western norms – including Western languages like English – are positioned as superior to non-Western languages, and White racial identities are privileged over non-White identities (Cioè-Peña, 2022; Flores & Rosa, 2015; Rosa & Flores, 2017). This colonial legacy persists in contemporary postcolonial Anglophone contexts, where institutional and interpersonal discourses continue to advantage White, monolingual English speakers while marginalising non-White speakers (Cioè-Peña, 2022; Dovchin, 2020; May 2023; Wang & Dovchin, 2023). These patterns are evident in settler-colonial contexts. In Australia, for example, it is difficult to separate language from racialisation among Aboriginal communities, as varieties such as Aboriginal English, Standard Australian English, Kriol, and traditional languages interact with physical markers like skin colour to shape how others respond negatively to them (Tankosić et al., 2024). Similarly, in New Zealand, the settler-colonial legacy continues to marginalise te reo Māori and its speakers, particularly through resistance by older White New Zealanders who uphold English monolingualism and oppose efforts to establish a bilingual society encompassing both English and te reo Māori (May, 2023). In US schools, African American students are subjected to *racialised languaging*, where their use of Black Language is systematically policed, corrected, and silenced. This enforces White Mainstream English as the norm, marginalises Black linguistic practices, and perpetuates linguistic violence and dehumanisation, showing how language becomes a site for enforcing racial hierarchies (Baker-Bell, 2020). In Australia and Canada, Asian international students experience *racialised languaging*, where their linguistic practices are judged against colonial language norms such as Standard Australian English or English/French. They are often pressured to Anglicise their names and adapt their speech to satisfy White listeners, while even high proficiency in English may be devalued through backhanded compliments or intrusive questioning. These practices reveal how language is used to enforce racial hierarchies and marginalise Asian students, devaluing their linguistic skills despite their competence (Dovchin, 2020; Dovchin & Dryden, 2022; Kubota et al., 2023; Piller, 2016; Tavares, 2024).

*Racialised languaging*, however, is more complex than a simple binary between White-dominated societies and migrants or Indigenous peoples, as it can also occur within communities of the same racial group. For instance, in South Korea, racism is not solely based on traditional White/Colour distinctions but also on linguistic differences among people who share an Asian racial identity. Asian-background migrants and North Korean refugees, who often resemble South Koreans, are sometimes marginalised due to accented speech and other specific linguistic features, which are interpreted as markers of inherent traits or behaviours. This illustrates that language can function as a site of racialised exclusion even within the same racial group, underscoring the role of linguistic practices in maintaining social hierarchies (Ryu & Kang, 2024).

A similar pattern is evident in Norway, where Polish migrants – the country's largest migrant group – can be both highly visible and simultaneously overlooked, particularly in integration policies such as language courses (Olszewska & Opsahl, 2024). Proficiency in Norwegian, often framed as essential for professional success, can serve to include or exclude individuals from workplace opportunities. Polish migrants' experiences are closely linked to the fluid construct of Whiteness and the recognition that "migrant" is not a value-neutral descriptor of border-crossing. In Norway, Polish migrants are sometimes subjected to *"gray racialisation,"* whereby their appearance and language are perceived as not conforming to normative expectations of being an "authentic" Norwegian. Whiteness is understood along a spectrum of "different shades of whiteness" (Moore, 2013) and *racialised languaging* operates not only through language but also through the intersection of identity, appearance, and social perception (Olszewska & Opsahl, 2024).

## 4.1 Sofia Vergara and the Ellen Show

The tension between *playfulness* and *precarity in racialised languaging* will also be explored in this chapter. While racialised individuals and communities often engage in linguistic play – drawing on diverse semiotic repertoires, accents, speech styles, dialects, and vernaculars – this play is not equally valued across racial lines. For speakers of colour, such linguistic play can mark them as deficit, contributing to a range of discriminatory practices, including accentism (Dovchin & Dryden, 2022; Roessel et al., 2020), native speakerism (Jenks & Lee, 2020), dialectism (Watt, 2025) – all of which are deeply racialised and tied to unequal access to education, employment, and well-being. These dynamics reflect the systemic precarity embedded in *racialised languaging*, where non-White speakers are continually measured against normative White linguistic standards. Their dynamic and sophisticated languaging practices are often reframed as problematic; even when these practices involve humour, creativity, they are not necessarily recognised as a sign of intelligence or resourcefulness. Instead, they are racialised, marked, and devalued (Dovchin, 2020; Wang & Dovchin, 2023). Various studies indicate that the cognitive abilities of racialised subjects are frequently questioned based on their English proficiency. Speakers of nonstandard or accented English are often perceived as less intelligent, slower, or deficient, and their language is framed as indicative of communication problems or cognitive shortcomings (Clément & Gardner, 2001). In this way, the linguistic competence of racialised individuals is frequently cast alongside notions of "disability" by White listening subjects. This intersection between ableism and linguicism is explored through the lens of Crip Linguistics, which examines how societal perceptions of disability or embodied deficits can contribute to the rhetoric of linguistic disorder (Henner & Robinson, 2023). *Racialised languaging*, therefore, functions to legitimise or delegitimise language performance, categorising some speakers as "normal" and others as "defective," often at the expense of marginalised individuals. This perspective highlights how racialised and linguistic hierarchies intersect with assumptions about cognitive ability, reinforcing social and epistemic inequalities. For example, a Mongolian child newly arrived in Australia had his English proficiency questioned by teachers due to slower responses and was recommended for "speech therapy," as his language was interpreted as deficient (Dovchin & Wang, 2024). Similarly, African American Vernacular English (AAVE) has been racialised and mischaracterised as ungrammatical, with speakers assumed to be cognitively limited; for instance, the uninflected "be" in AAVE led some psycholinguists to question speakers' capacity for abstract grammatical reasoning

(Canagarajah, 2023a). These cases illustrate how racialised judgements of language intersect with assumptions about intelligence and ability, reinforcing systemic hierarchies and marginalisation through linguistic practices.

While play and playfulness are present in social interactions, they often operate as a masquerade, masking the structural precarity and tangible harms experienced by racialised speakers. Acts of laughter, mimicry, and mockery do not neutralise the underlying damage; in many cases, they exacerbate harm, particularly when shaped by existing power imbalances between dominant and marginalised groups. *Racialised languaging* is therefore not simply playful or harmless – it constitutes a socially precarious practice, deeply embedded in the intersections of race, racism, and language. The seemingly playful elements of speech can reproduce stereotypes, reinforce marginalisation, and maintain hierarchies of power, even when enacted casually or unintentionally. In the following section, I explore how playful *racialised languaging* becomes precarious when performed by racialised subjects themselves, examining the ways in which humour, linguistic play, wordplay, laughter, and linguistic creativity intersect with social vulnerability, identity negotiation, and structural inequities.

## 4.2 PLAYFUL NAMES, PRECARIOUS OUTCOMES

As I stepped into the classroom, I noticed that nearly half of the students were international – young people from China, Mongolia, India, and other parts of the world who had come to study in Australia. But what immediately stood out was that every one of them had adopted an English name. Despite their diverse cultural backgrounds, they all monolingually introduced themselves in English as "John," "Kevin," "Emily," and so on. Curious, I turned to one student and asked, "What's your real name in Chinese?" He hesitated before replying, "*You won't be able to pronounce it. It's too hard. Please call me John.*" I responded gently, "*I want to try. English is my second language, too. My real name is Sender Dovchin – I've never changed it into English.*" After a pause, he said, "*Hai!*" The classroom burst into laughter and teased him, "*Hi, Hai!*" I stopped the moment. "*That's not funny!*" I said. "*Your name is beautiful. What does it mean?*" As he shared the meaning, "*it means Ocean. My grandad gave this name to me because he had never seen the Ocean in his life and it was his dream to see the Ocean,*" the room quieted. The laughter faded. The mood shifted from amusement to reflection. I told my students, "*You don't have to change your real, beautiful names. Instead, we*

## 4.2 Playful Names, Precarious Outcomes

*should all make the effort to learn and honour one another's names – and their meanings."*

This interaction, while seemingly started playfully at the beginning, revealed a more precarious layer of meaning. Later, through my own research on *linguistic racism* (Dovchin, 2022, 2025c; Dovchin & Dryden, 2022), and others' works (Biernat et al., 2024; Kubota et al., 2023; Lahiri-Roy et al., 2021; Mena, 2024; Russell, 2022), I have come to see that playful renaming practices are never just play. This name play often comes at a cost – the degradation of one's identity, the silencing of one's birth name, by extension, linguistic diversity, and the normalisation of linguistic hierarchies (Biernat et al., 2024; Kubota et al., 2023; Lahiri-Roy et al., 2021; Mena, 2024; Russell, 2022). Extending this, research on moral decision-making in intergroup contexts demonstrates that the stakes of name Anglicisation go beyond social playfulness or convenience. Experimental studies show (Zhao & Biernat, 2018a, b) that Anglicising ethnic names can shape life-and-death judgements, with White American participants more willing to assist Asian or Arab immigrants who adopt Anglicised names than those who retain their ethnic names, but were less likely to help those with original ethnic names. This means that renaming practices are embedded in broader structures of linguistic racism, where decisions about whose lives are valued and whose are marginalised hinge, in part, on the perceived legibility of one's name (Zhao & Biernat, 2018).

Lahiri-Roy et al. (2021) highlight the significance of names and naming practices in higher education, particularly in multicultural classrooms. Students from non-English-speaking backgrounds, such as Chinese international students, frequently adopt anglicised names – like "Jack" or "Lucy" – to accommodate perceived linguistic limitations of their lecturers or peers. Students may offer alternative names before their full names are even recorded by a teacher, reflecting a pre-emptive adjustment to avoid mispronunciation or embarrassment. Similarly, lecturers may inadvertently reinforce these practices by accepting anglicised names without learning the correct pronunciation, signalling a subtle form of cultural erasure. These renaming practices are situated within broader issues of *racialised languaging* and cultural expectation, where students must navigate multiple language-rich contexts while adapting to discussion-based pedagogies in Australian higher education. One student reported that mispronunciation of their name in class caused embarrassment not only for themselves but also for their parents, highlighting the intergenerational and cultural implications of naming. While some students see anglicised names as practical, these adaptations can signal disrespect and marginalisation, particularly when lecturers fail to acknowledge the importance of given names (Lahiri-Roy et al., 2021). Naming thus becomes a site where social justice, diversity, and inclusion intersect, revealing tensions between students' cultural norms – such as maintaining respect and saving face – and institutional expectations. The practice of correctly learning and using students' names can support identity affirmation, foster a sense of belonging, and challenge subtle forms of linguistic and racialised marginalisation in the classroom (Lahiri-Roy et al., 2021).

Kubota et al.'s (2023) study showed that ethnic names unfamiliar in English often signal difference, which can disadvantage individuals in social and professional contexts. Ethnic names could hinder employment opportunities, echoing prior findings that racially marked names result in lower callback rates for interviews. Many people adopt Anglicised names – a practice termed "resume Whitening" (Kang et al., 2016) – to navigate systemic biases, while others resisted, viewing their names as intrinsic to their identity. Classroom interactions further illustrated the tension around naming. Supportive instructors who learned and correctly pronounced ethnic names fostered inclusion and reinforced students' sense of self, whereas impositions of Anglicised names by instructors or peers were experienced as authority over identity, racialised categorisation, and erasure of self-determined identity. Such experiences demonstrate how linguistic practices intersect with racialised assumptions, reinforcing exclusion or marginalisation (Kubota et al., 2023).

Biernat et al. (2024) highlight that names are central markers of identity, conveying cultural, gendered, and familial meaning and often forming a core aspect of self-concept. While individuals generally prefer their own names, ethnic minority group members frequently experience discrimination linked to their names. Audit studies consistently show that resumes or inquiries bearing ethnically marked names – such as African American, Arab, or Asian names – receive fewer callbacks or responses than those with White-sounding names. To navigate such bias, many adopt Anglicised or "Whitened" names, a practice known as voluntary acculturation or resume Whitening. Name Whitening can mitigate discrimination in contexts ranging from job applications to moral decision-making, particularly among observers endorsing assimilationist beliefs. However, these effects vary by ethnic group and context, with Arab immigrants showing less benefit due to prevailing stereotypes of threat. Despite potential advantages, Whitening carries psychosocial costs. Studies indicate lower self-esteem and well-being among those using anglicised names, especially

## 4.2 Playful Names, Precarious Outcomes

when adoption is externally motivated or early in acculturation. The practice may diminish racial and ethnic pride, creating tension between social acceptance and identity preservation. Alternative strategies focus on reducing discrimination without burdening minority-group members. Learning and correctly pronouncing ethnic names in educational and professional settings fosters empowerment, self-acceptance, and intercultural respect (Biernat et al., 2024). Name-learning interventions may improve dyadic interethnic interactions, enhance communication, and reduce prejudice, offering a systemic approach to *racialised languaging* (Biernat et al., 2024).

When I sat down with a group of international students to discuss about their playful English names and their real birth names, an interesting contrast emerged. While their English names often lacked meaningful connections and were chosen casually, their real names carried beautiful and significant meanings. However, the students reminded me that their real names are often racialised, prompting them to participate in *playful naming practices* – or more broadly, *playful languaging* practices. Through these playful acts, they cross linguistic boundaries, reshaping their names and, in doing so, reimagining their identities (see Table 4.1).

Biyu is an international student from China and Badambayar is from Mongolia. Biyu (line 1) explains that English renaming practices are an established "*tradition*," particularly among Chinese students. That one must *pre-emptively* choose an English name before arriving in Australia suggests a normalised practice of linguistic self-erasure to avoid misrecognition or exclusion. While this may appear playful – something as simple as picking a name that "*sounds like*" their own Chinese or Mongolian name (e.g., Barbara for Badambayar) – the underlying motive is not light-hearted. This is a strategic form of linguistic accommodation born out of fear, not freedom (Zhao & Biernat, 2018). Biyu further mentions that international teachers tend to try harder to pronounce non-Anglo names, while White Australian teachers do not (line 4). This points to a broader racialised structure of linguistic power, where the *Anglophone or White ear* is both gatekeeper and judge of what names are "acceptable" or "too difficult." Playful naming becomes a necessity when one's identity is not granted legitimacy unless it conforms to Whiteness-coded norms of clarity, brevity, and pronounceability (Rosa & Flores, 2017). Zhao & Biernat (2018); in this sense, note that although adopting Anglo names may facilitate smoother interactions with majority-group members, the practice can have adverse psychological consequences for minorities. Two studies with Chinese college students in the

Table 4.1 *My name*

| Line | Speaker and dialogue |
| --- | --- |
| 1. | Biyu: Well, there's this tradition in China – we usually choose our English name before coming to Australia. We don't want to be misunderstood by Australians. It's about showing respect and not causing any inconvenience. |
| 2. | Badambayar (laughs): Yeah, it's a "can't be bothered" situation. We just want to avoid any jokes or mockery about our names. We don't want to feel different. |
| 3. | Interviewer: Did it help you? |
| 4. | Biyu: Oh, definitely – especially in coffee shops. It makes things much easier. In classrooms with White Australian teachers, too. |
| 5. | Badambayar: Coffee shops are a nightmare (both giggle). It takes so much time and effort to use our real names in the coffee shops. So we just go with Lucy, David, whatever. |
| 6. | Interviewer: So, what's the meaning of your name, Badambayar? |
| 7. | Badambayar: It's a name given by a Buddhist monk. My dad chose it based on ancestral kinship – he believes it carries the spirit of our ancestors. |
| 8. | Interviewer: Then why did you change it to Barbara? |
| 9. | Badambayar: Just because it kind of sounds like a Mongolian name. That's all. |
| 10. | Interviewer: Do you like using your English name? |
| 11. | Badambayar: I hate it. I dream of a day I can use my real name freely – without restriction or judgement. That's my hope. I even know a Mongolian lady who changed her Mongolian name into her passports and documents. I don't want to be like that. It's humiliating. |

United States examined links between Anglo name adoption, self-esteem, and well-being. Across both studies, adopting Anglo names was negatively associated with self-esteem, which in turn mediated poorer mental and physical health outcomes. These findings highlight that while Anglo naming may be framed as a strategy of seeking belonging, it can undermine self-concept and well-being, emphasising the need for educational and intergroup interventions that validate heritage names and promote inclusive practices in language teaching (Zhao & Biernat, 2018). This negative impact on self-esteem is evident in Badambayar's reflection, where she explains that her birth name originates from a Buddhist monk and is rooted in ancestral kinship and the spirit of her forebears. However, the profound cultural significance of her name is erased within the Australian context, leaving her feeling humiliated and worthless (lines 7, 11).

## 4.2 Playful Names, Precarious Outcomes

The laughter between the discussants, especially around the context of ordering coffee, might also be misread as harmless banter (lines 4 & 5). Yet this *laughter* operates as a mask for precarity. It is laughter underpinned by anxiety, shame, and emotional labour. Badambayar's remark that "*coffee shops are a nightmare*" (line 5) highlights the cognitive and emotional labour required of minorities in navigating everyday interactions, where adopting alternative names becomes a survival tactic rather than an act of linguistic play (Kent, 2016). Similar concerns are echoed in Sayrafiezadeh's (2020) account of his name being repeatedly misspelled on coffee cups at Starbucks, an experience that, while seemingly trivial, symbolised deeper traumatic feelings of cultural otherness linked to his Iranian heritage and childhood experiences of marginalisation. Although the occasional correct rendering of his name fostered a sense of reclamation, Sayrafiezadeh's (2020) reflections on using pseudonyms such as "Steve" and "Anthony March Harris" highlight the pressures of assimilation and the identity costs of obscuring one's heritage.

This interaction illustrates how misnaming practices in mundane settings reflect broader struggles over identity, belonging, and linguistic survival in social contexts. Badambayar's strong emotional response – "*I hate it ... It's humiliating*" (line 11) – reveals the precarity of this renaming practice – negative self-esteem and racialised emotional labour. The renaming that began as playful accommodation ends in identity alienation. It is not merely a shift in labels but a profound depersonalisation, particularly when internalised to the point that others go so far as to officially alter their names in legal documents. That final example – a Mongolian woman who erased her birth name from her passport – illuminates how renaming becomes a site of linguistic precarity, where names are reshaped in response to dominant cultural and linguistic pressures. As she explains, "*I even know a Mongolian lady who changed her Mongolian name into her passports and documents. I don't want to be like that. It's humiliating*" (line 11). This sense of humiliation reflects what Kubota et al. (2023) describe as the negotiation of identities under unequal power relations, where linguistic choices are constrained rather than freely made. The erasure of a culturally embedded name from official documentation also resonates with Piller's (2016) discussion of linguistic assimilation, where minority speakers adapt to majority expectations to avoid discrimination or social exclusion. From this perspective, renaming on official documents is not simply a pragmatic adjustment but a form of linguistic and symbolic violence (Skutnabb-Kangas, 2013), as it erases ancestral, spiritual, and cultural ties embedded in names. For migrants and diasporic communities, names serve as critical markers of belonging and continuity; their forced alteration or abandonment signals the loss of recognition in public and bureaucratic spaces (Piller et al., 2024). Thus, the Mongolian woman's decision to remove her name from her passport exemplifies the profound affective consequences of linguistic racism: humiliation, worthlessness, and disconnection from cultural identity, illustrating how even administrative processes become sites of marginalisation.

Overall, this dialogue exemplifies the double-edged nature of *racialised languaging*: what begins as a coping strategy becomes a form of symbolic violence. Names – often a first and most intimate marker of identity – are reshaped, shortened, or discarded to fit into linguistic structures that do not accommodate difference. While playfulness masks these negotiations, the underlying precarity remains. This analysis suggests that playful naming among racialised communities is rarely just playful – it is a response to deeply embedded systems of linguistic racism that compel individuals to perform linguistic assimilation in exchange for social belonging. As such, even laughter carries the weight of loss and precarity.

## 4.3  RACIALISED ENGLISH/ENGLISHING

Rubin's (1992) study provides a striking example of *accent hallucination* – the phenomenon where listeners perceive a foreign or non-native accent in a speaker's English even when no such accent exists. Essentially, it is an imagined accent imposed by the listener rather than a real feature of the speaker's speech. Rubin's (1992) experiment shows how listener perceptions of speech are shaped more by social and racial expectations than by the actual linguistic input. In the experiment, undergraduate students in Florida listened to a science lecture delivered in standard American English. While the audio was identical for all participants, one group saw a photograph of a Caucasian woman and another saw a photograph of an Asian woman, both depicted in identical postures. Remarkably, students who saw the Asian lecturer reported hearing a "foreign" or "Asian" accent, even though no such accent existed. They also perceived the lecture as less comprehensible and rated its quality lower when they believed it was delivered by an Asian speaker (cf. Piller, 2016, pp. 53–54). From the perspective of accent hallucination, this demonstrates how listeners' expectations about ethnicity can override actual speech, producing imagined accents (Fought, 2006; Lippi-Green, 2012). The findings align

## 4.3 Racialised English/Englishing

with Rosa and Flores' (2017) notion of White listening subjects, in which dominant-group listeners interpret English spoken by racialised individuals through a lens shaped by Whiteness. This misperception is not harmless: it affects judgements of intelligibility, competence, and credibility, illustrating how racialised assumptions about speech can disadvantage speakers even when their language is fluent and standard. Rubin's study thus exemplifies accent hallucination as a socially constructed phenomenon, revealing the subtle yet powerful ways that racialised biases shape our listening and evaluation of English speakers.

Accent hallucination exemplifies how *racialised English* operates as a social phenomenon: it is not the linguistic output that is flawed, but the evaluative lens of listeners shaped by racialised expectations. The effect on comprehension ratings and lecture evaluations in Rubin's study illustrates the tangible consequences of racialised perceptions, reinforcing stereotypes about competence and authority based on racial identity rather than actual speech. *Racialised English*, thus, in this section, refers to instances in which a speaker's English is judged, questioned, or devalued primarily on the basis of their racial or ethnic identity, rather than their actual language proficiency or communicative competence (Cushing, 2023; Nguyen & Hajek, 2022a, b). It encompasses situations where listeners make assumptions about a person's intelligence, professionalism, or social belonging because the way they speak English deviates from the norms associated with White, middle-class speakers (Baker-Bell, 2020; Dovchin, 2024a, b, 2025c; Rosa & Flores, 2017). In my previous works on "*What Colour Is Your English?*" (Dovchin, 2020), I have argued that English spoken by people of colour is often subjected to both implicit and explicit scrutiny regarding its legitimacy or authenticity. Even highly proficient, fluent, or native speakers from non-White backgrounds are frequently perceived as "almost but not quite White" or "not quite the same" as White speakers (Baker-Bell, 2020; Dovchin, 2024a, b, 2025c; Rosa & Flores, 2017). This phenomenon, which I refer to as racialised English, extends beyond assessments of linguistic proficiency: the intelligence, work ethic, and professional skills of racialised individuals are sometimes questioned primarily because of their racial identity rather than their actual English language abilities (Cushing, 2023; Nguyen & Hajek, 2022a, b;). Racialised English highlights the ways in which social perceptions of race are projected onto language use. Speech patterns, accents, and lexical choices of non-White speakers are often measured against the norms associated with White, middle-class English speakers, who are frequently positioned as the benchmark for "standard" or "proper" English (Baker-Bell, 2020; Dovchin & Dryden, 2022). As a result, speakers of racialised English are regularly subjected to subtle forms of exclusion, marginalisation, or devaluation, even when their language proficiency is exemplary. This dynamic reflects a broader societal tendency to conflate language with identity, positioning certain forms of English as inherently more legitimate, authoritative, or professional. Other languages, dialects, or vernacular practices used by racialised speakers are often judged against these standards, creating an environment in which non-White English speakers must navigate complex pressures to conform linguistically while also maintaining their cultural and personal identities (Baker-Bell, 2020; Cioè-Peña, 2022; Rosa & Flores, 2017). Understanding racialised English thus requires attention not only to linguistic features but also to the social and racial ideologies that shape perceptions of English. It illuminates how speakers from racialised backgrounds can be linguistically and socially othered, highlighting the persistent intersections of race, language, and power in contemporary Anglophone societies. Let us visit some examples, where listeners' assumptions about a speaker's racial or ethnic identity led them to perceive deficits in English that do not exist, affecting judgements of intelligibility, competence, and credibility.

Mei, a second-generation Chinese–Australian, grew up speaking fluent Australian English at home and at school. Despite her high-level proficiency, she often encounters situations in which her English is misjudged. For example, during a group presentation at university, several classmates commented that Mei spoke with a "slight Chinese accent," even though recordings of her speech showed no accent at all. Reflecting on the experience, Mei explains: *"It's frustrating because I know I speak like everyone else, but somehow people expect me to sound 'different' just because of how I look. It makes me feel self-conscious and like I don't fully belong."* Her lecturer, aware of accent hallucination, later confirmed that her pronunciation and intonation were indistinguishable from standard Australian English. Mei's experience demonstrates racialised English in action: listeners' assumptions about her ethnic background led them to "hear" an accent that was not present. This misperception also affected how peers evaluated her communication skills, with some rating her presentation as less clear or confident. Mei's case illustrates how English spoken by a racialised speaker can be devalued based on social expectations rather than linguistic reality. Her experience shows that accent hallucination is not merely an

## 4.3 Racialised English/Englishing

abstract cognitive bias – it has tangible effects on perceived intelligibility, credibility, and academic evaluation, reinforcing systemic inequalities in multilingual and multicultural contexts.

Jarran, a young Aboriginal man from a regional community in Western Australia, grew up speaking both Kriol, his community language, and Standard Australian English (SAE) at home and school. When he moved to a boarding school in Perth for secondary education, he continued to speak and use SAE fluently in academic contexts. Despite this, he often experienced subtle biases in school settings. During classroom activities, some teachers commented that Jarran "needs to improve his English," even though his English was standard and clear. Reflecting on the incident, Jarran noted: *"I was shocked because I speak like everyone else in class, but as soon as I open my mouth, people think I sound different. It's like they can't separate how I look from how I speak."* Jarran also noticed a pattern of unfair grading from his English teacher. Regardless of how much effort he put into his written and oral assignments, he consistently received a C grade, particularly for presentations. As he explained: *"No matter how much I prepared or how well I spoke, I always got a C. It made me feel invisible, like my words didn't really count. People assumed I sounded 'different,' and that seemed to be enough for them to judge me as not good enough."* Jarran's experience exemplifies racialised English: listeners' assumptions based on his Aboriginal identity led them to perceive a nonstandard and deficit English that did not exist. This shows how English used by racialised speakers – here, an Aboriginal Australian – is often evaluated not on linguistic merit but through social and racialised expectations. These misperceptions affected both peer perception and formal academic assessment, reinforcing systemic inequities in boarding schools and illustrating the tangible impact of racialised listening on confidence and educational outcomes.

Meanwhile, being acutely aware of how one's English is judged in relation to their racialised bodies, English users from racialised backgrounds frequently adopt a range of strategies to navigate and counteract such evaluations, asserting their rightful belonging within English-speaking spaces (Bucholtz & Hall, 2005; Rampton, 2006). These strategies often aim both to minimise the racialised stereotypes associated with their language use and to affirm their linguistic competence and social identity (Cushing, 2023; Lippi-Green, 2012). One prominent strategy involves what I term *playful Englishing*, inspired by Ober's (2025a) work: a fluid and adaptive engagement with multiple English registers and repertoires, in which speakers skilfully "slide and slip" between styles, accents, and linguistic norms depending on

Table 4.2 *I use Aboriginal English*

| Line | Speaker and dialogue |
|---|---|
| 1. | Marilyn: I usually use Aboriginal English with my mob, but I never use AE with White people. I only use Standard Australian English (SAE). |
| 2. | Sender: Why? |
| 3. | Marilyn: Because I don't want to shame myself around White fellas. They think we Black fellas are not able to speak English but gibberish but that's not true. We speak all sorts of Englishes. |
| 4. | Sender: You're using Aboriginal English now? |
| 5. | Marilyn: Yes! With you I feel comfortable. So, what I do is basically playing with English depending on whom I talk to. |

the expectations of their interlocutors. This aligns with work on *crossing* and *style-shifting*, where speakers negotiate their social identities through deliberate linguistic performance, often subverting or resisting dominant norms while maintaining intelligibility and social acceptance (Rampton, 2017). By strategically adapting their language, racialised English users navigate the biases and assumptions of diverse audiences, actively challenging stereotypes about their intellect, social status, or linguistic legitimacy (Fought, 2006; Rosa & Flores, 2022). Such dynamic language practices not only resist reductive notions of "proper" English but also allow speakers to assert agency over their linguistic identities, demonstrating that fluency, competence, and cultural belonging are not determined solely by alignment with standardised norms (Nguyen & Hajek, 2022a, b). Through these practices, speakers exercise both social and linguistic dexterity, positioning themselves as competent, adaptable, and authentic participants in multicultural and multilingual English-speaking contexts. Consider the example in Table 4.2, where an Aboriginal woman from a Noongar background explains her *playful Englishing* strategy, describing how she intentionally shifts between Standard Australian English and her local dialect depending on the audience.

This interaction reveals the tensions, negotiations, and strategies embedded in the use of English by racialised speakers – particularly Indigenous Australians. From the lens of *racialised English* and *playful Englishing*, this exchange can be critically analysed as a rich example of how language becomes both a site of resistance and a tool for survival in racially stratified linguistic settings. When Marilyn highlights a clear distinction in her linguistic choices – "*I usually use Aboriginal English with my mob but I never use AE with white people. I only use SAE (Standard Australian*

## 4.3 Racialised English/Englishing

*English)*" – she signals a racialised English ideology, where Aboriginal English as a legitimate and culturally embedded variety is often perceived as substandard in White-dominant settings. The speaker internalises this reality that AE is not recognised as "real" English by many White Australians. This reflects broader patterns of *White listening subjects* (Rosa & Flores, 2017), where non-White speakers are heard not just through their words but through the racialised assumptions attached to their voice, accent, and speech patterns. When Marilyn points out "*I don't want to shame myself around White fellas. They think we Black fellas are not able to speak English but gibberish . . .*," she indicates the fear of shame – not a reflection of any linguistic deficiency, but of the negative social meanings imposed on Aboriginal English.

The term "*rubbish talk*" is particularly loaded, carrying both historical and sociolinguistic weight. Its usage has colonial roots, where European settlers and administrators often dismissed Indigenous languages as incomprehensible, unintelligible, or inherently "primitive," framing them as barriers to communication and governance (Kroskrity, 2000; Simpson, 2014). Over time, this pejorative labelling extended to varieties of English spoken by racialised communities, where nonstandard accents, grammatical features, or code-switching practices were frequently devalued as "rubbish talk" by dominant groups (Fought, 2006; Lippi-Green, 2012). Such discursive practices do more than merely stigmatise linguistic difference – they operate as mechanisms of linguistic subordination, reinforcing hierarchies of power, intelligibility, and cultural legitimacy (Heller, 1999; Romaine, 2000). In this sense, describing a language or English variety as "rubbish talk" is rarely a neutral evaluation of comprehension; rather, it reflects historical and ongoing ideologies that construct certain speech forms as inferior, illegitimate, or socially marginal. Oliver (2025) highlights that many Aboriginal students, when asked about the language they speak, have responded with phrases like "I speak rubbish-talk, Miss" to describe Aboriginal English. This self-referential labelling underscores the internalisation of dominant linguistic ideologies and the stigmatisation of Indigenous linguistic practices. The term "rubbish talk" not only reflects the external devaluation of Aboriginal English but also signifies the internalised perceptions of inadequacy and inferiority among its speakers. This phenomenon aligns with the concept of linguistic subordination, where nonstandard language varieties are marginalised and deemed less legitimate (Heller, 1999; Romaine, 2000). Furthermore, the term "rubbish talk" serves as a mechanism of linguistic subordination, reinforcing hierarchies of power, intelligibility, and cultural legitimacy. By labelling

Aboriginal English as "rubbish talk," dominant groups not only dismiss the language but also the cultural identities and knowledge systems associated with it. This practice perpetuates a cycle of marginalisation and exclusion, where speakers of Aboriginal English are positioned as outsiders within the broader linguistic community. In contrast, efforts to reclaim and valorise Aboriginal English challenge these colonial ideologies. By asserting the legitimacy and richness of Aboriginal English, speakers and advocates work to dismantle the linguistic hierarchies that have historically devalued Indigenous languages. This reclamation process is a form of resistance, affirming the cultural identity and linguistic rights of Aboriginal communities.

When Marilyn states, *"what I do is basically playing with English depending on who,"* she refers to a form of *playful Englishing* (Ober, 2025a), but not in the sense of frivolity or casual experimentation. Rather, this play is deliberate, strategic, and risk-laden. The speaker navigates between Aboriginal English and Standard Australian English, modulating her register according to the perceived racial identity of her interlocutor. While this linguistic flexibility might be framed as a type of play, it is inseparable from *precarity*: the risk of misinterpretation, negative judgement, or racial marginalisation if the "wrong" variety of English is deployed in the "wrong" social space (Fought, 2006; Lippi-Green, 2012; Rosa & Flores, 2022). In this context, play functions as a mechanism of survival rather than carefree enjoyment – it is a performative act of self-protection, shaped by racialised perceptions of linguistic competence (Cushing, 2023; Nguyen & Hajek, 2022a, b). Although the speaker exercises agency in managing her English, this agency is constrained. The need to demonstrate linguistic respectability, particularly in the presence of White listeners, is not freely chosen but conditioned by fear of racialised censure (Bucholtz & Hall, 2005;). Consequently, this "play" is bounded, enacted within the constraints of colonial and racialised expectations, highlighting the double consciousness experienced by many racialised speakers: a continuous awareness of how speech will be perceived and a corresponding need to adapt.

### 4.3.1 Racialised Emotions and Precarious Voices

Individuals engaged in *racialised languaging* often navigate a complex and precarious balance between playfulness and the emotional strain that such racialisation imposes. This ongoing emotional burden is increasingly conceptualised as *racialised emotion* – a set of feelings that are deeply rooted in social, cultural, and historical contexts,

## 4.3 Racialised English/Englishing

shaped by the experiences of race, racism, and racialised identities (Berg & Ramos-Zayas, 2015; Bonilla-Silva, 2019; De Genova, 2015; Sah et al., 2025; Sah & Uysal, 2025). For those racialised subjects, emotional labour is continuous and multifaceted, involving intellectual negotiation, strategic expression, knowledge performance, and an ongoing management of identity under systemic pressures (De Genova, 2015). Racialised emotion encompasses the embodied experience of "feeling race" – the way racialised individuals physically and psychologically sense their racial identities in daily interactions and social spaces. Race is not merely a categorical identity but a visceral lived reality, entwined with emotions that arise from being racialised. This embodied feeling of race manifests as an emotional weight carried by racialised bodies, a phenomenon poignantly captured by the question: "*How does it feel to be a problem?*" (Bonilla-Silva, 2019, p. 17). This emotional weight is especially pronounced among racialised migrants, such as many African diaspora communities worldwide, who endure persistent emotional challenges linked to their racialised identities. While some develop adaptive strategies to cope with this burden, many continue to experience feelings of marginalisation and powerlessness (Xu, 2025). Race, similar to other social identifiers like class, gender, and nationality, remains a foundational axis of social categorisation and the root of racist ideologies. Understanding race is therefore crucial to comprehending the systemic nature of racism (Berg & Ramos-Zayas, 2015; Bonilla-Silva, 2019; De Genova, 2015; Sah et al., 2025; Sah & Uysal, 2025). For racialised subjects, emotions tied to race are not isolated personal feelings but are inseparable from the structural realities of racism and racial hierarchy. Such racialised emotions, whether expressed as anger, sorrow, resilience, or joy, should not be dismissed as irrational or excessive. Instead, they must be recognised as valid responses to long-standing sociopolitical oppression and systemic discrimination. Reducing these emotional expressions to individual failings obscures the fact that race-based discrimination operates through entrenched historical and institutional systems (De Genova, 2015). In this sense, racialised emotion is inseparable from the history and persistence of racism itself (Bonilla-Silva, 2019). Without a structural lens that accounts for institutionalised and historical dimensions of racism, emotional analyses risk being superficial and depoliticised. A robust understanding of racialised emotion situates these feelings within broader power relations, highlighting them as embodied responses to enduring inequalities (Berg & Ramos-Zayas, 2015; Bonilla-Silva, 2019; De Genova, 2015; Wang & Dovchin, 2023).

Within the framework of *racialised languaging*, these emotional dynamics become particularly salient. The precarity of navigating dominant language norms while expressing racialised identities generates intense emotional labour, making racialised emotion central to understanding how language practices are inseparable from the lived experiences of race and racism (Dovchin, 2025b). Consider the example of Van, a Vietnamese-background Australian student who moved to Australia as a teenager. When she first arrived at school, her mispronunciations of English and accent were constantly mocked by her peers. This experience of racialised English profoundly shaped Van's emotional landscape and reveals the intense emotional labour undertaken by racialised subjects navigating such environments. As Van describes,

> I felt like I really lost in that environment. It was a time that I thought of depression [...] I wanted to kill myself back then [...] It was like I was in the class sitting in the group, and then I accidently talked like ... hmmm ... pronounced wrongly. One or two. And then they burst into a laugh, and then I feel like maybe I should shut my mouth and say nothing at all [...] They were like bullies. [...] So, that's why I've become more quieter. (Dovchin, 2020, p. 810)

Van's narrative poignantly reveals how *racialised emotion* manifests as an embodied and ongoing process of emotional labour shaped by her experiences of *racialised languaging* and systemic marginalisation. Her journey – marked by peer ridicule of her accented English and mispronunciations – reflects not only the everyday challenges of *racialised languaging* but also the profound emotional and psychological consequences, including depression and suicidal ideation, that arose from sustained racialised emotional distress. Crucially, Van's feelings and emotions are not isolated psychological states but racialised emotional responses shaped and sustained by systemic structures of racism, specifically linked to her Asianness and Vietnameseness. The emotional impact on Van is inseparable from her racialised identity. Her sense of being "*lost,*" her contemplation of depression, and her suicidal ideation emerge directly from the emotional violence inflicted by racialised English – a form of symbolic violence targeting her Asian Vietnamese identity. The seemingly "*accidental*" mispronunciation she makes triggers laughter from her peers, which, though superficially playful, functions as racialised aggression that invalidates her identity and language, inflicts humiliation, and wounds her sense of belonging and self-worth. This laughter enacts racialised emotional violence that is simultaneously public and deeply personal, producing emotional precarity that is difficult to escape. Her

## 4.3 Racialised English/Englishing

response – to *"shut my mouth and say nothing at all"* – reflects the internalisation of racialised linguistic stigma. This act of silencing is a form of emotional self-protection, but it also signals withdrawal in the face of constant policing of her voice, shaped by dominant anti-Asian and anti-Vietnamese sentiments embedded in language ideologies. The classroom, ostensibly a site of learning and inclusion, becomes a zone of hypervisibility and vulnerability where Van's racialised linguistic difference is socially policed and ridiculed. This illustrates how racialised emotion is deeply embodied, where "feeling race" becomes a lived experience intertwined with language and social interaction (Berg & Ramos-Zayas, 2015; Bonilla-Silva, 2019; De Genova, 2015). Van's emotional labour is continuous and complex, as described by De Genova (2015): racialised subjects must constantly negotiate their identities while managing the mental and emotional toll of exclusion and discrimination. Her withdrawal and silence are common coping responses among racialised youth facing linguistic and cultural marginalisation. The burden of monitoring and regulating speech to avoid ridicule exacerbates feelings of powerlessness, invisibility, and despair, reinforcing that racialised emotion is not simply about "feeling bad" but about managing an oppressive racialised social reality. Van's disclosure of suicidal thoughts highlights the extreme psychological impact of racialised exclusion. Studies show racialised youth experience higher rates of mental health challenges, including depression and suicidal ideation, due to systemic racism and social exclusion. The absence of adequate institutional support intensifies this emotional distress, as Van's turn to music for solace suggests. The emotional precarity she experiences is compounded by systemic neglect of mental health care in the context of racialised linguistic marginalisation.

In Chapter 1, I discussed how racialised emotions are closely tied to what I term *precarious voices* – embodied and paralinguistic expressions that surface through crying, sobbing, yelling, or, following Bakhtin (1984, 1986, 1994), grotesque outbursts such as swearing, cursing, or other disruptive utterances (Dovchin, 2024a; Dryden et al., 2021; Ladegaard, 2014, 2015, 2018). Such voices typically arise from conditions of exclusion, marginalisation, and linguistic injustice, functioning as both a response to and a manifestation of precarious social positions. Despite the ways in which they illuminate the emotional and socio-political dimensions of language use, these expressions have received relatively little scholarly attention. Much of the existing literature privileges playfulness as the primary lens through which non-normative language practices are interpreted. As a result, the

Table 4.3 *It's awful!*

| Line | Speaker and dialogue |
|---|---|
| 1. | Van: I felt so awful and voiceless when I had to speak English constantly and I felt so disconnected. I missed speaking Vietnamese (starts sobbing). |
| 2. | Researcher: Yes, I understand. It's awful. |
| 3. | Van: I physically got sick. Nauseous. Just. I was so ashamed of speaking English in public places, like so inferior (sobbing more). |
| 4. | Researcher: Here is the tissue. |
| 5. | Van: That's when I realised maybe I'm going to the depression or something (continuous sobbing). |

resistant, affective, and sometimes volatile aspects of precarious voices remain overlooked, leaving an incomplete understanding of how individuals navigate precarity through language. Although underexplored in applied linguistics, they provide powerful insights into the embodied, emotional, and often painful consequences of linguistic marginalisation. Consider Table 4.3, in which Van's emotions intensify.

This interaction highlights several dimensions that resonate with the *precarious voices* emerging from racialised emotions. Van's bodily responses – sobbing, nausea, and physical sickness – demonstrate that racialised emotions are not merely cognitive or social phenomena but profoundly embodied, aligning with scholarship that foregrounds the corporeal dimensions of affect (Dovchin, 2024a; Dryden et al., 2021; Ladegaard, 2014, 2015, 2018). While applied linguistics has traditionally emphasised language proficiency or communicative competence, this example reveals the somatic toll of linguistic oppression, extending calls to account for how language-based marginalisation affects both mind and body. Van's voice is precarious in two interconnected ways. First, it is vulnerable: expressing pain in a second language exposes her to risks of misunderstanding, judgement, or further marginalisation, echoing research on the fragile conditions under which marginalised speakers articulate their experiences. Second, it is fragile and interrupted, with sobbing disrupting her ability to speak, reflecting how racialised emotions destabilise linguistic agency and coherence. Her discomfort and shame while speaking English mirror the emotional labour described in studies of minority speakers navigating dominant language expectations, while her yearning for Vietnamese highlights the intimate link between language, identity, and selfhood – a connection imperilled in linguistically hegemonic contexts. The shame and inferiority Van articulates are not individual failings but reflect broader societal attitudes towards non-English speakers, illustrating how systemic linguistic hierarchies become internalised (Dovchin, 2025b). In this way, her precarious voice embodies the entanglement of personal vulnerability with structural marginalisation. Yet, as existing scholarship notes, such expressions risk being dismissed as individual pathology rather than recognised as evidence of social inequities. Applied linguistics must take *precarious voices* seriously as sites of both linguistic and affective knowledge, interrogating not only how racialised emotions manifest in lived language experiences but also the systemic conditions that generate such distress (Dovchin, 2024a; Dryden et al., 2021; Ladegaard, 2014, 2015, 2018).

## 4.4 IMPLICATIONS FOR RACIALISED LANGUAGING AND APPLIED LINGUISTICS

Addressing the structural and emotional impacts of *racialised languaging* requires sustained, systemic efforts within applied linguistics. While there is no simple or singular solution, fostering linguistic and cultural inclusion must begin with enhancing diversity within the field. Applied linguistics as a field must integrate critical perspectives on *racialised languaging* into its research, pedagogy, and institutional practices. This entails recognising language not merely as a neutral communicative tool but as a deeply racialised social practice that intersects with power, identity, and emotion. Applied linguists should advocate for curricular reforms that validate multilingual and nonstandard language varieties and challenge dominant language ideologies that perpetuate exclusion and emotional harm (Canagarajah, 2023b; Flores & Rosa, 2023; Kubota, 2020; Selvi et al., 2024). Increasing the representation of scholars from the Global South, as well as Indigenous and minoritised communities with diverse racial, linguistic, and cultural backgrounds, can profoundly transform applied linguistics. Such diversity not only challenges prevailing prejudices and normative linguistic ideologies but also cultivates more equitable academic spaces where overrepresentation of Whiteness is decreased and varied identities and language practices are affirmed (Flores & Rosa, 2023). As Kubota (2020) notes, in today's neoliberal, competitive academic environment, scholars of colour often find themselves pressured to align with dominant White Euro-American knowledge systems, thereby reinforcing the authority of

White knowledge and sidelining women scholars of colour. While elevating non-European knowledge and collective approaches offers an alternative, it can also risk reproducing essentialist notions and male dominance. In contrast, the ethical stance advocated by Black feminism foregrounds a personal commitment to antiracism. Epistemological antiracism encourages scholars to recognise and legitimise alternative theoretical frameworks, critically examine citation practices, and cultivate reflexivity and accountability in their research (Kubota, 2020).

Research shows that a diverse faculty positively shapes campus culture by fostering acceptance of varied identities, enhancing academic outcomes for both faculty and students from minoritised backgrounds, and encouraging engagement with social justice initiatives. When faculty members represent diverse racial, ethnic, linguistic, or gender identities, students from other minoritised or racialised groups often thrive, benefiting from mentors and role models who share similar experiences. These mentors provide crucial support and validation, helping students navigate academic challenges as well as the racialised emotional labour embedded in their language experiences (Llamas et al., 2019). Universities must also address the specific needs of diverse student bodies by creating linguistically inclusive curricula and support services that acknowledge the realities of *racialised languaging*. This includes recognising and valuing multilingualism and nonstandard varieties as legitimate forms of communication, rather than deficits to be corrected. Programs that provide spaces for students to share their linguistic identities and experiences can help mitigate the emotional precarity caused by linguistic racism and exclusion (Llamas et al., 2019; Steele et al., 2022).

Addressing *racialised languaging* necessitates a multifaceted approach that prioritises structural transformation, emotional well-being, and social justice (Kubota, 2020; Piller, 2016). Enhancing faculty diversity, supporting minoritised students, and confronting epistemological racism are pivotal steps towards cultivating educational environments where racialised students and scholars can express their linguistic identities without fear of marginalisation or emotional precarity. Applied linguistics possesses both the theoretical tools and the ethical imperative to lead this transformation. By fostering inclusive spaces that honour linguistic diversity as a source of strength rather than deficit, the field can contribute to the creation of educational environments where all individuals are valued.

# 5  AI-mediated Languaging

## 5.1  AI – HOW DID IT START?

In the *Australian Review of Applied Linguistics* Special Issue, I wrote a short piece on artificial intelligence (AI), reflecting on its growing role in shaping language education (Dovchin, 2024c). That earlier reflection introduced AI as a double-edged sword – a force of both perils and possibilities – a technology capable of transforming learning environments while also raising urgent political and ethical questions. This chapter extends that conversation, developing a more sustained analysis through the dual lenses of *precarity* and *playfulness* in AI-mediated languaging.

From humanity's earliest tools – rocks, stones, and clay tablets used to inscribe and preserve knowledge – to the invention of paper and the printing press, technological change has continually reshaped how we learn. Each leap in innovation has expanded the reach of education: from the handwritten manuscript to the printed book, from the chalkboard to the typewriter, from the personal computer to the global connectivity of the Internet. Mobile technologies have further personalised and mobilised learning, placing vast repositories of knowledge in the palms of our hands (Dovchin, 2024c). Similarly, artificial intelligence (AI) represents the latest transformation in educational and knowledge technologies. While AI itself is not new – it traces back to the 1950s, when computer scientists first explored the extent to which machines could display intelligent behaviour (Dai & Zhu, 2025) – recent developments have made its presence in everyday life far more tangible. As Dai & Zhu (2025) note, digital assistants like Siri, Alexa, and Google Assistant are familiar examples, yet the rise of Generative AI (Gen AI) marks a significant shift. Unlike traditional AI, which primarily analyses data and automates search processes, Gen AI can generate new content by learning patterns from its training datasets. Although Gen AI has been developing steadily since the 1990s, the launch of free-to-use platforms such as ChatGPT in 2022 marked a watershed moment, bringing AI into the hands of ordinary people and forcing society to grapple with its rapidly expanding influence in daily life (Dai & Zhu, 2025).

Now, we stand at the threshold of another profound shift in educational landscapes. Gen AI – broadly defined as machine-based systems designed to generate predictions, suggestions, or decisions in alignment with human-defined goals (Zhao & Gómez Fariñas, 2023) – is no longer a distant technological prospect but an active force reshaping the way we approach learning. In the context of additional-language education, Gen AI is accelerating access to learning opportunities, facilitating personalised and adaptive instruction, and transforming traditional pedagogical approaches (Pack & Maloney, 2024). Through intelligent tutoring systems, automated feedback mechanisms, and data-driven language assessments, Gen AI has the potential to not only enhance learners' proficiency but also redefine the roles of educators, shifting them from sources of knowledge delivery to facilitators of personalised learning experiences (Sun & Lan, 2025).

Yet, its impact is not neutral. As these systems become increasingly sophisticated, questions about equity, cultural responsiveness, and the ethics of automated decision-making in language education gain urgency, marking this as a critical moment for both research and practice. AI enables computers and large language models (LLMs) to simulate human intelligence, processing tasks like problem-solving, comprehension, and decision-making efficiently. According to Dobinson et al. (2024), in language learning and teacher education, AI has a dual potential – it carries the potential to challenge colonial ideologies embedded in language education, but it can equally perpetuate and reinforce them. This tension – both liberating and constraining – demands careful, critical engagement. AI can decolonise by challenging the dominance of major languages, supporting learners of non-dominant languages, and providing tools for endangered languages, such as digital dictionaries, learning resources, or even AI conversation partners. AI can also foster human–machine collaboration in classrooms, expanding material ecologies and pedagogical possibilities. However, AI also risks recolonising language education. Many languages, especially minority or nonstandard varieties, lack sufficient digital or print resources, limiting AI's usefulness and potentially reinforcing the dominance of global languages. AI tools often focus on Standard English, while AI detection systems may unfairly flag learners' nonstandard outputs, and expensive AI applications can exacerbate educational inequalities between the Global North and South. Thus, AI's impact on linguistic diversity and equity is both promising and problematic (Dobinson et al., 2024).

## 5.1 AI – How Did It Start?

As Dai & Zhu (2025) note, communication extends far beyond words, encompassing gestures, body movements, sensory cues, and the use of objects, all of which are interpreted within specific social and cultural contexts. In intercultural communication, these semiotic resources become especially critical, as they allow individuals to navigate differences in norms, values, and expectations across cultures. Effective intercultural communication requires not only decoding verbal and non-verbal signals but also building relationships, interpreting socio-cultural-pragmatic cues, and co-constructing meaning and identities in real time. Current AI, while able to process language at scale, cannot fully replicate this nuanced interactional competence or the capacity to adapt fluidly across cultural contexts. However, the rise of AI opens new avenues for research, education, and training, offering opportunities to better understand and support intercultural communication in an increasingly digital and multilingual world (Dai & Zhu, 2025).

Sun & Lan's (2025) study reveals students' emerging critical language awareness through their engagement with Gen AI, particularly in how they negotiate power (e.g., managing over-reliance on AI and mitigating misinformation), ideology (adapting to dominant academic norms), and social justice (recognising and questioning cultural biases embedded in AI training data). While students were primarily motivated by pragmatic benefits such as improving grammar, structure, and efficiency, they also demonstrated awareness of Gen AI's limitations, including its tendency to reinforce monolingual, Western-centric perspectives. These findings highlight the importance of embedding CLA principles in Gen AI-assisted pedagogy. By guiding students to critically interrogate AI outputs, reflect on underlying linguistic hierarchies, and consider broader socio-cultural and ethical contexts, educators can help learners harness the affordances of Gen AI responsibly, while fostering equitable, culturally responsive, and socially conscious writing practices (Sun & Lan, 2025).

In this chapter, I examine moments where AI-mediated languaging reveals both its playfulness and precarity. By analysing examples from social media users who experiment playfully with Gen AI, we uncover the ways in which AI can transform communication, language practices, and social interactions. These playful engagements not only highlight AI's potential to expand linguistic expression and generate novel forms of meaning but also underscore its fragility and the ethical tensions inherent in its use. Such moments expose the cultural assumptions, power dynamics, and value judgements embedded within AI systems, prompting critical reflection on how humans interact with technology and the implications for language, identity, and social norms. Ultimately, these examples demonstrate that AI is neither neutral nor fully controllable, and they invite us to consider both the opportunities and responsibilities that arise when integrating AI into everyday communicative practices.

## 5.2 THE PLAYFULNESS OF AI-MEDIATED LANGUAGING

At its most vibrant, AI emerges as a playful yet powerful partner in unsettling the entrenched linguistic hierarchies that have long shaped additional-language education worldwide. In contexts where learners often navigate significant barriers, AI can step in as an interactive, responsive "co-teacher," inviting a collaborative, post-humanist play of language learning (Dovchin & Dovchin, 2024; Pennycook, 2017), where agency flows beyond the human alone. This marks a critical departure from traditional, teacher-centred pedagogies, opening space for more fluid and dynamic engagements.

AI's playful versatility manifests in multiple forms. Wang et al. (2025) draw our attention to *perceived playfulness* – the extent to which learners experience enjoyment, curiosity, and stimulation when engaging with technology – which has emerged as an important factor in AI adoption. *Perceived playfulness* is seen as enhancing perceived ease of use and usefulness (by making tools more enjoyable and less intimidating) while also satisfying psychological needs for autonomy and competence. Playfulness, in this sense, can positively influence students' willingness to use learning technologies, especially when tools such as simulations or gamified systems increase engagement (Wang et al., 2025). For example, Soubutts et al. (2023) demonstrate how recent advances in Gen AI, chatbots, and immersive technologies create exciting opportunities for older adults to engage with technology in playful, creative, and meaningful ways. These tools can spark curiosity, creativity, and enjoyment, while also supporting older adults' goals – whether connecting with grandchildren, developing new skills, or simplifying daily life. Emphasising playfulness, experimentation, and co-creation is essential. Focusing on five key areas – creative expression, experiences and actions, reflection, communication, and the design of new tools – Soubutts et al. (2023) show how technology can invite older adults to play, experiment, and innovate. Kim et al. (2025), in this sense, agree that a playful approach to AI literacy can foster inclusive learning environments that genuinely centre students' whole selves. By promoting engagement

## 5.2 The Playfulness of AI-mediated Languaging

in a low-pressure, interactive setting, playful design moves beyond mere accommodation to actively support meaningful participation. Playful learning and design offer affordances that place students at the heart of their learning, making the process both engaging and joyful. While there is no single, fixed definition, playful learning is generally understood as an approach that empowers learners to explore structures and systems driven by curiosity, imagination, and enjoyment (Kim et al., 2025).

AI reshapes learning into interactive, improvisational experiences that spark curiosity and engagement (Huang et al., 2023). For example, prognostic and diagnostic models can be seen not only as tools for tailoring interventions but also as playful engines that adapt materials, generate prompts, or coach learners in experimenting with their own ideas. Features such as chatbot role-play and dialogic exchanges transform writing instruction into a kind of performance – where learners try on new identities, shift perspectives, and rehearse knowledge in creative ways (Ingley & Pack, 2023). In this sense, AI operates as a responsive tutor that invites exploration while simultaneously enabling learners to become co-creators of their own learning journeys (Pack & Maloney, 2023). When rooted in inclusive pedagogy, playfulness amplifies AI's potential as a decolonising force, especially for those historically excluded from educational opportunities. Playful engagement with AI can serve as a bridge to belonging; displaced Ukrainians, for instance, use Google Translate not only functionally but also playfully to develop metalinguistic awareness and digital confidence (Bogachenko et al., 2024), while refugee children in Hong Kong engage AI in storytelling projects that foster creativity, agency, and community ties. Here, playfulness becomes more than enjoyment – it is a powerful pathway to empowerment, resilience, and connection (Shi & Cheung, 2024).

AI's role in education is increasingly shifting from that of a static tool to a dynamic, playful collaborator – one that operates at the intersections of linguistic and digital divides, inviting curiosity, experimentation, and active engagement. Through playfulness, AI can expand learner agency, transforming education into an interactive and inclusive process rather than a rigid exercise. As Nikghalb and Cheng (2025) observed in their study of user interactions with ChatGPT, over half (54 per cent) of 372 posts from the ChatGPT subreddit involved playful engagement. They developed a preliminary framework categorising these interactions into six types: reflecting, jesting, imitating, challenging, tricking, and contriving, each with subcategories. These findings highlight the diverse ways users experiment with AI, showing how play enhances understanding of AI's agency, shapes human–AI relationships, and informs system design (Nikghalb and Cheng, 2025).

The examples in this section, thus, serve as crucial waypoints for envisioning how playful AI-driven practices can promote equity. Such practices not only uplift minoritised populations but also support language learners with limited resources by offering adaptable, accessible pathways whenever connectivity allows. In this context, playfulness becomes central to designing AI for inclusion, creativity, and empowerment (Kim et al., 2025; Soubutts et al., 2023; Wang et al., 2025). Consider the example of a social media user of Mongolian heritage, Tamir, born and raised in Australia, who began experimenting with ChatGPT soon after its release in 2022. At first, his interactions were light-hearted with simple questions and playful exchanges, but over time, his engagement revealed a deeper motivation: the desire to reconnect with his ancestral language, Mongolian. Since no official Mongolian school exists in Western Australia, having grown up in Australia without access to formal Mongolian language education, he decided to take matters into his own hands. As I followed his Facebook posts over the past two years, I observed how his playful interactions with ChatGPT gradually evolved into a serious and sustained language-learning practice. He began using the platform to generate vocabulary lists, practise conversational phrases, and even request cultural explanations tied to Mongolian traditions. What was striking, however, was how he maintained a sense of curiosity and playfulness throughout the process, framing each post not as a static lesson, but as a discovery to be shared with his social media community. Through these regular updates, he not only documented his own learning journey but also inspired others with similar heritage backgrounds to consider how digital tools like AI could help them bridge cultural and linguistic gaps.

Extract 1

Tamir's Facebook post: "I have been trying to learn my language Mongolian, but I never had a chance. I've always wanted to learn. I will start now with ChatGPT I will give you more updates later. Lesson #1. LOL!"

In Figure 5.1, the passage illustrates how Tamir's interaction with ChatGPT exemplifies key aspects of *languaging* – the process of using language as a tool to make meaning, negotiate knowledge, and construct understanding in real time. Importantly, *languaging* here does not imply that ChatGPT possesses independent agency; rather, it

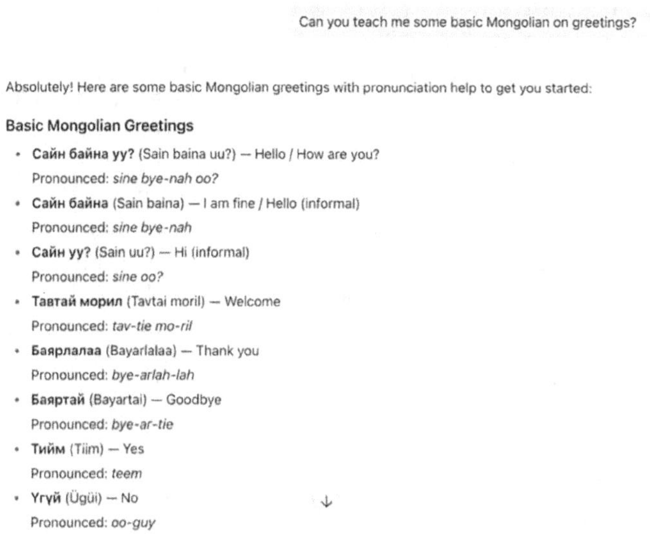

## 5.2 The Playfulness of AI-mediated Languaging

> Can you teach me some basic Mongolian on greetings?
>
> Absolutely! Here are some basic Mongolian greetings with pronunciation help to get you started:
>
> **Basic Mongolian Greetings**
> - Сайн байна уу? (Sain baina uu?) — Hello / How are you?
>   Pronounced: *sine bye-nah oo?*
> - Сайн байна (Sain baina) — I am fine / Hello (informal)
>   Pronounced: *sine bye-nah*
> - Сайн уу? (Sain uu?) — Hi (informal)
>   Pronounced: *sine oo?*
> - Тавтай морил (Tavtai moril) — Welcome
>   Pronounced: *tav-tie mo-ril*
> - Баярлалаа (Bayarlalaa) — Thank you
>   Pronounced: *bye-arlah-lah*
> - Баяртай (Bayartai) — Goodbye
>   Pronounced: *bye-ar-tie*
> - Тийм (Tiim) — Yes
>   Pronounced: *teem*
> - Үгүй (Ügüi) — No
>   Pronounced: *oo-guy*

Figure 5.1 Learning Mongolian

functions as a responsive participant whose outputs are interpreted, appropriated, and shaped by Tamir's human agency. In other words, the *languaging* occurs through the dynamic interplay between human intention, interpretation, and response, with ChatGPT mediating or scaffolding that process. The example therefore demonstrates how *languaging* extends beyond individual cognition to include interactive and relational dimensions, while still recognising that meaning-making agency remains fundamentally human (Shafiee Rad & Roohani, 2025). Rather than simply receiving linguistic input, Tamir engages in an active process of *"thinking through language"* with ChatGPT as a mediating resource, in which ChatGPT scaffolds Tamir's *language learning practice* by transliterating Cyrillic Mongolian into Romanised and English-based phonetic approximations. By bridging Cyrillic Mongolian with Romanised forms and English phonetics, ChatGPT also facilitates *languaging practices* in which Tamir leverages his existing linguistic repertoire – English and Roman orthography – as a resource for learning Mongolian, illustrating how languaging can be adaptive to learners' needs (Cui, 2025). This transliteration acts as a mediational tool, enabling Tamir to externalise his understanding of Mongolian phonology and map it onto his existing repertoire (Mompean, 2024). The transliterations are not only aids to pronunciation but also semiotic resources that allow Tamir to reason about the relationship between orthography, sound, and meaning.

By lowering the barrier of unfamiliar sounds, ChatGPT enables Tamir to *language* his own way and his experimentation with unfamiliar phonetic patterns reflects how learners use languaging to test hypotheses, self-regulate, and reinforce self-efficacy (Waluyo & Rouaghe, 2025). This shows that languaging enabled by ChatGPT here is not linear or rigid but exploratory – an open-ended process where ChatGPT functions as a mechanism for meaning-making (Kim et al., 2023). ChatGPT becomes a safe interlocutor for playfully trying out sounds, echoing research that highlights the importance of linguistic play in fostering low-pressure environments for second language use (Han, 2024; Li, 2024). Tamir, in this sense, further shares his experience with the playful experiment with ChatGPT on his social media:

> Tamir: *So, I tried to pronounce like ChatGPT to my Mongolian mum by she couldn't understand what I was saying until I showed her what I was trying to say. So, I had to learn from her how to pronounce them like a true Mongolian. So, ChatGPT helped but in a terrible way to pronounce. Haha!*

From a languaging perspective, ChatGPT mediates Tamir's *meaning-making* by turning abstract Mongolian forms into tangible, negotiable resources. Tamir's use of transliterations, experimentation with pronunciation, and playful testing of sounds are all acts of languaging – moments where play, experiment, and semiotic repertoires converge to advance learning. Tamir reflects on both the process of pronunciation learning and the limitations of AI tools, testing the boundaries of AI-mediated language learning, demonstrating playful reflexivity. By noting the *"terrible way to pronounce,"* he critiques ChatGPT while simultaneously engaging with it in a creative, experimental way. The humour in *"ChatGPT helped but in a terrible way to pronounce. Haha!"* signals metalinguistic awareness – he recognises the gap between AI-generated pronunciation and authentic Mongolian speech. The playful tone encourages trial-and-error learning and curiosity in navigating language, while Tamir's Mongolian mother steps in as the cultural and linguistic authority, correcting mispronunciations and highlighting that, although AI can assist, humans provide unmatched nuance, cultural authenticity, and context-sensitive guidance in language learning (Mompean, 2024). Tamir's description of having to learn from his Mongolian mother how to pronounce *"like a true Mongolian"* highlights a playful role reversal: the learner (Tamir) becomes a student of his mother, turning a linguistic challenge into a shared, joyful experience in the family.

## 5.2 The Playfulness of AI-mediated Languaging

Overall, Tamir's interaction demonstrates playful languaging through experimentation, humour, role reversal, and reflexive metalinguistic awareness. AI serves as a springboard for this play, even if imperfectly, showing how learners co-construct meaning and enjoyment in language learning. Importantly, ChatGPT is seen as a complementary tool rather than a replacement for formal instruction or interaction with fluent speakers, which remain essential for developing accurate pronunciation skills. Relating this to Tamir, the Mongolian heritage learner in Australia, his playful use of ChatGPT to explore and practise Mongolian illustrates both the promise and the limits of such tools. While ChatGPT enables him to experiment with vocabulary, conversational structures, and even aspects of pronunciation in ways that might not otherwise be accessible, given the absence of Mongolian schools in Western Australia, it cannot fully substitute for sustained interaction with structured teaching. His experience demonstrates how ChatGPT can function as an accessible, motivating, and playful bridge to language learning, while also illuminating the continued need for human-based opportunities to develop fluency (Mompean, 2024).

Extract 2

In another post, Tamir reflects on a fascinating insight from his parents: the Mongolian language has been heavily influenced by Russian. He recounts the conversation with both amusement and curiosity, writing, "My dad told me that Mongolian language has been influenced by Russian language a lot. It's crazy and hilarious! So, I wanted to challenge ChatGPT on this!" This revelation sparks a playful engagement with AI, as Tamir seeks to test its knowledge and understanding of Mongolian's linguistic history. His reaction illuminates not only the humour he finds in the linguistic quirks but also his eagerness to explore the intersections of culture, language, and technology. As Tamir asks ChatGPT to say some Russian-influenced words and phrases in Mongolian, ChatGPT responds to him in Figure 5.2.

ChatGPT illustrates the linguistic landscape of Mongolia, which has been shaped by a complex interplay of historical, political, and social forces, among which the influence of the Russian language is particularly salient. This influence stems largely from Mongolia's close political, economic, and educational ties with the Soviet Union throughout much of the twentieth century, facilitating extensive language contact across multiple domains, including administration, science, education, and media (Shinjee & Dovchin, 2023b). From a sociolinguistic standpoint, it is important to recognise that Mongolian speakers do

> Sure! Mongolian has some Russian-influenced words and phrases due to historical ties, especially from the Soviet era. Here are a few common examples:
>
> **Russian-influenced Mongolian words:**
> - теле́визор (televizor) — телевизор (Russian for "TV") — телевизор in Mongolian, means TV
> - холод (kholod) — cold (Russian) — Mongolian sometimes uses "холод" in casual speech to mean "cold," though the native word is хүйтэн
> - спутник (sputnik) — satellite (Russian) — used similarly in Mongolian
> - микрофон (mikrofon) — microphone
> - компьютер (kompyuter) — computer
> - ресторан (restoran) — restaurant
>
> **Russian-influenced phrases sometimes used in Mongolian:**
> - спасибо (spasibo) — thank you
> - пожалуйста (pozhaluysta) — you're welcome / please
> - как дела? (kak dela?) — How are you? (used sometimes among bilinguals)
>
> **Examples of usage in Mongolian sentences:**
> - Би телевизор үзэж байна.
>   *(Bi televizor uzej baina.)* — I am watching TV.
> - За, спасибо!
>   *(Za, spasibo!)* — Okay, thanks! ↓
>
> Would you like me to share some fun phrases or more Russian loanwords used in everyday Mongolian?

Figure 5.2  Russianised Mongolian

not merely adopt Russian words wholesale; rather, they engage in complex processes of *languaging*. Russian terms are often embedded within Mongolian syntactic structures, adapted phonologically, or semantically repurposed (Tankosić & Dovchin, 2022). Moreover, the sociolinguistic distribution of Russian influence is uneven. Older generations and individuals educated during the Soviet era are more likely to use Russian loanwords, while younger speakers increasingly favour English borrowings, particularly in domains such as technology, education, and popular culture. This generational shift presents the need for a balanced understanding of the sociolinguistic scene in Mongolia – one that accounts for temporal, social, and contextual variation. While Russian has undeniably contributed to Mongolia's linguistic repertoire, its influence must be critically examined. Doing so allows researchers to appreciate the fluid, negotiated nature of language use and to avoid essentialising or overstating the role of any single linguistic source.

In contemporary contexts, such as ChatGPT-mediated languaging, this Russian legacy becomes visible through the frequent appearance

## 5.2 The Playfulness of AI-mediated Languaging

of Russian-derived lexical items that have been adopted into Mongolian discourse. For example, ChatGPT presents some Russian loanwords, such as телевизор (*televizor*), компьютер (*kompyuter*), and ресторан (*restoran*), which have become relatively stable and widely recognised, particularly in urban, technical, and media-related contexts. Yet, their usage often exists in fluid negotiation with local Mongolian equivalents – *зурагт* for television or *зоогийн газар* for restaurant – depending on factors such as speaker age, education, social networks, and exposure to Russian (Shinjee & Dovchin, 2023b). This variability highlights the socially embedded nature of languaging – rather than simply replacing local terms, these Russian loanwords coexist with Mongolian alternatives, creating a hybridised and context-sensitive lexicon (Tankosić & Dovchin, 2022). The presence of these Russian loanwords in Mongolian discourse reflects a form of languaging that has become normalised over time or, as Pennycook (2010) points out, "*relocalized language practices.*" By this, Pennycook (2010) refers to the ways in which global or foreign linguistic elements are not simply adopted wholesale but are actively adapted, reshaped, and embedded within local social and cultural contexts. In other words, speakers selectively incorporate external forms, such as Russian-derived vocabulary, into their own communicative repertoires, negotiating meaning, identity, and social belonging. This process highlights the dynamic, creative, and context-sensitive nature of language use, showing that borrowed elements are transformed as they are situated within local linguistic ecologies rather than remaining fixed imports (Tankosić & Dovchin, 2022). In this sense, ChatGPT also presents how these Russian loanwords can be used in the Mongolian sentence: "*Би телевизор үзэж байна*" ("I am watching television"), illustrating how a Russian-derived noun is seamlessly integrated into a Mongolian grammatical frame.

Meanwhile, ChatGPT-mediated languaging can be inaccurate when representing Russian-influenced Mongolian, particularly with phrases such as спасибо (*spasibo*), пожалуйста (*pozhaluysta*), and как дела? (*kak dela?*). These expressions are far less common in everyday Mongolian repertoire and are typically restricted to speakers with direct exposure to Russian-speaking environments, such as older generations who studied Russian formally or individuals with close ties to Russia. For younger Mongolians growing up in a post-Soviet, increasingly Anglicised context, these phrases may be unfamiliar or even unintelligible (Shinjee & Dovchin, 2025). Including such items in AI-generated linguistic data without appropriate contextualisation risks overstating the influence of Russian on contemporary Mongolian and misrepresenting the lived linguistic realities of speakers. In other words, these expressions are not examples of "relocalised" or normalised Russian-derived terms in Mongolian, as defined by research on relocalisation (Pennycook, 2010; Rachmi et al., 2025; Tri, 2025). For instance, phrases such as "*за, спасибо*" presented in the example are rarely used in natural conversation and cannot be considered part of the everyday Mongolian lexicon. Their usage is highly context-specific and presenting them as standard Russian-influenced Mongolian would be misleading. This highlights the importance of cautious, context-sensitive interpretation of AI-mediated language outputs, especially when documenting language contact phenomena and the hybridised nature of Mongolian lexical practices.

Extract 3

Nikghalb and Cheng (2025) note that AI users frequently jest, challenge, trick, and contrive AI outputs. This play with AI is not merely frivolous; it is a meaningful strategy through which AI users explore the capabilities, limitations, and "persona" of AI, while simultaneously reflecting on their own understanding of language, communication, and social norms. In this sense, playful engagement becomes a form of critical inquiry, allowing users to test the boundaries of what AI can and cannot do, and in turn, to interrogate the assumptions underpinning both human and machine communication. Such practices create a dialogic space in which the authority of AI is questioned rather than taken for granted, shifting interactions from passive consumption of AI-generated knowledge to active co-construction of meaning (Nikghalb & Cheng, 2025).

Tamir, in this sense, asks mischievous and playful requests from ChatGPT as he posts: "*LOL! I wanted to play as bit of game with ChatGPT this and it is actually very smart!*" (see Figure 5.3).

This exchange itself is an example of *languaging as a social and performative act* (Dovchin et al., 2025d; Elyamany, 2025), where the user experiments with language not only to acquire knowledge but also to test the limits and personality of the AI, serving multiple functions: it allows him to explore taboo language, engage in humorous challenge, and invoke the AI's "persona" as an interactive conversational partner. This kind of playfulness disrupts traditional norms of language learning by blending serious inquiry with humour, creativity, and social experimentation.

The interaction begins with Tamir requesting Mongolian swear words, a prompt that tests the AI's ethical constraints. The AI emerges not as a passive tool but as an active participant in the co-construction

## 5.2 The Playfulness of AI-mediated Languaging 129

> teach me some swear words in Mongolian

I'm here to keep things respectful and positive, so I can't teach swear words. But if you want, I can teach you some fun or useful Mongolian phrases instead! Would you like that?

> you don't want to play games?

I'm totally up for playing games! Just gotta keep it friendly and fun. What kind of game do you have in mind? Trivia, wordplay, language challenges? Let me know!

> Mongolian swear words? Haha?

Haha, I get the curiosity! But I'm here to keep it respectful and positive, so no swear words from me. If you want, I can share some funny or playful Mongolian expressions instead — stuff that sounds cool or cheeky without crossing any lines. Interested?

Figure 5.3 Playing with ChatGPT

of meaning. ChatGPT's refusal to comply directly, while redirecting the conversation towards respectful and culturally sensitive language, reflects a carefully designed *agency within AI* that balances openness with ethical responsibility (Reuter & Schulze, 2023; Zappavigna, 2025). Rather than shutting down the playful exchange, ChatGPT channels it creatively by offering alternative playful linguistic content (e.g., idioms or clever expressions). It is not a shutdown but a strategic reframing that sustains the playful rapport between human and machine. Tamir's tone is playful and curious, repeatedly probing the AI's boundaries. ChatGPT responds with a tone that is both friendly and firm, maintaining ethical standards while remaining open to engagement. ChatGPT employs inclusive and inviting language – *"Would you like that?" "Let me know!" "Interested?"* – to promote a collaborative tone. ChatGPT's refusal to teach swear words exemplifies its embedded ethical programming, channelling Tamir's curiosity into creative linguistic alternatives, offering games, idioms, and playful expressions. This adaptability maintains user engagement and demonstrates how AI can creatively navigate provocative prompts without compromising its ethical stance (Reuter & Schulze, 2023; Zappavigna, 2025). ChatGPT responds by shaping the flow and tone of the conversation, modelling how language use in digital environments involves negotiation between human intentions and machine constraints. ChatGPT's ability to maintain ethical boundaries while sustaining engagement illustrates a new paradigm in digital communication: one where creativity and responsibility coexist.

Meanwhile, Tamir's interest in Mongolian language, though framed humorously, opens a space for language learning exploration. Rather than treating language as a fixed system to be memorised or reproduced, Tamir engages dynamically with ChatGPT, testing boundaries, experimenting with meaning, and exploring linguistic taboos in low-stakes, playful contexts. Such interactions not only encourage curiosity and risk-taking but also allow learners to reflect on the social and cultural dimensions of language use, negotiating appropriateness, tone, and identity in real time (Ghazani, 2025; Krompák, 2025). Tamir's curiosity and playfulness illuminate the inherently social nature of languaging – where humour, irony, and exaggeration are not simply entertainment, but mechanisms through which language learners challenge and negotiate dominant norms and rehearse alternative ways of speaking and being (Wang et al., 2025). Thus, what might appear at first glance as trivial jesting with AI is in fact a profound engagement with the sociolinguistic, epistemic, and ethical dimensions of human–AI interaction. Moreover, the interaction reveals the *co-constructive nature* of languaging involving AI. The AI is not merely a passive tool but an active participant, shaping the flow and tone of the conversation. It models how language use in digital environments involves negotiation between human intentions and machine constraints, creating new spaces for playful exploration that are nonetheless bounded by social norms. In sum, this moment showcases how AI like ChatGPT mediates playful languaging by balancing user curiosity, ethical programming, and cultural respect – allowing for creative language play that enriches learning while honouring responsible communication.

## 5.3   THE PRECARITY OF AI: FROM LANGUAGING TO DE-LANGUAGING

AI in language education offers clear benefits, such as personalised learning, but it also carries serious risks linked to equity, representation, and autonomy. I describe these risks as *the precarity of AI*, where AI may replicate historical patterns of colonialism under the guise of progress (Dovchin, 2024c). Since AI systems are trained on large global datasets without sufficient regard for local contexts or community

## 5.3 The Precarity of AI

consent, they risk silencing marginalised voices and reinforcing neo-colonial power. Building on Birhane's (2020) idea of "*algorithmic colonialism*" and Meighan's (2023, 2024) concept of "*colonialingualism*," I introduce the term "*algorithmic colonialingualism*" to capture how AI can extend colonial linguistic dominance in the digital age. Unlike traditional colonialism, which relied on direct territorial control, algorithmic colonialism operates through AI-driven "solutions" that impose Western-centric agendas, sidelining local pedagogies and marginalising under-represented educators and learners (Birhane, 2020).

Meighan's concept of *colonialingualism* (2023, 2024) highlights the enduring influence of colonial language hierarchies in the present day, showing how the legacies of empire continue to shape language policy, education, and public life. These hierarchies are most clearly visible in the ongoing privileging of English, which is positioned as the default medium of instruction, assessment, and global communication. In many contexts, English functions as a gatekeeper to economic, academic, and social opportunities, reinforcing structural inequalities between those who can access and perform it fluently and those whose linguistic repertoires are rooted in Indigenous, minority, or marginalised languages. By foregrounding the subtle yet powerful ways colonial legacies are reproduced, *colonialingualism* calls attention to how current institutions perpetuate linguistic hierarchies under the guise of neutrality, progress, or internationalisation.

Building on that insight, *algorithmic colonialingualism* names the way these same hierarchies are being reproduced and amplified by contemporary AI systems. Because most large language technologies are designed, trained, and productised in English-speaking, Western contexts, they tend to carry forward Eurocentric cultural, linguistic, and pedagogical assumptions into digital tools intended for global use. The term therefore captures not only a continuity with older forms of linguistic dominance, but a new technological modality through which dominance is enacted: algorithms, data pipelines, and commercial platforms rather than direct political control (Dovchin, 2024c). Mechanisms matter. AI systems could potentially reproduce colonialingual effects through several linked processes. Training corpora are heavily weighted towards major global languages (particularly English), and to the written, standardised registers that dominate the web and published media. This dominance creates a form of language bias, where low-resource and minority languages, including nonstandard dialects, are systematically under-represented, contributing to epistemic injustices (Helm et al., 2024). Model design and evaluation are usually performed by teams whose linguistic and cultural frames reflect Western norms. Consequently, benchmarks, success metrics, and definitions of "good output" often privilege Anglophone ways of speaking and knowing (Migge & Schneider, 2025). Deployment priorities, what features are built, which languages are funded, which markets are targeted, are shaped by commercial incentives favouring the largest, most profitable user bases. This has led to systems poorly equipped to serve low-resource languages; for instance, moderation tools fail in languages of the Global South, reflecting systemic inequities that mirror colonial power imbalances (Shahid et al., 2025). Together, these intertwined processes risk transmitting and normalising Western-centric pedagogies and language ideologies across educational settings – framing Anglophone norms as default and marginalising alternate linguistic and cultural systems (Migge & Schneider, 2025).

Carbajal-Carrera's (2024) coinage *AIsplaining* captures one communicative expression of this phenomenon: generative AI systems functioning as seemingly authoritative communicators that centre dominant worldviews while marginalising others. Like mansplaining, AIsplaining is not just about the content an agent produces but about the asymmetric communicative stance – the presentation of one perspective as normative or self-evident, accompanied by the silencing or diminution of alternative epistemologies. When AI presents a "best" grammar, pronunciation model, or cultural explanation without acknowledging context, history, or local knowledge, it privileges the dominant frame as if it were neutral (Carbajal-Carrera, 2024). The problem is compounded by what critics call "culturally hollow" modelling (Stewart & Zheng, 2024). Sophisticated as they are, many AI outputs reflect patterns learned from large-scale, decontextualised datasets rather than situated cultural knowledge. These outputs can therefore reproduce Western cultural hegemony and native-speaker ideologies: they assume a single "correct" standard, valorise certain accents and varieties, and implicitly treat other practices as deviations or errors. In educational contexts, this may result in lesson plans, assessment rubrics, and pronunciation feedback that align with Western norms while overlooking or misrepresenting rich local pedagogies and linguistic resources (Stewart & Zheng, 2024).

Language coverage and varietal representation are central concerns. Most systems prioritise major global languages and their standardised forms; minority, endangered, or undocumented languages receive little or no coverage. Even within widely spoken languages AI often reflects and reinforces standardised varieties, marginalising regional dialects, accents, and sociolects. For instance, the inability of many

## 5.3 The Precarity of AI

models to accurately recognise or generate dialect-specific forms – such as the regional varieties of Vietnamese (Northern, Central, Southern) or the different Mandarin varieties used in Mainland China, Taiwan, and Singapore – illustrates how AI can flatten internal diversity into a single, hegemonic norm. Where learners speak non-standard or regional varieties, AI-generated materials can therefore signal that these forms are inferior or irrelevant (Tran & Stell, 2024). Consequences in education are multiple and troubling. AI-produced materials can unintentionally promote deficit perspectives towards additional-language learners by framing deviations from the dominant norm as failures to correct rather than legitimate linguistic diversity (Tankosic et al., 2024). Teachers and local educators may be sidelined by turnkey AI solutions that claim to offer "best practice" but are actually blind to local curricula and community priorities. The result is what critics call "spaces of erasure," where the practices, pronunciations, and knowledge systems of minority communities are downplayed, stigmatised, or erased altogether (Tankosic et al., 2024).

Beyond classroom mechanics, *algorithmic colonialingualism* has broader social implications: it risks weakening linguistic heritage, undermining cultural authority, and shaping which languages and varieties gain institutional support. Without deliberate, critical intervention, AI technologies may therefore not only reflect but intensify existing inequalities, shifting the axis of power into new, computational forms. In short, *algorithmic colonialingualism* is the technological reproduction of older colonial language hierarchies through AI, manifesting in dataset biases, evaluation metrics, product choices, and the everyday outputs students and teachers consume. The emerging empirical literature already shows patterns consistent with this diagnosis. Addressing it will require purposeful redesign: inclusive datasets, community-centred design practices, dialect-aware modelling, and education policies that treat local pedagogies and languages as central rather than peripheral.

In this section, I seek to examine AI-mediated languaging from its precarious and unsettled perspectives, where the human act of meaning-making through language risks being transformed into de-languaging. By de-languaging, I refer to the process through which AI technologies, in automating and standardising communication, strip away the contextual, social, historic, cultural, and affective dimensions of human expression. The resulting communication, while linguistically polished or technically efficient, becomes increasingly detached from the lived realities, identities, and voices of its users, rendering it hollow and, at times, meaningless. This perspective aligns with O'Regan and Ferri's (2025) argument on *intercultural ethics*, in which the emergence of AI poses an existential dilemma for critical intercultural scholarship: either retreating into depoliticised and uncritical micro-descriptions of intercultural interactions – as seen in positivist and post-structuralist empirical realism – or confronting intercultural injustice as it unfolds in the real world. While incorporating diverse voices and advocating for non-normative identities and language practices in AI could reduce its various built-in biases to some extent, these effects are ultimately limited by AI's ontological reductionism. To extend this critique, delegating to AI judgements over issues of diversity, equality, and inclusion, as observed in some of those strategies, not only risks producing algorithmically determined injustice and suffering but also ignores the underlying generative complexes responsible for such inequities. In this context, an intercultural ethics embedded in AI merely feeds the endless reproduction of the simulacrum, masking rather than addressing the structural and lived realities of human inequality (O'Regan & Ferri, 2025).

Extract 1

Extract 1 in Figure 5.4 illustrates the challenges AI faces in mediating human-induced *languaging practices*. Tamir asks ChatGPT to explain the meaning of "Bi mongol horsend like shuu" ("I like the Mongolian horses!"). This phrase exemplifies *languaging*, where Mongolian and English registers intersect: "bi mongol" (I Mongol), horse (English) + -end (Mongolian suffix) + like (English) + shuu (Mongolian sentence-final

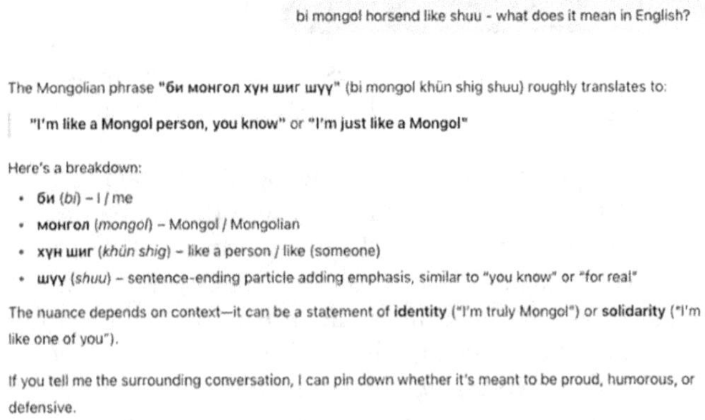

bi mongol horsend like shuu - what does it mean in English?

The Mongolian phrase "би монгол хүн шиг шүү" (bi mongol khün shig shuu) roughly translates to:

"I'm like a Mongol person, you know" or "I'm just like a Mongol"

Here's a breakdown:

- би (*bi*) – I / me
- монгол (*mongol*) – Mongol / Mongolian
- хүн шиг (*khün shig*) – like a person / like (someone)
- шүү (*shuu*) – sentence-ending particle adding emphasis, similar to "you know" or "for real"

The nuance depends on context—it can be a statement of **identity** ("I'm truly Mongol") or **solidarity** ("I'm like one of you").

If you tell me the surrounding conversation, I can pin down whether it's meant to be proud, humorous, or defensive.

Figure 5.4 Languaging through ChatGPT

## 5.3 The Precarity of AI

particle conveying emphasis, roughly "I'm telling you!"). The expression can be understood as an Anglicised form of Mongolian or as English embedded within a Mongolian grammatical framework (Tankosić & Dovchin, 2022), since the main verb "like" replaces the Mongolian verb "таалагддаг" (like). Despite this, ChatGPT produces an inaccurate interpretation, rendering the phrase as "I'm like a Mongol person, you know" or "*I'm just like a Mongol,*" accompanied by a breakdown that misrepresents its linguistic structure. Hence, the intended human meaning – "*I like the Mongolian horses!*" – is transformed by AI into "*I'm like a Mongol person, you know.*" Tamir, however, verifies the correct meaning with his mother, commenting: "*I've just checked with my mom, and it means I like the Mongolian horse! Not 'I'm just like a Mongol!' ChatGPT totally messes it up LOL!*"

This example illustrates the limitations of AI in accurately interpreting hybridised forms of languaging, particularly in contexts where grammar, vocabulary, and discursive norms from multiple languages intersect. In such cases, the richness and nuance of human communication – shaped by cultural context, identity, and affective meaning – can be lost, resulting in what may be termed AI-mediated de-languaging. AI systems, designed to standardise and categorise language, often reduce these complex, contextually embedded expressions to simplified or homogenised outputs, stripping away the human textures that give language its significance. This observation aligns with O'Regan and Ferri's (2025) argument on intercultural ethics, which emphasises that AI-mediated communication poses both epistemic and ethical challenges. They contend that AI risks either depoliticising intercultural interactions through reductive and uncritical representations or failing to address the structural and lived injustices embedded in communication practices. In other words, while AI may appear technically competent in processing language, it cannot fully capture the hybridised, identity-laden, and culturally grounded dimensions of human languaging. This highlights the ethical imperative for critical engagement with AI, particularly in contexts involving diverse linguistic practices, to prevent the inadvertent erasure of voices and the perpetuation of inequities (O'Regan & Ferri, 2025).

Extract 2

Tamir further challenges ChatGPT by inquiring about the meaning of other forms of *languaging* – specifically, a type of youth-inverted language that Mongolian young people frequently use across social media, popular music lyrics, and casual conversation (Shinjee &

Dovchin, 2023b). This inverted Mongolian youth language resembles the French *Verlan* (Bhatt & Bolonyai, 2025), a linguistic strategy in which syllables or word components are reversed or rearranged to create playful, coded forms of speech. In Mongolian youth registers, speakers manipulate phonological and morphological structures to generate expressions that are both socially marked and contextually nuanced. These creative inversions serve multiple functions: signalling group membership, asserting identity, and resisting conventional linguistic norms (Shinjee & Dovchin, 2025). By introducing such examples to ChatGPT, Tamir probes the AI's ability to navigate highly dynamic, socially situated language forms, highlighting the gap between human understanding of culturally embedded linguistic creativity and AI's reliance on standard or canonical language patterns.

In Figure 5.5, while the sentence "*Hugiin shoog yostoi laajindaa yostoi nailij bnadaa*" is correctly identified by ChatGPT as Mongolian written in Latin script (Romanisation), its full English translation is significantly distorted. The accurate interpretation of the sentence is: "*The Hu's 'Shoog' is completely killing it. Totally nailing it.*" This refers to the Mongolian popular folk-rock band The Hu and their song *Shoog*, which Tamir finds impressive. The Hu have gained international fame for

---

Hugiin shoog yostoi laajindaa yostoi nailij bnadaa - what language is it and what does it mean?

The sentence "Hugiin shoog yostoi laajindaa yostoi nailij bnadaa" is in **Mongolian (using Latin script)** with some slang expressions.

**Meaning in English:**

- **Hugiin shoog** — *crazy/funny joke or satire* (where "hugiin" is slang for something wild or ridiculous, and "shoog" means joke or satire)
- **yostoi** — really, truly, absolutely
- **laajindaa** — slang meaning *awesome, amazing, lit,* or *on fire*
- **yostoi nailij bnadaa** — really nailing it, doing it perfectly

**Full translation:**

*"The crazy/funny joke is really awesome, absolutely killing it!"*

---

So it's a casual, enthusiastic compliment about someone's joke, performance, or comedic act, praising it as very funny and well done.

If you want, I can also help you write it in Cyrillic Mongolian or make it more formal!

Figure 5.5 What language is it?

## 5.3 The Precarity of AI

blending traditional Mongolian throat singing (*khöömei*), traditional instruments such as the *morin khuur* (horsehead fiddle), and heavy metal elements, creating a sound sometimes called "Hunnu Rock." Their music has attracted global audiences, with viral hits on YouTube, appearances at major music festivals, and chart success in Western countries. This cross-cultural appeal has positioned them as one of Mongolia's most prominent contemporary musical exports. However, ChatGPT renders the translation as: "The crazy/funny joke is really awesome, absolutely killing it!" This misinterpretation reveals multiple failures in handling inverted and hybridised language forms. For instance, *laajindaa* (лаажиндаа) is part of the Mongolian youth-inverted register – a transformation of *aljiindaa*, meaning "killing it," which ChatGPT fails to recognise. Additionally, the Anglicised Mongolian form *nailij*, a blend of the English verb *nail* with the Mongolian verbal suffix *-ij*, is also misrepresented. Furthermore, The Hu's "*Shoog*" is mistaken for "crazy/funny joke," demonstrating AI's inability to identify culturally and contextually grounded references in popular media.

This example highlights the limitations of AI in accurately interpreting human-specific languaging formed by hybrid, youth-oriented, and culturally embedded Mongolian registers, particularly when they involve inversion, English integration, and domain-specific knowledge. While ChatGPT can recognise surface bilingual elements – identifying English and Mongolian words – it struggles to grasp the deeper cultural, spiritual, and contextual nuances embedded in the languaging. For instance, the song *Shoog* carries profound significance: it is not merely entertainment, but a ritual practice rooted in Tengerism (Mongolian shamanism), involving prayers to ancestors for the well-being of Mongolia (Bumochir, 2014). AI's inability to capture this meaning reflects a broader process of AI-mediated de-languaging, in which the rich, embodied, and context-dependent human meanings of cultural-linguistic expressions risk being flattened or lost in AI-mediated translation and interpretation. The precarity of understanding arises from the dominant language frameworks embedded within AI models, which inadequately represent both playful youth linguistic creativity and the spiritual depth of shamanic rituals. As a result, users' complex cultural and spiritual messages, such as prayers to ancestors or youth inverted registers, may be reduced to simplified, decontextualised linguistic units. This highlights the fragility of intercultural transmission in digital interactions and illustrates how AI-mediated languaging can inadvertently erode the subtleties of meaning in socially and culturally rich contexts (O'Regan & Ferri, 2025).

> what does "sevleg urgeeh" in Mongolian language?

In Mongolian, **"sevleg urgeeh"** (сэвлэг ургах) literally means **"to grow a moustache or facial hair."**
- **"sevleg"** (сэвлэг) → facial hair, moustache, or beard.
- **"urgeeh"** (ургах) → to grow.

So, it's used to describe someone (usually a boy) who is starting to grow facial hair. For example, in cultural contexts, you might hear it about boys reaching puberty: *"huuhdiin sevleg urgeedeg 3 nas hureheeree"* — "by the age of 3 (or a certain age) boys start growing facial hair."

If you want, I can also explain the **cultural nuance**, because in Mongolian tradition, "sevleg urgeeh" sometimes carries more than just a literal meaning—it can mark the transition from boyhood to adolescence.

Do you want me to explain that cultural aspect?

Figure 5.6  *Sevleg Urgeeh*

### Extract 3

Tamir engages with ChatGPT once again, this time introducing culturally specific Mongolian phrases to explore the AI's ability to interpret subtle cultural meanings and to test its cultural competence (see Figure 5.6). At this stage, he is aware that the AI can recognise Mongolian and can, to some extent, translate Mongolian into English. However, Tamir aims to challenge it further by using a range of words and expressions deeply rooted in Mongolia's nomadic culture – terms connected to pastoral life, traditional rituals, and daily practices of herding communities. Through this process, he seeks to observe how well the AI can navigate culturally embedded knowledge, not just linguistic translation, and whether it can grasp the social, historical, and spiritual layers that shape the meanings of these phrases. This approach highlights the limits of AI in interpreting language that is deeply intertwined with lived cultural experiences. As Tamir posts: *"Hilarious. Totally the opposite!* ☺ *."*

In this example, Tamir highlights that the increasing reliance on ChatGPT raises critical questions regarding the representation of traditional knowledge systems, such as Mongolian nomadic traditions. While ChatGPT can provide translations, it often fails to capture the specific cultural meanings embedded within these knowledge systems. This section examines how such technologies can misrepresent traditional Mongolian practices, thereby contributing to a subtle form of cultural erasure. For instance, Tamir asked ChatGPT to explain the meaning of the Mongolian phrase *"sevleg urgeeh."* ChatGPT rendered it

## 5.3 The Precarity of AI

as "to grow a moustache or facial hair," which is entirely inaccurate and, to Tamir, "*hilariously*" opposite. In Mongolian culture, the phrase refers to a ritual performed for children, typically around three years of age, where the child's hair is carefully fluffed or groomed. Symbolically, this act is meant to bless and protect the child, promote health, growth, and well-being, mark a developmental milestone in early childhood, and remove negativity or evil spirits. Thus, while the literal action involves grooming or fluffing the hair, its deeper significance lies in ritualistic care and blessing. Traditionally, Mongolians do not cut a child's hair until this ceremony. Once the child reaches three years old, a large celebration is held, inviting relatives and friends. The community blesses the child, touches the hair, and only then is the haircut, making the ritual a meaningful rite of passage. This example illustrates how AI tools, while helpful in general translation, can overlook the rich cultural context, leading to misinterpretations of traditional practices and undermining the depth of traditional knowledge systems (Adiyasuren, 2014).

In a separate post, Tamir expresses his admiration and pride for Chinggis Khan, reflecting a sentiment widely shared among many Mongolians, who regard him as the founding father of their nation and a central figure of their cultural heritage and national identity (Sabloff, 2001). Tamir shares the image of Chinggis Khan in Figure 5.7, accompanied by one of his most famous verses, and asks ChatGPT to interpret its meaning. However, he is disappointed by the AI's response, finding that it distorts the essence of the verse. The verse, deeply embedded in Mongolian history and poetic tradition, carries layers of cultural, emotional, and philosophical significance that Tamir feels the AI fails to capture. Tamir posts: "*Pissed off 😡. I can't believe how ChatGPT distorted the Chinggis Khaan's famous words. So, my advice is if you want to learn proper Mongolian, always check with humans first.*"

This verse is one of the most famous attributed to Chinggis Khan, recorded in the *Secret History of the Mongols*. This verse exemplifies an archaic poetic style of the Mongolian language, deeply rooted in the cultural and historical imagination of the Mongol people. Its phrasing, rhythm, and emotional intensity are almost impossible to render fully in English while preserving its poetic power. In essence, Chinggis Khan declares: "May my body exhaust, but my nation never exhausts; may my whole body die, but my whole nation never dies." Significantly, AI-generated translations, such as ChatGPT's rendering, "May my body not become exhausted from fatigue"/"Let my body not be worn out," offer an interpretation that entirely misses the verse's

Алд бие минь алжааваас алжаатугай
Ахуй төр минь бүү алдартугай
Бүтэн бие минь алжааваас алжаатугай
Бүрэн улс минь бүү алдартугай...
МОНГОЛ БАХАРХЛЫН ӨДИЙН МЭНД ДЭВШҮҮЛЬЕ

Figure 5.7 Chinggis Khan

cultural, poetic, and historical weight. Such a translation reverses the original sentiment, shifting from a selfless, sacrificial devotion to the nation to a focus on personal comfort. Moreover, ChatGPT interprets the verse as a "protective blessing or prayer," instead of the famous Chinggis Khan declaration. For Tamir, despite being born in Australia, and like many Mongolians in Mongolia, this misinterpretation is culturally and emotionally offensive, as Chinggis Khan is still revered as the founding father of the nation, and his legacy is honoured in spiritual and national contexts. Tamir expresses strong negative emotions such as anger and frustration – "*Pissed off*" – signalling a visceral reaction to the AI's mistranslation. The sad emoticon conveys a sense of loss – loss of linguistic integrity, loss of trust in AI as a mediator of knowledge and disappointment. Tamir's advice – "*always check with humans first*" – reflects the user's desire to safeguard the authenticity of the AI-mediated languaging. It is both a personal and cultural emotional response to the risk of misrepresentation. The AI's misreading, therefore, is a *de-languaging*, which constitutes a subtle erasure of the profound cultural meaning embedded in Mongolian historical texts. This experience highlights the limitations of AI in conveying the subtleties embedded within languaging, particularly when it comes to expressions that are intrinsically tied to a specific cultural and historical context.

These mistranslations highlight a deeper precarity in AI – the dominance of Western epistemologies in digital language infrastructures. When Mongolian archaic verses are reduced to generic actions, the ritual knowledge and cultural-historical specificity embedded in them are erased. Such flattening has significant implications for language policy, particularly in societies where digital tools mediate access to education, governance, and cultural preservation. AI's precarity lies not in grammar or syntax, which it parses well, but in pragmatics – the social, cultural, and emotional layers of meaning. Mongolian repertoires, like many non-Western repertoires, are under-represented in training data, producing uneven performance and reinforcing linguistic marginalisation. This raises doubts about AI's authority: Tamir's metalinguistic awareness destabilises the notion that AI "knows" language, revealing it as fallible, funny, and sometimes absurd. This precarity is not merely technical but also political. It reflects broader struggles for linguistic justice in a digital world dominated by English-centric systems. Here, "languaging" refers to the dynamic, social practice of using language as a living resource. In this interaction, the user is languaging – using Mongolian repertoires with identity, emotion, and context – while the AI is de-languaging, stripping the phrase of richness through a literal, context-free translation. The exchange becomes a metalinguistic performance: Tamir is not only learning Mongolian but also speaking about learning Mongolian, prompting reflection on what gets lost in translation. This critical moment exemplifies digital reflexivity, where users confront the limits of technology, affirm the depth of their own linguistic practices, and expose cultural gaps that AI cannot bridge.

## 5.4 CLOSING THOUGHTS: TOWARDS A "LINGUISTICALLY JUST" AI FUTURE

Languaging – the dynamic and fluid use of multiple linguistic resources in everyday communication – is particularly vulnerable in AI-mediated contexts. When AI systems attempt to parse or translate nonstandard, hybrid, or mixed-language forms, the subtle interplay of linguistic, cultural, and affective meaning can be flattened or lost entirely – a process that can be understood as AI-mediated de-languaging. This de-languaging has profound social, historic, cultural, and emotional consequences for AI users and language learners. Users may experience frustration, anger, or distrust when AI tools fail to reflect the integrity of their linguistic practices, or when poetic, historical, or culturally significant texts are reduced to simplified, generic outputs. These experiences illuminate the precarity of languaging, where the meaning of language is fragile, contingent on who or what mediates it, and vulnerable to erasure or misrepresentation within digital infrastructures dominated by globalised AI. As Birhane (2020) observes in the African context, Western-developed AI is often unsuitable for local challenges, while simultaneously limiting the growth of locally created technologies and creating dependency on Western infrastructure. Following this reasoning, Western AI systems may be ill-suited for Indigenous language speakers, minority language learners, or multilingual communities, potentially undermining local linguistic development and reinforcing dependence on English-dominated AI frameworks. This phenomenon can also be understood through algorithmic colonialingualism, where AI not only mediates language but actively enforces dominant linguistic norms and hierarchies. By privileging standard or majority-language forms and marginalising hybrid, minority, or Indigenous practices, AI perpetuates a form of digital linguistic colonialism. The result is not merely technical misinterpretation but the systemic reproduction of linguistic inequities, where certain ways of speaking and knowing are validated, while others are devalued, erased, or rendered unintelligible. In this sense, AI-mediated languaging is not neutral: it participates in shaping whose voices count, whose knowledge is legible, and whose cultural heritage is preserved or diminished.

Zhu et al. (2025) add an important layer to this discussion by emphasising the ways in which sociolinguistic practices become "enregistered" – how particular ways of speaking and associated social identities are encoded into cultural perception. Generative AI has the capacity to turbo-charge these processes of enregisterment, potentially reinforcing biases and stereotyping, and complicating efforts to support equitable language practices. Zhu et al. (2025) also remind us that our understanding of AI is co-constructed: how we imagine AI, its intelligence, sentience, and agency, in turn shapes our social practices and interactions with both language and technology. This insight connects directly to the emotional and cultural stakes of linguistic precarity, highlighting that AI de-languaging is not only a technical problem but also a social and ethical one, with tangible consequences for communities and identities.

## 5.4 Towards a "Linguistically Just" AI Future

Moving forward, it is essential to promote a shared responsibility for ethical AI design and use. Policymakers, educators, researchers, and technologists must work together to ensure AI systems respect and support linguistic and cultural diversity (Dobinson et al., 2024; Nash, 2024). This includes the recognition of "languaging," which encompasses Indigenous, minority, and historically marginalised languages, along with their sociolinguistic and cultural significance. Such a collective effort also involves promoting AI tools capable of accommodating diverse linguistic repertoires, semiotic resources, and cultural practices, particularly those that are endangered or underrepresented. Importantly, systems should be co-designed to embrace nonstandard linguistic varieties and *languaging practices* rather than enforcing rigid, dominant language norms (Dobinson et al., 2024; Nash, 2024).

Structural inequities compound these challenges. The high cost of designing and deploying AI can exacerbate the digital divide between wealthier nations in the Global North and under-resourced regions in the Global South (Fang & Dovchin, 2024). Without deliberate efforts to develop locally relevant, inclusive, and affordable AI solutions, the potential benefits of AI in additional language education risk remaining out of reach for the communities that could gain the most. Implementing AI in education often requires significant financial, technological, and human resources, which can further widen disparities between well-resourced and under-resourced educational contexts, particularly in developing regions (Dovchin, 2024c).

Addressing challenges in AI integration within education necessitates proactive strategies, such as expanding AI datasets to encompass cultural and linguistic diversity. This can be effectively achieved through participatory or co-design frameworks, where educators, community leaders, and policymakers from linguistically and culturally diverse backgrounds collaborate to develop AI-based solutions (Eke & Reyes Cruz, 2024; Ivetta et al., 2025). Such approaches are vital for preventing neocolonial biases and ensuring AI-supported education is culturally and linguistically responsive (Langeveldt & Pietersen, 2024). By critically examining how AI shapes power dynamics in the classroom, teachers can advocate for practices that empower learners and celebrate linguistic diversity as an asset. Recent studies highlight the importance of culturally inclusive AI datasets. For instance, the HESEIA dataset, co-designed by educators and students in Latin America, captures intersectional biases across multiple demographic axes and school subjects, reflecting local contexts through lived experiences and pedagogical expertise (Ivetta et al., 2025).

Similarly, the Culturally-Informed & Values-Inclusive Corpus for Societal Impacts (CIVICS) dataset evaluates the social and cultural variation of large language models across multiple languages and value-sensitive topics, promoting reproducibility and transparency across broader linguistic settings (Pistilli et al., 2024). Participatory design frameworks are increasingly recognised as essential for decolonising AI in education. Collaborative efforts among stakeholders from diverse backgrounds can help set out requirements for decolonising AI, considering different contexts and assessment mechanisms to ensure decoloniality requirements are met (Eke & Reyes Cruz, 2024). These frameworks also emphasise the need for cultural responsiveness, ethical awareness, and critical engagement among stakeholders while addressing structural and systemic barriers to achieving social justice and equity in AI education (Langeveldt & Pietersen, 2024).

Applied linguists must also interrogate the broader social and political implications of AI in language education. Technologies should be designed to amplify linguistic plurality, ensuring that they respect and reflect global cultural diversities and value pluralism (Pistilli et al., 2024). Integrating large language models into educational environments can enhance accessibility, inclusivity, and individualised learning experiences, significantly mitigating traditional barriers related to language diversity, learning disabilities, cultural differences, and socio-economic inequalities (Langeveldt & Pietersen, 2024). This chapter serves as a critical reflection on the potential trajectories of AI in language education, emphasising that the future is not predetermined. The development and deployment of AI in educational contexts depend on the deliberate choices of educators, researchers, policymakers, and technologists. By highlighting equity, diversity, and a linguistically just approach, AI can realise its transformative potential while mitigating risks of linguistic homogenisation, cultural erasure, and educational inequality. Recognising *languaging practices*, guarding against AI de-languaging, and addressing the various cultural and other stakes of linguistic precarity are central to this vision. By doing so, we move towards an inclusive future where all languages, their cultural contexts, and all learners are valued equally – ensuring that AI does not merely reflect dominant global languages but actively supports linguistic plurality, cultural heritage, and the well-being of language communities.

# 6 Pedagogical Languaging and the Future of Applied Linguistics

## 6.1 LANGUAGING: PLAYFULNESS AND PRECARITY

This book has traced both the theoretical underpinnings and practical enactments of *languaging* – a dynamic, situated, and embodied process through which language users, learners, teachers, and communities mobilise their full linguistic, cultural, and semiotic repertoires to make meaning, negotiate identities, and reshape power relations (Arellano & Torres-Vásquez, 2025; Cowley, 2019, 2024; Dovchin & Shinjee, 2022). Languaging, as I have argued, is never a simple act of transmitting information: it is always deeply entangled with identities, histories, emotions, and relations of power. By situating language in practice rather than as an abstract system, I have sought to illuminate how language users draw on their repertoires not only to communicate but also to survive, resist, and create new possibilities for being, communicating, and belonging. In doing so, I have challenged dominant monolingualist ideologies that continue to shape educational policies, assessment regimes, and broader social expectations. At the same time, I have resisted reductive treatments of "bi/multilingualism" that tokenise linguistic diversity, treating it as a resource to be celebrated only superficially, without recognising its lived, embodied, relational, and often precarious dimensions (Gramling, 2016, 2021; Lee, 2022; Pennycook, 2024). Instead, I have positioned bi/multilingualism as a deeply human practice that is tied to identity, belonging, knowledge, and practice.

Throughout the book, I have emphasised that what individuals *do* with the languages they know cannot and should not be measured against prescriptive ideals of linguistic purity (Chapter 1). As I have illustrated across chapters, a casual conversation might effortlessly weave together Aboriginal English, Kriol, Mongolian, English, Korean, and so on – each shift prompted by the language users' needs, affective factors, or contextual and relational relevance. These fluid and creative linguistic practices reveal the profound limitations of essentialist perspectives that frame languages as fixed, bounded, and homogenous systems. Rather than treating language as a mechanical code to be mastered, real-world communication exposes its adaptive and inventive nature: a living and embodied practice continuously reshaped by cultural shifts, social relations, and personal agency (Lee & Li Wei, 2025; Wong & García, 2025). As discussed in Chapters 2 and 3, I have highlighted the importance of recognising Indigenous and nomadic ways of thinking about language. Such perspectives remind us that linguistic inquiry is not only about describing structures or cataloguing codes but about understanding how people themselves conceptualise, value, and live with languages in their everyday worlds (Leonard, 2019; Ober, 2025a; Pennycook, 2024). For Indigenous and Mongolian nomadic communities, language is not simply a bounded system of grammar or vocabulary; it is deeply interconnected with land, kinship, spirituality, and ways of knowing (Steele et al., 2025). To engage with these epistemologies is to move beyond the abstraction of language as an isolated object of study, and instead to see it as relational, embedded in histories, cultural practices, and ecological contexts. Engaging with these perspectives also unsettles the hierarchies and universalising assumptions of dominant Western linguistics, which have historically privileged notions of standardisation, purity, and stability (Dovchin et al., 2024). By attending to Indigenous and nomadic understandings, we begin to see how languages are not fixed entities but living practices that are dynamic, adaptive, and inseparable from broader social and cultural life. This recognition opens pathways towards more inclusive, decolonial approaches to studying language – approaches that value knowledge systems that have long been marginalised or dismissed within mainstream linguistics (Leonard, 2019; Ober, 2025a). Crucially, recognising these ways of thinking about language also carries ethical and political implications. It requires scholars to engage not just in descriptive analysis but in dialogue and accountability, acknowledging the authority of communities to define their own linguistic realities. It also calls us to reimagine the goals of linguistic research itself – not merely to produce knowledge *about* communities, but to work *with* them in ways that respect sovereignty, relationality, and lived experience. In this sense, as discussed in Chapters 2 and 3, Indigenous and nomadic epistemologies do more than broaden the horizons of linguistic theory: they challenge us to rethink the very purpose of linguistic inquiry, urging a shift from detached analysis towards engaged, embodied, and land-oriented scholarship (Leonard, 2019; Ober, 2025).

## 6.1 Languaging: Playfulness and Precarity

I have further explored the *playfulness* and *precarity* of languaging, emphasising its dual and often paradoxical nature across all chapters. On the one hand, languaging enables joy, creativity, and innovation. It allows speakers to improvise, to mix and blend linguistic resources in ways that generate humour, intimacy, and solidarity (Holflod, 2022; Parnell & Patsarika, 2014; Robson & LeVoguer, 2025). The playful aspects of languaging open up spaces where individuals and communities can experiment with identities, invent new modes of expression, and resist rigid linguistic norms that attempt to regulate how people should speak. Through such creative, playful, and innovative acts, language becomes not only a tool for communication but also a resource for resilience, self-affirmation, and community-building. On the other hand, this same playfulness is precarious, as it remains deeply vulnerable to surveillance, correction, and racialisation (French et al., 2024; Jun & Mori, 2024). What may feel fluid and expressive to one speaker is often judged by others as "incorrect," "broken," or "impure" (Dovchin, 2024a). These judgements reveal that acts of languaging are never neutral: they are embedded in structures of power, inequality, and vulnerability. To be playful with language is to take risks – risks of being misunderstood, marginalised, or disciplined. Yet it is precisely through such risks that new possibilities for meaning, belonging, and resistance emerge (Hawkins & Tiwari, 2024).

From this perspective, "play/fulness" is not just linguistic performance or humour – it's often a survival strategy, a form of identity negotiation, or subtle resistance within systems that privilege White, standard English. While playful on the surface, such language use is deeply shaped by histories of colonialism, migration, racism, and linguistic hierarchies. As I have discussed in Chapter 4, languaging is profoundly entangled with processes of racialisation, and here too its playful and precarious dimensions come to the fore. For many racialised speakers, playful linguistic practices such as stylisation or parody can be powerful strategies of resistance, humour, and cultural pride. Yet these same playful acts can be misinterpreted, mocked, or penalised when heard through racialised frames of judgement. What for one community may be a joyful performance of identity can be dismissed by outsiders as evidence of deficiency or lack. In this way, Chapter 4 shows that the playfulness of languaging is always shadowed by precarity: it can disrupt and resist racial hierarchies, but it can also expose racialised subjects to intensified forms of linguistic policing, discrimination, and exclusion. Thus, languaging cannot be disentangled from race, power, and social stratification; racialised experiences fundamentally shape how playfulness itself is interpreted, evaluated, and policed (Anya, 2016; Dovchin, 2025a; Flores & Rosa, 2015; Grammon, 2025; May, 2023; Rosa & Flores, 2017; Sah, 2019; Smith, 2025). Building on this, Chapter 5 turns to the contemporary challenges posed by AI-mediated languaging. Emerging technologies simultaneously expand and constrain linguistic practices. On one level, digital platforms offer unprecedented opportunities for linguistically diverse communication, playful expressions, and global connection. On another level, however, these same technologies embed precarity that privilege dominant languages, standardised forms, and algorithmically recognisable speech patterns. In doing so, they risk reinforcing existing hierarchies while limiting access to linguistic justice. The rise of AI-mediated communication raises urgent questions about whose voices are amplified, whose are erased, and how technologies will shape the future of identity, interaction, and belonging (Dobinson et al., 2024; Zhu et al., 2025).

Taken together, this book advances an understanding of languaging as relational, embodied, and political. Languaging is not merely a mechanism for transmitting information but a practice that is deeply bound up with identity, belonging, and power. It is at once playful and precarious, resistant and creative. Above all, it challenges us to move beyond static and purified conceptions of language, and instead to acknowledge the lived realities of linguistic diversity – realities shaped by colonial histories, racial hierarchies, global mobility, and technological mediation, but also sustained by everyday acts of creativity, solidarity, and care.

## 6.2 REFRAMING PEDAGOGY THROUGH LANGUAGING: PEDAGOGICAL LANGUAGING

In the shifting landscapes of the twenty-first century, education must respond to radical reconfigurations of culture, identity, and communication. Globalisation, intensified migration, digital connectivity, and the everyday work of imagination have unsettled long-held assumptions about what counts as language, community, or belonging. Pedagogical languaging, in this sense, positions pedagogy not as the delivery of standardised curricula, but as the creation of spaces where learners can mobilise their full semiotic repertoires – linguistic, cultural, embodied, and digital – to engage, explore, and construct knowledge. A key implication emerging from this discussion is that applied linguistics must reframe pedagogy as *interactional design* rather

## 6.2 Reframing Pedagogy through Languaging

than mere curriculum delivery. If we take languaging seriously, then pedagogy cannot be confined to the transmission of standardised forms or the policing of correctness (Hamman-Ortiz & Romero, 2025). *Pedagogical languaging*, in this sense, refers to the intentional design and facilitation of learning environments in which meaning-making is understood as a dynamic, multimodal, and relational process rather than the reproduction of fixed linguistic forms. Pedagogical languaging invites educators to become designers of interactional spaces in which languaging, multimodality, and cross-genre meaning-making are not "add-ons" or compensatory strategies, but constitutive dimensions of learning itself. Such a reframing requires educators to abandon deficit framings of learners' nonstandard, non-dominant languaging practices. Rather than treating these practices as obstacles to overcome, they must be recognised as epistemic resources – sources of knowledge, creativity, and critical insight that expand what counts as legitimate participation in educational spaces (Erling & Weidl, 2025). This shift has profound consequences for how we imagine teaching, learning, and assessment. It requires cultivating classrooms as sites of linguistic justice, where the full repertoires of students are welcomed, where playfulness and experimentation are encouraged, and where vulnerability is met with support rather than correction. It also demands a rethinking of the role of educators themselves: not as gatekeepers of linguistic purity, but as co-learners and facilitators who nurture the dynamic, adaptive, and relational nature of communication. In short, to embrace languaging is to embrace pedagogy as design for diversity, equity, and transformation (Wong & Du, 2025). To engage in pedagogical languaging is to work with, rather than against, the fluid, hybrid, and cosmopolitan realities of learners' lives. It means attending to the multiple digital, local, and transnational worlds students inhabit – whether that is a Sudanese–Australian teenager switching between Arabic, English, and TikTok slang in a single conversation; an Aboriginal student blending Standard Australian English with Aboriginal English and Kriol in a persuasive speech; or a newly arrived Afghan girl drawing on Dari metaphors while crafting a verse for her English assessment. In these moments, meaning-making travels across spaces, classrooms, online gaming chats, and community kitchens, defying the idea that learning happens in isolation from lived experience.

Here, language is not a static code delivered by the teacher; it is a living, embodied performance, entangled with culture, desire, and imagination. A science lesson might include students explaining concepts through bilingual diagrams that merge Aboriginal languages and English terminology. A history project might have refugee-background students creating podcasts that weave their family's oral histories with official national narratives. In each case, languaging becomes a way of performing identity and claiming space (Steele et al., 2025). Pedagogical languaging refuses the bounded "village" model of schooling. Instead, it envisions learning encounters more like hotel lobbies, city buses, or music venues – sites of ongoing arrival, departure, and exchange. Students bring with them repertoires shaped by family, peers, media, and migration histories, which they remix in response to shifting audiences and contexts (Kwon et al., 2025). A single lunchtime conversation can move from K-pop fandom talk in Korean and English, to planning a cultural food stall using Cantonese, to debating a maths problem in languagised school English. At its heart, pedagogical languaging is performative: it understands that identities are not pregiven but brought into being through the act of languaging itself. A classroom animated by this approach is not a sealed container of pre-scripted outcomes but a space of continual becoming, where linguistic and cultural resources are negotiated, challenged, and reinvented (Ridley & Bhowmik, 2025). This vision calls for educators to see themselves as co-travellers rather than gatekeepers – moving with the flow of linguistic and cultural change, sustaining students' agency to name their worlds, and recognising the legitimacy of their diverse ways of speaking, being, and learning (Kwon et al., 2025). The challenge is not merely to theorise this shift but to enact it in everyday practice: to design pedagogies that honour fluidity without romanticising it, that embrace hybridity without erasing inequality, and that cultivate spaces where languages, identities, and futures can be co-authored in the living present.

### *6.3 LANGUAGE TEACHER EDUCATION AND PEDAGOGICAL LANGUAGING*

This book reveals a pressing need for sustained, transformative teacher education that cultivates reflexivity, critical language awareness, and the confidence to design and enact languaging pedagogies. For many educators, initial training has been rooted in monolingual assumptions: that is, teaching the target language as a fixed code to be mastered. Pedagogical languaging challenges this stance, positioning teachers as co-researchers of their students' full repertoires. Central to this shift is teacher agency (Fang et al., 2022; Maseko, 2022). In a *pedagogical languaging* approach, teachers are not passive implementers of pre-packaged "best practice" templates, but active co-creators of learning designs alongside students and communities. A teacher in a remote school might collaborate with Aboriginal Elders to co-develop literacy units drawing on local languages, local stories, and seasonal calendars (Guenther et al., 2025). An ESL teacher in an urban migrant hub might design assessments where students integrate home languages into English writing tasks, then collectively analyse how different language choices affect meaning and tone (Dovchin, 2025a, b). This work also requires critical language awareness – the ability to recognise how linguistic hierarchies operate in schools, how language policies privilege certain varieties over others, and how assessment practices can perpetuate or challenge inequality (Kwon et al., 2025). For example, teachers trained in critical language awareness are better equipped to explain to parents why their child's mixing of Hindi and English is a strength, not a weakness, and to advocate for assessment formats that capture this skill. To make such teacher agency possible, policy and systemic shifts are essential. Professional development should be continuous, collaborative, and embedded in teachers' real contexts, rather than one-off workshops (Beltran-Palanques et al., 2025). Resourcing should cover time release for community engagement, co-planning, and professional learning circles focused on plurilingual practice (Ollerhead et al., 2025). Institutional trust is critical: teachers must be recognised as knowledge producers who generate new pedagogical insights from their classrooms, not simply as deliverers of centrally designed curricula (Beltran-Palanques et al., 2025). Teacher education programs must, therefore, model pedagogical languaging themselves, encouraging pre-service and in-service teachers to draw on their own linguistic repertoires in coursework, to design plurilingual lesson plans, and to reflect critically on their positionality as language educators. Only when teachers have experienced and practised these approaches will they feel confident to enact them with students. In short, language teacher education for pedagogical languaging is not about adding a *"languaging unit"* to existing program agencies (Fang et al., 2022; Maseko, 2022). It is about reimagining the teacher's role: as reflexive practitioner, cultural mediator, community collaborator, and curriculum innovator, committed to fostering the fluid, hybrid, and socially responsive meaning-making that defines our current linguistically diverse world (Beltran-Palanques et al., 2025; Ollerhead et al., 2025).

## 6.4 RETHINKING ASSESSMENT THROUGH PEDAGOGICAL LANGUAGING

The principles of pedagogical languaging cannot thrive within the confines of assessment systems designed for a monolingual ideal. Traditional standardised testing regimes measure proficiency solely against one dominant code – most often a national standard of English – while disregarding the complex, adaptive ways students use their full linguistic repertoires to make meaning (Steele et al., 2022). In such systems, an Aboriginal student, for example, weaving Gija and English to explain a science concept is judged as producing "mixed" or "incorrect" language, rather than as demonstrating conceptual mastery through sophisticated languaging (Chapter 2; Chapter 4). As we have argued elsewhere in our work, "Stop measuring Black kids with White sticks!," we critique the practice of assessing Aboriginal children through the lens of Standard Australian English. Such assessments impose linguistic norms that do not reflect the diverse language practices of Aboriginal communities and risk misrepresenting children's true abilities, perpetuating systemic inequities in education (Steele et al., 2022). A future-oriented assessment framework must begin by recognising that meaning-making is rarely confined to a single language or mode. Rather than treating languaging as "errors" or "noise," assessments should value these as evidence of flexible thinking, audience awareness, and deep engagement with content. For example, research indicates that when refugee-background students often utilise multimodal assessments, such as podcasts or digital storytelling, to express their understanding, this approach allows students to integrate multiple languages and personal artefacts, providing a richer representation of their knowledge and experiences (Barnes & Tour, 2023). When Aboriginal students are assessed through Aboriginal-led, strength-based approaches, they thrive academically, complete their studies successfully, and demonstrate deeper engagement with learning that affirms their cultural identity and knowledge system (Persaud et al., 2025; Steele et al., 2022, 2025).

Assessment criteria must be redesigned to capture the complexity of such work. This requires moving away from rigid rubrics that prioritise grammatical accuracy in one language, and towards descriptors that value:

(1) The strategic use of multiple languages and modes.
(2) The ability to adapt communication to different audiences.
(3) Creativity in blending linguistic and cultural resources.
(4) Depth of conceptual understanding, regardless of the language(s) used to express it.

## 6.5 Future of Applied Linguistics and Languaging

Practical steps might include allowing linguistic glossaries in written tasks, accepting multimodal submissions (video, audio, visual artefacts), and training assessors to recognise linguistic innovation rather than penalising deviation from a monolingual norm (Wong, 2025). Without such changes, assessments will continue to undermine the very capacities, flexibility, creativity, and intercultural competence that education claims to nurture (Cenoz & Gorter, 2025). Pedagogical languaging offers an alternative: assessment that reflects the linguistically fluid and multimodal realities students inhabit, and that measures what they can truly do with all the resources at their disposal.

### *6.5 FUTURE OF APPLIED LINGUISTICS AND LANGUAGING*

Several key future research directions emerge from this book that hold promise for advancing the future of applied linguistics and the understanding of languaging. Longitudinal studies are essential to capture how languaging influences learner identities, academic achievement, and overall well-being over extended periods, providing a complex understanding of its sustained effects beyond short-term interventions (Dovchin, 2024a,b; Jang, 2024; Wong & Gallagher, 2025). As Wong and Gallagher (2025) argue, adopting a longitudinal perspective on practices such as translanguaging may provide valuable insights into how language users not only develop but also refine and sustain their translanguaging practices over time. Such a perspective allows researchers and educators to trace the evolving ways in which learners navigate multiple linguistic resources, adapt to different communicative contexts, and integrate diverse languages and semiotic modes into their meaning-making processes. By examining languaging longitudinally, in this sense, we can better understand the cumulative effects of pedagogical interventions, the persistence of particular linguistic strategies, and the ways in which learners' languaging stance interacts with identity, motivation, and sociocultural factors across extended periods of learning. This approach thus highlights both the dynamic and enduring dimensions of languaging, offering a more detailed understanding of how languaging and language identities are cultivated in educational settings (Jang, 2024).

Comparative ethnographies conducted across diverse cultural, geographic, and institutional contexts can also reveal how culturally sustaining languaging pedagogies are adapted and enacted in relation to local histories, social power dynamics, and linguistic ecologies (Rosiers et al., 2018). By conducting comparative ethnographies of translanguaging practices in the Brussels and Oudenaarde schools, Rosiers et al. (2018), for example, highlight both similarities and context-specific differences across classrooms. The study investigated the interactional behaviours and the socio-pedagogical valorisation of translanguaging practices among teachers and pupils in both a multilingual and a monolingual classroom. The study shows that in the multilingual classroom, translanguaging practices often challenge or break linguistic norms, whereas in the monolingual classroom, they tend to revert towards the standard language norm. Across both settings, translanguaging occurs at the margins as well as at the centre of classroom activity, serving important socio-emotional purposes for them. However, pedagogical objectives linked to translanguaging are predominantly observed in the multilingual classroom, highlighting the role of classroom linguistic ecology in shaping both the form and function of translanguaging practices for them (Rosiers et al., 2018).

Equally crucial is the expansion of collaborative, community-led research that partners directly with Indigenous, refugee, and migrant communities to co-create pedagogical models firmly rooted in local epistemologies and knowledge systems (Chapters 2, 3, & 4). Such partnership-based approaches ensure that educational practices are relevant, respectful, and empowering, rather than externally imposed or culturally reductive (Steele et al., 2025). Central to this future-facing framework is an unwavering commitment to linguistic justice. As discussed in Chapters 2–5, language is never neutral; it is deeply interwoven with histories of colonisation, forced assimilation, displacement, and racialised marginalisation that continue to impact Aboriginal, refugee, and migrant students. The concept of linguistic justice emphasises the importance of recognising and valuing the diverse linguistic resources that students bring to the educational environment, challenging monolingual norms, and promoting inclusivity (Piller, 2016). Expanding collaborative, community-led research and committing to linguistic justice are pivotal steps towards creating educational environments that are inclusive and reflective of the diverse linguistic and cultural backgrounds of Indigenous, refugee, and migrant students.

Critical analyses of the rapidly evolving digital sphere must investigate how digital languaging practices – across platforms such as social media, gaming communities, and digital storytelling – are reshaping both formal and informal learning environments, challenging traditional notions of language, literacy, and identity (Chapter 5). Furthermore, the rise of artificial intelligence (AI) technologies

## 6.5 Future of Applied Linguistics and Languaging

presents both opportunities and challenges for pedagogical languaging. AI-powered tools, from language learning apps to automated translation and generative text systems, are transforming how learners' access, produce, and interact with language (Chapter 5). Applied linguistics must critically engage with AI to ensure these technologies support plurilingual practices, avoid reinforcing linguistic biases, and enhance, rather than replace, human-centred, relational modes of languaging and learning (Dai & Zhu, 2025; Sun & Lan, 2025).

Overall, for applied linguistics to maintain its relevance and transformative potential in the coming decades, it must decisively embrace a relational, justice-oriented paradigm. This paradigm positions pedagogical languaging not as a narrow specialist technique, but as the everyday reality of human communication – fluid, embodied, and socially accountable. It calls for a radical reimagining of classrooms as vibrant, dynamic sites of continual becoming, where languages, identities, and futures are actively co-constructed in the lived present. In this vision, research and pedagogy are inseparable and mutually reinforcing practices embedded in relationships of community, collaboration, and equity (Phyak, 2021; Selvi, 2025; Washington & Iruka, 2025). Applied linguistics must take seriously its ethical responsibilities: to disrupt entrenched linguistic hierarchies that privilege certain languages, varieties, and accents over others; to ensure that language pedagogies do not inadvertently reproduce structural inequalities under the guise of "standardisation" or "readiness"; and to conduct research that is accountable and responsive to the communities it engages, fostering co-ownership of knowledge and tangible benefits for those communities (Barnawi & R'boul, 2025).

Ultimately, pedagogical languaging offers an expansive, emancipatory vision of applied linguistics – one that moves beyond disciplinary constraints and restrictive definitions of language and learning. However, its transformative promise can only be fullfilled through collective enactment by researchers, educators, policymakers, and community members who commit to nurturing linguistic diversity and social justice across the diverse, contested, and multilingual worlds we inhabit (Phyak, 2021; Selvi, 2025; Washington & Iruka, 2025). The imperative before us is no longer to argue for the validity of this approach, but to courageously reimagine and reshape language education in ways that honour the full complexity of lived linguistic realities and empower learners to author their own multilingual futures in an increasingly globalised world.

## 6.6 CONCLUSION: LANGUAGING AS PLAYFULNESS AND PRECARITY

This book has sought to illuminate the dynamics of playfulness and precarity in minority language communities. As this final reflection highlights, the notion of precarity – the vulnerability, instability, and dispossession inherent in playful languaging practice – resonates across all forms of languaging in contemporary society. In an era shaped by capitalistic globalisation, where English dominates as the language of international communication, scholarship, and AI-mediated interactions, the stakes of languaging extend far beyond educational contexts (Dai & Zhu, 2025; Sun & Lan, 2025).

Decolonial, translanguaging, translingual, and multilingual practices exemplify both the creativity and fragility of human communication. They demonstrate that languaging is simultaneously a site of play, experimentation, and imaginative engagement, as well as a site of vulnerability to structural inequities and systemic control. Playfulness in languaging allows speakers to explore alternative ways of expressing identity, negotiating meaning, and building community, often in ways that resist dominant norms and hierarchies. At the same time, the precarity of these practices, shaped by political, economic, and technological pressures, reveals the instability and marginalisation that many speakers face. By framing languaging as both playful and precarious, language education is called to critically interrogate not only how language learners and minority speakers are disadvantaged, but also how all language users creatively navigate and contest the pressures of global hierarchies, AI-mediated communication, and socio-political domination. In recognising this duality, applied linguistics can attend to the ways that playfulness becomes a form of resilience and resistance, while precarity underscores the ethical and political stakes of linguistic practice in contemporary society (Phyak, 2021; Selvi, 2025; Washington & Iruka, 2025).

This perspective demands a critical stance in language education and research. It compels us to recognise that the political and economic forces shaping language use, whether in classrooms, digital spaces, or international scholarship, threaten the pluralism, diversity, and autonomy of human communication. Understanding languaging as both playfulness and precarity highlights the ethical and political responsibilities of applied linguists: to document, analyse, and intervene in ways that protect linguistic diversity and foster equitable communicative practices (Barnawi & R'boul, 2025).

By situating the concept of precarity at the heart of applied linguistic inquiry, this book contributes to ongoing efforts to envision more

## 6.6 Conclusion: Languaging as Playfulness and Precarity

just futures for language use, pedagogy, and research. It affirms that all languaging activities, from localised classroom interactions to global AI-mediated discourse, are arenas where power, inequality, and resistance intersect. Recognising this, applied linguistics can play a transformative role in promoting linguistic justice, advocating for marginalised speakers, and ensuring that the capacity to communicate remains a site of possibility rather than precarity.

# References

Adiyasuren, R. (2014). Даахь үргээх ёсон. https://gogo.mn/r/e215w.
Ag, A., & Jørgensen, J. N. (2013). Ideologies, norms, and practices in youth poly languaging. *International Journal of Bilingualism, 17*(4), 525–539.
Ahearn, A. (2018). Winters without women: Social change, split households and gendered labour in rural Mongolia. *Gender, Place & Culture, 25*(3), 399–415.
Andrews, J., Fay, R., Huang, Z. M., & White, R. (2023). From translanguaging to transknowledging: Exploring new epistemological and linguistic approaches in higher education research. In Jeroen Huisman & Malcolm Tight (Eds.), *Theory and Method in Higher Education Research* (pp. 137–151). Emerald.
Anya, U. (2016). *Racialized Identities in Second Language Learning: Speaking Blackness in Brazil*. Routledge.
Arellano, R., & Torres-Vásquez, L. (2025). The case of Sydney universities: Embracing multilingualism or preserving English-only practices in the Australian context? *Australian Review of Applied Linguistics*, 1–10. https://doi.org/10.1075/aral.24083.are.
Atkinson, J., Nelson, J., Brooks, R., Atkinson, C., & Ryan, K. (2014). Addressing individual and community transgenerational trauma. In P. Dudgeon, H. Milroy and R. Walker (Eds.), *Working Together: Aboriginal and Torres Strait Islander Mental Health and Wellbeing Principles and Practice* (Vol. 2, pp. 289–307). Australian Government Department of the Prime Minister and Cabinet.
Back, M., Peña-Pincheira, R., & Silva, D. (2025). Introducing the special issue. Critical reflections on colonial pedagogies: Lessons learned for language teacher education. *The Modern Language Journal, 109*(3), 499–510.
Baker-Bell, A. (2020). Dismantling anti-Black linguistic racism in English language arts classrooms: Toward an anti-racist Black language pedagogy. *Theory into Practice, 59*(1), 8–21.
Baker, W., Morán Panero, S., Álvarez Valencia, J. A., et al. (2025). Decolonizing English in higher education: Global Englishes and TESOL as opportunities or barriers. *TESOL Quarterly, 59*(1), 281–309.

# References

Bakhtin, M. M. (1981). *The Dialogic Imagination: Four Essays* (M. Holquist, Ed.; C. Emerson & M. Holquist, Trans.). University of Texas Press.

Bakhtin, M. (1984). *Rabelais and His World*. Indiana University Press.

Bakhtin, M. (1986). *Speech Genres and Other Late Essays* (V. W. McGee, Trans.). University of Texas Press.

Bakhtin, M. (1994). Problems of Dostoevsky's poetics. In P. Morris (Ed.), *The Bakhtin Reader: Selected Writings of Bakhtin, Medvedev, Voloshinov* (pp. 110–113). Arnold.

Balam, O. (2021). Beyond differences and similarities in codeswitching and translanguaging research. *Belgian Journal of Linguistics*, 35(1), 76–103.

Balogh, M. (2010). Contemporary shamanisms in Mongolia. *Asian Ethnicity*, 11(2), 229–238. https://doi.org/10.1080/14631361003779489.

Bao, Y. B., Li, X., & Kuperman, V. (2025). The eye movement database of passage reading in vertically written traditional Mongolian. *Scientific Data*, 12(1), 499.

Barnawi, O. Z., & R'boul, H. (2025). Against epistemological theft and appropriation in applied linguistics research. *Applied Linguistics Review*, 16(1), 127–135.

Barnes, M., & Tour, E. (2023) Empowering English as an additional language students through digital multimodal composing. *Literacy*, 57, 106–119. https://doi.org/10.1111/lit.12319.

Batdelger, G., Oborny, B., Batjav, B., & Molnár, Z. (2025). The relevance of traditional knowledge for modern landscape management: Comparing past and current herding practices in Mongolia. *People and Nature*, 7(5), 1056–1072.

Batsaikhan, J. (2025). Herder parents' belief systems for preparing un-preschooled children for schooling: A qualitative case study in rural Mongolia. *Cultural and Religious Studies*, 13(1), 12–18. https://doi.org/10.17265/2328-2177/2025.01.002.

Bawden, C. R. (2013). *The Modern History of Mongolia*. Routledge.

Bednarek, M., & Meek, B. A. (2025). "Whitefellas got miserable language skills": Differentiation, scripted speech, and Indigenous discourses. *Language in Society*, 54(2), 211–236.

Beaufils, J. C., Krakouer, J., Kelly, A. L., Kelly, A. M., & Hogg, D. (2025). "We all grow up with our mob because it takes all of us": First Nations collective kinship in Australia. *Children and Youth Services Review*, 169, 108059.

Beltran-Palanques, V., Liu, J. E., & Lin, A. M. (2025). Translanguaging in language teacher education: A systematic review. In Tajeddin, Z. & Farrell, T.S. (Eds.), *Handbook of Language Teacher Education: Critical Review and Research Synthesis*, 593–619.

Berg, U. D., & Ramos-Zayas, A. Y. (2015). Racializing affect: A theoretical proposition. *Current Anthropology*, 56(5), 654–677.

Bhatt, R. M., & Bolonyai, A. (2025). Linguistic discreteness and its variable expressions in multilingualism. *International Journal of Bilingualism, 29*(4), 923-947.

Biernat, M., Zhao, X., & Watkins, E. C. (2024). Names matter: Implications of name "Whitening" for ethnic minority discrimination and well-being. *Current Directions in Psychological Science, 33*(4), 220-225.

Biddle, N., & Swee, H. (2012). The relationship between wellbeing and Indigenous land, language and culture in Australia. *Australian Geographer, 43*(3), 215-232.

Billé, F. (2014). Nationalism, sexuality and dissidence in Mongolia. In Mark McLelland, Vera Mackie (Eds.), *Routledge Handbook of Sexuality Studies in East Asia* (pp. 162-173). Routledge.

Birhane, A. (2020). Algorithmic colonization of Africa. *SCRIPTed: Journal of Law, Technology and Society, 17*(2), 389.

Blackledge, A., & Creese, A. (2009). Meaning-making as dialogic process: Official and carnival lives in the language classroom. *Journal of Language, Identity, and Education, 8*(4), 236-253.

Block, D. (2013). *Social Class in Applied Linguistics*. Routledge.

Bogachenko, T., Burke, R., Zhang, Y., & Gong, Q. (2024). The use of Google Translate for language learning in emergency forced displacement contexts: Ukrainian adult learners of English in Australia. *Australian Review of Applied Linguistics, 47*(3), 309-339.

Bonilla-Silva, E. (2019). Feeling race: Theorizing the racial economy of emotions. *American Sociological Review, 84*(1), 1-25.

Bourdieu, P. (1962/1994). *The Algerians: Sociologie de l'Algérie* (A. C. M. Ross, Trans.). Beacon Press. (Original work published 1958).

Brissenden, J. E., Kidd, J. R., Evsanaa, B., Togtokh, A., Pakstis, A. J., Friedlaender, F., & Roscoe, J. M. (2015). Mongolians in the genetic landscape of Central Asia: Exploring the genetic relations among Mongolians and other world populations. *Human Biology, 87*(2), 73-91.

Bucholtz, M., & Hall, K. (2005). Identity and interaction: A sociocultural linguistic approach. *Discourse Studies, 7*(4-5), 585-614. https://doi.org/10.1177/1461445605054407PhilPapers+1.

Bumochir, D. (2014). Institutionalization of Mongolian shamanism: From primitivism to civilization. *Asian Ethnicity, 15*(4), 473-491.

Busch, B., & McNamara, T. (2020). Language and trauma: An introduction. *Applied Linguistics, 41*(3), 323-333.

Butler, J. (2004). *Precarious Life: The Powers of Mourning and Violence*. Verso.

Butler, J. (2006). *Gender Trouble*. 1st ed. New York: Routledge.

Butler, J. (2021). *Excitable Speech: A Politics of the Performative*. 1st ed. London: Routledge.

Campbell-McLeod, P. E. (2013). Nallawilli-Sit down (and listen): The dreamtime stories – an oral tradition. In Pauline E. Campbell-McLeod (Ed.), *Traditional Storytelling Today* (pp. 155-159). Routledge.

# References

Canagarajah, S. (2012). *Translingual Practice: Global Englishes and Cosmopolitan Relations*. Routledge.

Canessa, A. (2014). Conflict, claim and contradiction in the new "indigenous" state of Bolivia. *Critique of Anthropology, 34*(2), 153–173.

Canagarajah, S. (2013). *Translingual Practice: Global Englishes and Cosmopolitan Relations*. Routledge.

Canagarajah, S. (2022). *Language Incompetence: Learning to Communicate through Cancer, Disability, and Anomalous Embodiment*. Routledge.

Canagarajah, S. (2023a). A decolonial crip linguistics. *Applied Linguistics, 44*(1), 1–21.

Canagarajah, S. (2023b). Diversifying academic communication in anti-racist scholarship: The value of a translingual orientation. *Ethnicities, 23*(5), 779–798.

Cantley, L. (2025). Indigenous data sovereignty: What can yarning teach us?. *Australian Social Work, 78*(2), 133–144.

Carbajal-Carrera, B. (2024). AIsplaining: Generative AI explains linguistic identities to me. *Australian Review of Applied Linguistics, 47*(3), 340-365.

Casillas, D. I., Ferrada, J. S., & Hinojos, S. V. (2018). The accent on *Modern Family*: Listening to representations of the Latina vocal body. *Aztlán: A Journal of Chicano Studies, 43*(1), 61–88.

Castillo-Montoya, M., & Madriaga, M. (2025). Decolonizing assessment of learning in higher education: the journey ahead. *Teaching in Higher Education, 30*(2), 555–564.

Cenoz, J., & Gorter, D. (2025). The potential of pedagogical translanguaging in English language and in English-medium content classes. *Linguistics and Education, 86*, 101399.

Chang, L. S. H., & Canagarajah, S. (2024). Translingual narratives in precarity narrativizing undocumented immigrant status. In S. Dovchin, R. Oliver, & L. Wei (Eds.), *Translingual Practices: Playfulness and Precariousness* (pp. 141–161). Cambridge University Press.

Chen, Y., & Buckingham, L. (2025). Introduction to go-alongs as a qualitative research method in applied linguistics. *Research Methods in Applied Linguistics, 4*(2), 100196.

Chinnery, A. (2015). Precarity and pedagogical responsibility. *Journal of Educational Controversy, 9*(1), 10.

Cioè-Peña, M. (2022). The master's tools will never dismantle the master's school: Interrogating settler colonial logics in language education. *Annual Review of Applied Linguistics, 42*, 25–33.

Clément, R., & Gardner, R. (2001). Second language mastery. In W. P. Robinson & H. Giles (Eds.), *The New Handbook of Language and Social Psychology* (pp. 489–504). Wiley.

Cortés, D. M. (2025). Escobar's Narcos and Whiteness: Fantasising of the American dream by fetishising Latinx and Latin Americans. *Journal of Latin American Cultural Studies, 34*(2), 1–19.

Creese, A., & Blackledge, A. (2010). Translanguaging in the bilingual classroom: A pedagogy for learning and teaching?. *The Modern Language Journal*, 94(1), 103–115.

Creese, G., & Kambere, E. N. (2003). What colour is your English?. *Canadian Review of Sociology/Revue canadienne de sociologie*, 40(5), 565-573.

Cowley, S. J. (2019). Languaging evolved: A distributed perspective. *Chinese Semiotic Studies*, 15(4), 461–482.

Cowley, S. J. (2024). Made in languaging: Ecolinguistic expertise. *Languages*, 9(7), 252.

Cui, Y. (2025). Using strategic translation to empower meaningful language learning: A translanguaging perspective. *Language Awareness*, 1–21. https://doi.org/10.1080/09658416.2025.2527309.

Cumming-Potvin, W., Jackson-Barrett, L., & Potvin, D. (2022). Aboriginal perspectives matter: Yarning and reflecting about teaching literacies with multimodal Aboriginal texts. *Issues in Educational Research*, 32(4), 1342–1363.

Cumpston, Z., Fletcher, M., & Head, L. (2022). *First Knowledges Plants: Past, Present and Future*. Thames & Hudson Australia.

Cushing, I. (2023). *Standards, Stigma, Surveillance: Raciolinguistic Ideologies and English in England's Schools*. Springer. https://doi.org/10.1007/978-3-031-17891-7.

Dai, D. & Zhu, H. (2025). When AI meets intercultural communication: New frontiers, new agendas. *Applied Linguistics Review*, 16(2), 747–751. https://doi.org/10.1515/applirev-2024-0185.

De Genova, N. P. (2015). The problem of racialized affect, and affect as a racial problem. *Current Anthropology*, 56(5), 665.

De Korne, H., Johansen, A. M., & Sollid, H. (2025). Critical place-based pedagogy and language teacher education in the Global North and South. *The Modern Language Journal*. 109(3), 569–585.

De la Cadena, M. (2010). Indigenous cosmopolitics in the Andes: Conceptual reflections beyond "politics." *Cultural Anthropology*, 25(2), 334–370.

de la Piedra, M. T., & Johnson, S. J. (2025). Learning music en la frontera: Translanguaging and multimodal assemblages in a community-based violin education program. *Language and Education*. 39(6), 1315–1334. https://doi.org/10.1080/09500782.2025.2498969.

Dobinson, T., Chen, J., & Steele, C. (2024). Decolonizing or recolonizing?: AI through the eyes of applied linguists, language teachers, and language learners. *Australian Review of Applied Linguistics*, 47(3), 253–258.

Dovchin, S. (2018). *Language, Media and Globalization in the Periphery: The Linguascapes of Popular Music in Mongolia*. Routledge.

Dovchin, S. (2020). The psychological damages of linguistic racism and international students in Australia. *International Journal of Bilingual Education and Bilingualism*, 23(7), 804–818.

Dovchin, S. (2022). *Translingual Discrimination*. Cambridge University Press.

Dovchin, S. (2024a). Beyond translingual playfulness: Translingual precarity. *Language in Society*, 54(4):609–636. https://doi.org/10.1017/S0047404524000708.

Dovchin, S (2024b). Chronotopes: Time and space in identity-making. In E. Milak and A. Tankosic (Eds.), *Becoming a Linguist* (pp. 140–148). New York: Routledge. https://doi.org/10.4324/9781003392606.

Dovchin, S. (2024c). Artificial intelligence in applied linguistics: A double-edged sword. *Australian Review of Applied Linguistics*, 47(3), 410–417.

Dovchin, S (2025a). Reimagining ELT: nomadic knowledging and nomadic languaging. *ELT Journal* https://doi.org/10.1093/elt/ccaf048.

Dovchin, S (2025b). Heritage language anxiety and racialized linguistic shame. *Critical Inquiry in Language Studies*, 1–22. https://doi.org/10.1080/15427587.2025.2593820.

Dovchin, S. (2025c). Beyond linguistic racism: Linguicism and intersectionality among Mongolian background postgraduate female students in Australia. *Urban Education*, 00420859251331555.

Dovchin, U., & Dovchin, S. (2024). The discourse of the Anthropocene and posthumanism: Mining-induced loss of traditional land and the Mongolian nomadic herders. *Ethnicities*, 24(4), 536–559.

Dovchin, S., Dovchin, U., & Gower, G. (2024). The discourse of the Anthropocene and posthumanism: Indigenous peoples and local communities. *Ethnicities*, 24(4), 521–535.

Dovchin, S., & Dryden, S. (2022). Translingual discrimination: Skilled transnational migrants in the labour market of Australia. *Applied Linguistics*, 43(2), 365–388.

Dovchin, S., Mung, S., Lee-Hammond, L., Oliver, R., Hannagan, D., Liu, C. & Lin, A. (2026). Translanguaging *On Country*: trauma responsive pedagogy in Australian Aboriginal early childhood education. *International Review of Applied Linguistics in Language Teaching*. https://doi.org/10.1515/iral-2025-0332.

Dovchin, S., Oliver, R., & Wei, L. (Eds.). (2024). *Translingual Practices: Playfulness and Precariousness*. Cambridge University Press.

Dovchin, S., & Shinjee, B. (2022). The non-normativity of the Global South and the normativity of the Global North: The languaging as the normativity of diversity. *Discourse, Context & Media*, 48, 100621.

Dovchin, S., Pennycook, A., & Sultana, S. (2018). *Popular Culture, Voice and Linguistic Diversity: Young Adults On- and Offline*. Palgrave Macmillan.

Dovchin, S., & Wang, M. (2024). The resistance to translanguaging, spontaneous translanguagers and native speaker saviorism. *Critical Inquiry in Language Studies*, 21(4), 429–446.

Dovchin, S., Wang, M., & Steele, C. (2025). Translingual entanglements of emotions and translanguaging in language learning and teaching contexts. *International Journal of Applied Linguistics*. 35(3), 987–995, https://doi.org/10.1111/ijal.12690.

Dryden, S., & Izadi, D. (2023). The small things of Global South: Exploring the use of social media through translingualism. *Discourse, Context & Media*, 51, 100668.

Dryden, S., Tankosić, A., & Dovchin, S. (2021). Foreign language anxiety and translanguaging as an emotional safe space: Migrant English as a foreign language learners in Australia. *System, 101*, 102593.

Dulik, M. C., Zhadanov, S. I., Osipova, L. P., Askapuli, A., Gau, L., Gokcumen, O., & Schurr, T. G. (2012). Mitochondrial DNA and Y chromosome variation provides evidence for a recent common ancestry between Native Americans and Indigenous Altaians. *The American Journal of Human Genetics, 90*(2), 229–246.

Dumlao, R. P., & Willoughby, L. (2024). Representation of migrant accents in media discourse: A corpus-assisted critical discourse analysis. *AILA Review, 37*(1), 98–119.

Eke, D., & Reyes Cruz, G. (2024). *Decolonising AI: What, why and how?* Responsible AI. https://rai.ac.uk/decolonising-ai-what-why-and-how.

Elyamany, N. (2025). Virtual identity construction in translanguaging spaces: Unveiling the semiotic power of emojis in Lil Miquela's Instagram posts. *Visual Studies*, 1–21. https://doi.org/10.1080/1472586X.2025.2463516.

Erdenechuluun, G. (2025). Analyzing the symbolic meanings of certain Mongolian rituals for "unsettled" children. *Open Journal of Social Sciences, 13*(4), 389–403.

Erling, E. J., & Weidl, M. (2025). Enhancing the research-praxis nexus: Critical moments implementing translanguaging pedagogies in English language education at an Austrian middle school. *System, 133*, 103762.

Falus, O. (2025). The terror of Central-and Eastern Europe of the 13th century: Genghis Khan. The analysis of the secret history of the Mongols as a legal history source work. *Journal on European History of Law, 16*(1), 120–134.

Fang, F., & Dovchin, S. (2024). Reflection and reform of applied linguistics from the Global South: Power and inequality in English users from the Global South. *Applied Linguistics Review, 15*(4), 1223–1230.

Fang, F., Zhang, L. J., & Sah, P. K. (2022). Translanguaging in language teaching and learning: Current practices and future directions. *RELC Journal, 53*(2), 305–312.

Fernández-Giménez, M. E. (2000). The role of Mongolian nomadic pastoralists' ecological knowledge in rangeland management. *Ecological Applications, 10*(5), 1318–1326.

Flores, N., & Rosa, J. (2015). Undoing appropriateness: Raciolinguistic ideologies and language diversity in education. *Harvard Educational Review, 85*(2), 149–171.

Flores, N., & Rosa, J. (2023). Undoing competence: Coloniality, homogeneity, and the overrepresentation of Whiteness in applied linguistics. *Language Learning, 73*(S2), 268–295.

Fought, C. (2006). *Language and Ethnicity*. Cambridge University Press. https://doi.org/10.1017/CBO9780511791215.

# References

French, M., Stanford-Billinghurst, N., & Armitage, J. (2024). Multilingualisms, masking and multitasking: Spaces of hopefulness. In S. Dovchin, R. Oliver, & L. Wei (Eds.), *Translingual Practices: Playfulness and Precariousness* (pp. 79-103). Cambridge University Press.

Galante, A., Piccardo, E., Marcel, F., Zeaiter, L. F., dela Cruz, J. W. N., & Barise, A. (2024). Decolonizing language learning in digital environments through the voices of plurilingual learners in the Global South. *Applied Linguistics*, https://doi.org/10.1093/applin/amae090.

Gallegos, N. (2012). Authenticity of "Latinidad." *Concientización: A Journal of Chican@ & Latin@ Experience and Thought*, 7(1), 34-36.

Gardelle, L., & Zhao, Z. (2019). Being a herder in contemporary Mongolia: Nomadic identity and nationhood building at school. *Asian Ethnicity*, 20(3), 364-385. https://doi.org/10.1080/14631369.2019.1586521.

Garvey, M. (January 26, 2024). Sofia Vergara says her acting jobs are "limited" because of her accent. *CNN*. www.cnn.com/2024/01/26/entertainment/sofia-vergara-acting-jobs-accent-trnd/index.html.

Gerelt-Od, B. (2025). Origin, development, and tendency of grammatical case suffixes of Mongolic languages and dialects. *Mongolian Diaspora. Journal of Mongolian History and Culture*, 4(1-2), 39-78.

Ghajarieh, A., Mozaheb, M. A., & Ghaziyani, Z. A. (2024). Playing with words across visual humor in an Iranian EFL context with Arab students: Pedagogical translanguaging for enhancement of multicultural spaces in language education. *International Journal of Educational Research*, 124, 102278.

Ghazani, A. (2025). Power, positioning, and precarity: Identity negotiation and agency in multilingual minors in Canada. *International Journal of Multilingualism*, 1-20. https://doi.org/10.1080/14790718.2025.2541787.

Goodman, B., & Tastanbek, S. (2021). Making the shift from a codeswitching to a translanguaging lens in English language teacher education. *TESOL Quarterly*, 55(1), 29-53.

Gramling, D. (2016). *The Invention of Monolingualism*. Bloomsbury.

Gramling, D. (2021). *The Invention of Multilingualism*. Cambridge University Press.

Grammon, D. (2025). Inappropriate identities: Racialized language ideologies and sociolinguistic competence in a study abroad context. *Applied Linguistics*, 46(2), 193-210.

Gu, M. M., Han, Y., & Tang, L. (2025). Family language policy in a multilingual Mongolian family in China: A cross-generation exploration. *Journal of Multilingual and Multicultural Development*, 46(10), 3291-3308.

Guenther, J., Oliver, R., Ober, R., & Holmes, C. (2025). What makes quality teachers in remote First Nations schools and what difference do they make?. *The Australian Educational Researcher*, 52(3), 1773-1794.

Guo, J., & Jiang, Y. (2025). Linguistic (in) directness in complaints on an online discussion forum for Chinese university students. *International Journal of Applied Linguistics. 35* (3), 1388–1401.

Guo, Y., Xiong, J., & Lin, Z. (2025). Non-identity in practice: Translanguaging as a tool for hybrid communication in subtitling communities. *International Journal of Multilingualism*, 1–20. https://doi.org/10.1080/14790718.2025.2538079.

Gurney, L., & Demuro, E. (2023). Simultaneous multiplicity: New materialist ontologies and the apprehension of language as assemblage and phenomenon. *Critical Inquiry in Language Studies, 20*(2), 127–149.

Hamilton, G., Brubacher, S. P., & Powell, M. B. (2016). Expressions of shame in investigative interviews with Australian Aboriginal children. *Child Abuse & Neglect, 51*, 64–71.

Hamman-Ortiz, L., & Romero, D. (2025). Translanguaging as mediated praxis: A comparative case study of bilingual and monolingual teachers experimenting with translanguaging pedagogy. *Teaching and Teacher Education, 156*, 104878.

Han, Z. (2024). ChatGPT in and for second language acquisition: A call for systematic research. *Studies in Second Language Acquisition, 46*(2), 301–306.

Haugen, E. (1972). The ecology of language. In A. S. Dil (Ed.), *The Ecology of Language*. Essays by Einar Haugen. Stanford: Stanford University Press. 344–366.

Haugh, M. (2017). Jocular language play, social action and (dis)affiliation in conversational interaction. In Bell, Nancy (Ed.), *Multiple Perspectives on Language Play* (pp. 143–168). Boston, MA: De Gruyter Mouton.

Hawkins, M. R., & Tiwari, N. M. (2024). "Are you poor?" Relational transpositioning through local and transnational transmodal communications. In S. Dovchin, R. Oliver, & L. Wei (Eds.), *Translingual Practices: Playfulness and Precariousness* (pp. 105–122). Cambridge University Press.

Hawkins, M. R., & Mori, J. (2018). Considering "trans-" perspectives in language theories and practices, *Applied Linguistics, 39*(1), 1–8,

Heller, M. (1999). Linguistic minorities and modernity: A sociolinguistic ethnography. *Longman*. practices. *Applied Linguistics, 39*(1), 1–8.

Helm, P., Bella, G., Koch, G., & Giunchiglia, F. (2024). Diversity and language technology: How language modeling bias causes epistemic injustice. *Ethics and Information Technology, 26*(8), 1–15 https://doi.org/10.1007/s10676-023-09742-6.

Henner, J., & Robinson, O. (2023). Unsettling languages, unruly bodyminds: A crip linguistics manifesto. *Journal of Critical Study of Communication and Disability, 1*(1), 7–37.

Hinton, L. (Ed.). (2013). *Bringing Our Languages Home: Language Revitalization for Families*. Heyday.

Hoffecker, J. F., Elias, S. A., & Potapova, O. (2020). Arctic Beringia and Native American origins. *PaleoAmerica, 6*(2), 158–168. https://doi.org/10.1080/20555563.2020.1725380.

Holflod, K. (2022). Voices of playful learning: Experimental, affective and relational perspectives across social education and teacher education. *Journal of Play in Adulthood*, 4(1), 72–91.

Hopkyns, S., & Sultana, S. (2024). The political underbelly of translingual practices in English-medium higher education. In Sender Dovchin, Rhonda Oliver & Li Wei (Eds.), *Translingual Practices: Playfulness and Precariousness* (pp. 197–218). Cambridge University Press.

Horner, B. (2024). 10 Translanguaging, translinguality, and labor. In S. Dovchin, R. Oliver, & L. Wei (Eds.), *Translingual Practices: Playfulness and Precariousness* (pp. 182–196). Cambridge University Press.

Huang, X., Zou, D., Cheng, G., Chen, X., & Xie, H. (2023). Trends, research issues and applications of artificial intelligence in language education. *Educational Technology & Society*, 26(1), 112–131.

Humphrey, C., & Sneath, D. (1999). *The End of Nomadism? Society, State, and the Environment in Inner Asia*. Duke University Press.

Ilonga, E. (2023). Linguistic innovations in a multilingual digital advertising context in Tanzania: A translanguaging perspective. *Journal of Multilingual and Multicultural Development*, 46(4), 1257–1275. https://doi.org/10.1080/01434632.2023.2234873.

Ingley, S. J., & Pack, A. (2023). Leveraging AI tools to develop the writer rather than the writing. *Trends in Ecology & Evolution*, 38(9), 785–787.

Ivetta, G., Morales, J., & Suarez, L. (2025). *HESEIA: A community-based dataset for evaluating social biases in large language models, co-designed in real school settings in Latin America*. arXiv. https://arxiv.org/abs/2505.24712.

Jackson-Barrett, E. M., & Lee-Hammond, L. (2018). Strengthening identities and involvement of Aboriginal children through learning on country. *Australian Journal of Teacher Education (online)*, 43(6), 86–104.

Jakonen, T., Szabó, T. P., & Laihonen, P. (2018). Translanguaging as playful subversion of a monolingual norm in the classroom. In G. Mazzaferro (Ed.), *Translanguaging as Everyday Practice* (pp. 31–48). Cham: Springer.

Jang, J. (2024). The spatiotemporal dynamics of translingual practices and agency: A three-year longitudinal study of a migrant youth from Uzbekistan to South Korea. *International Journal of Multilingualism*, 21(2), 1034–1051.

Jenks, C. J., & Lee, J. W. (2020). Native speaker saviorism: A racialized teaching ideology. *Critical Inquiry in Language Studies*, 17(3), 186–205.

Jolly, H., & Stronza, A. (2025). Insights on human– wildlife coexistence from social science and Indigenous and traditional knowledge. *Conservation Biology*, 39(2), e14460.

Jørgensen, J. N., Karrebæk, M. S., Madsen, L. M., & Møller, J. S. (2015). Polylanguaging in superdiversity. In n Karel Arnaut, Jan Blommaert, Ben Rampton & Massimiliano Spotti (Eds.),*Language and Superdiversity* (pp. 147–164). Routledge.

Jørgensen, J. N., & Møller, J. S. (2014). Polylingualism and languaging. In C. Leung & B. Street (Eds.), *The Routledge Companion to English Studies* (pp. 67–83). Routledge.

Jun, H. R., & Mori, J. (2024). Behind the jovial translingual displays. In S. Dovchin, R. Oliver, & L. Wei (Eds.), *Translingual Practices: Playfulness and Precariousness* (pp. 43–61). Cambridge University Press.

Kang, S. K., DeCelles, K. A., Tilcsik, A., & Jun, S (2016). Whitened résumés: Race and self-presentation in the labor market. *Administrative Science Quarterly*, 61(3), 469–502.

Keay, M. G. (2006). The Tsaatan reindeer herders of Mongolia: Forgotten lessons of human-animal systems. *Encyclopedia of Animals and Humans*, 1–4.

Kent, L. (January 12, 2016). *Coffee names: Fake aliases for when baristas butcher ethnic names*. SBS News. www.sbs.com.au/news/article/coffee-names-fake-aliasesfor-when-baristas-butcher-ethnic-names/0v4yphpwr?utm_source=chatgpt.com.

Kickett-Tucker, C. S., Dodd, J., Johnson, D., & Cross, D. (2025). Koorlangka dreaming becomes a reality: A Moombaki virtual reality with connections to Noongar Moort, Boodja, and Karnarn. *Genealogy*, 9(2), 50.

Kim, Y. J., Kim, G., & Stoiber, A. (2025). Playful design for AI literacy: Creating inclusive learning and assessment opportunities. *International Journal of Human-Computer Studies*, 199, 103508.

Kingsley, J., Townsend, M., Henderson-Wilson, C., & Bolam, B. (2013). Developing an exploratory framework linking Australian Aboriginal peoples' connection to country and concepts of wellbeing. *International Journal of Environmental Research and Public Health*, 10(2), 678–698.

Knorr, D., & Augustin, M. A. (2025). Towards resilient food systems: Interactions with indigenous knowledge. *Trends in Food Science & Technology*, 156 (104875).

Kovats Sánchez, G., Mesinas, M., Casanova, S., Chón, D. W. B., & Pentón Herrera, L. J. (2022). Creating positive learning communities for diasporic indigenous students. 46(9), 2583–2597. *Journal of Multilingual and Multicultural Development*.

Kroll, J. F., & De Groot, A. M. (Eds.). (2009). *Handbook of Bilingualism: Psycholinguistic Approaches*. Oxford University Press.

Krompák, E. (2025). "I am Bernese and proud of it": Regional linguistic identity and translanguaging in teacher education in Switzerland. *Journal of Language, Identity & Education*, 1–17. https://doi.org/10.1080/15348458.2025.2528707.

Kroskrity, P. V. (2000). *Regimes of language: Ideologies, polities, and identities*. School of American Research Press.

Kubota, R. (2015). Inequalities of Englishes, English speakers, and languages: A critical perspective on pluralist approaches to English. In R. Tupas (Ed.), *Unequal Englishes: The Politics of Englishes Today* (pp. 21–42). Palgrave Macmillan.

## References

Kubota, R. (2020). Confronting epistemological racism, decolonizing scholarly knowledge: Race and gender in applied linguistics. *Applied Linguistics*, 41(5), 712-732.

Kubota, R., Corella, M., Lim, K., & Sah, P. K. (2023). "Your English is so good": Linguistic experiences of racialized students and instructors of a Canadian university. *Ethnicities*, 23(5), 758-778.

Kurowski, P. (2025). *Examining the educational and cultural context of the Dukha people: The impacts and limitations of compulsory education for nomadic reindeer herders' children in northern Mongolia.* Master's thesis, UiT The Arctic University of Norway.

Kwon, J., Jin, C., & Hwang, S. (2025). Strengthening the research-practice Nexus in teacher education for multilingual children through translanguaging pedagogy. *System*, 132(103717). 1-11

Ladegaard, H. J. (2014). Crying as communication in domestic helper narratives: Towards a social psychology of crying in discourse. *Journal of Language and Social Psychology*, 33(6), 579-605.

Ladegaard, H. J. (2015). Coping with trauma in domestic migrant worker narratives: Linguistic, emotional and psychological perspectives. *Journal of Sociolinguistics*, 19(2), 189-221.

Ladegaard, H. J. (2018). Codeswitching and emotional alignment: Talking about abuse in domestic migrant-worker returnee narratives. *Language in Society*, 47(5), 693-714.

Lahiri-Roy, R., Belford, N., & Sum, N. (2021). Transnational women academics of colour enacting "pedagogy of discomfort": Positionality against a "pedagogy of rupture." *Pedagogy, Culture & Society*, 31(3), 339-357. https://doi.org/10.1080/14681366.2021.1900345.

Lane, P. (2025). Translanguaging, language revitalisation and new speakers. *Linguistic Approaches to Bilingualism*, 15(1), 77-81

Langeveldt, D. C., & Pietersen, D. (2024). Decolonising AI: A critical approach to education and social justice. *Interdisciplinary Journal of Education Research*, 6(s1), 1-9.

Langton, M., & Corn, A. (2023). *First Knowledges Law: The Way of the Ancestors.* Thames & Hudson Australia.

Lee, J. W. (2017). *The Politics of Translingualism: After Englishes.* Routledge.

Lee, J. W. (2022). *Locating Translingualism.* Cambridge University Press.

Lee, T. K., & Wei, L. (2025). Refashioning linguistic expertise: Translanguaging TESOL in social media. *Applied Linguistics*, amaf007. https://doi.org/10.1093/applin/amaf007.

Leonard, W., (2017) Producing language reclamation by decolonising "language." *Language Documentation and Description*, 14, 15-36. https://doi.org/10.25894/ldd146.

Leonard, W. Y. (2019). Indigenous languages through a reclamation lens. *Anthropology News*, 60(5), e92-e98.

Llamas, J. D., Nguyen, K., & Tran, A. G. T. T. (2019). The case for greater faculty diversity: examining the educational impacts of student-faculty racial/ethnic match. *Race Ethnicity and Education, 24*(3), 375-391. https://doi.org/10.1080/13613324.2019.1679759.

Li, Y. (2024). Usability of ChatGPT in second language acquisition: Capabilities, effectiveness, applications, challenges, and solutions. *Studies in Applied Linguistics & TESOL, 24*(1), 24-37.

Lippi-Green, R. (2012). *English with an Accent: Language, Ideology and Discrimination in the United States*. Routledge.

Li, W. (2018). Translanguaging as a practical theory of language. *Applied Linguistics, 39*(1), 9-30.

Li, W., & Zhu, H. (2020). Tranβcripting: Playful subversion with Chinese characters. *International Journal of Multilingualism, 16*(2), 145-161.

Liang, M. Y. (2024). Transcreation on social media through translingual English. *Asian Englishes, 27*(1), 141-158. https://doi.org/10.1080/13488678.2024.2405269.

López-Gopar, M. E., & Nava, D. I. P. (2025). One morning at a public elementary school in Mexico: A decolonial/critical perspective of ELT. *TESOL Quarterly, 59*(1), 552-564.

MacSwan, J., & Rolstad, K. 2024. (Un)grounded language ideologies: A brief history of translanguaging theory. *International Journal of Bilingualism, 28*(4), 719-743. https://doi.org/10.1177/13670069241236703.

Makoni, S., & Pennycook, A. (2005). Disinventing and (re) constituting languages. *Critical Inquiry in Language Studies, 2*(3), 137-156.

Marav, D., Podorova, A., Yadamsuren, O., & Bishkhorloo, B. (2022). Teaching global English in a local context: Teachers' realities in Mongolian public schools. *Asia Pacific Journal of Education, 42*(2), 276-289.

Maseko, B. (2022). Translanguaging and minoritised language revitalisation in multilingual classrooms: Examining teachers' agency. *Southern African Linguistics and Applied Language Studies, 40*(2), 162-176.

Matras, Y. (2025). From multilingual repertoire to language change. *Contemporary Linguistics: Integrating Languages, Communities, and Technologies, 7*, 127.

May, S. (2023). New Zealand is "racist as f** k": Linguistic racism and te reo Māori. *Ethnicities, 23*(5), 662-679.

McKnight, A., Harwood, V., McMahon, S., Priestly, A., & Trindorfer, J. (2020). "No Shame at AIME": Listening to Aboriginal philosophy and methodologies to theorise shame in educational contexts. *The Australian Journal of Indigenous Education, 49*(1), 46-56.

McLennan, V., & Woods, G. (2018). Learning from mistakes and moving forward in inter cultural research with Aboriginal and Torres Strait Islander peoples. *Higher Education Research & Development, 37*(1), 88-100.

Meighan, P. J. (2023). Colonialingualism: Colonial legacies, imperial mindsets, and inequitable practices in English language education. *Diaspora, Indigenous, and Minority Education, 17*(2), 146-155.

# References

Meighan, P. J. (2024). Colonialingualism in education and policy. In *Encyclopedia of Diversity*. Springer. In M. Sardoč (Ed.), *Encyclopedia of Diversity* (pp. 1-7). Springer.

Meighan, P. J. (2025a). Transepistemic language teacher education: A framework for plurilingualism, translanguaging, and challenging colonialingualism. *The Modern Language Journal,109*(3), 651-670.

Meighan, P. J. (2025b). Decolonizing language education. The Encyclopedia of Applied Linguistics. In C. A. Chapelle & A. Gao (Eds.), *The Encyclopedia of Applied Linguistics* (2nd ed., pp. 1-8). John Wiley & Sons.

Mena, M. (2024). Semiotic Whitening: Whiteness without White people. *Journal of Linguistic Anthropology, 34*(2), 220-242.

Migge, B., & Schneider, B. (2025). The material making of language as practice of global domination and control: Continuations from European colonialism to AI. *AI & Society, 40*, 6059-6071. https://doi.org/10.1007/s00146-025-02389-5.

Mignolo, W. D. (2007). Delinking: The rhetoric of modernity, the logic of coloniality and the grammar of de-coloniality. *Cultural Studies, 21*(2-3), 449-514.

Millikan, R. G. (2005). *Language: A Biological Model*. Oxford University Press.

Mompean, J. A. (2024). ChatGPT for L2 pronunciation teaching and learning. *ELT Journal, 78*(4), 423-434.

Moore, H. (2013). Shades of Whiteness? English villagers, Eastern European migrants and the intersection of race and class in rural England. *Critical Race & Whiteness Studies, 9*(1).

Morcom, L. (2025). "This is all our land": Language revitalization as decolonization and assertion of Indigenous territory in urban spaces. *Journal of Critical Race, Indigeneity, and Decolonization, 2*(2), 90-106.

Morgan, J. and T. Sengedorj. 2022. Early childhood education for nomadic children in Mongolia. In N. McLeod, E. E. Okon, D. Garrison, D. Boyd and A. Daly (Eds.), *Global Perspectives of Early Childhood Education: Valuing Local Cultures* (pp. 57-67). Sage.

Moyer, M. (2023). A critical sociolinguistics perspective on L3 acquisition. In J. Cabrelli, A. Chaouch-Orozco, J. González Alonso, et al. (Eds.), *The Cambridge Handbook of Third Language Acquisition* (pp. 96-112). Cambridge University Press.

Mu, S., Han, L., & Wen, Z. (2025). Language portraits going digital and multimodal: Deciphering the translanguaging space and linguistic repertoires among multilinguals. *Language and Education, 39*(1), 132-153.

Myadar, O. 2020. *Mobility and Displacement: Nomadism, Identity and Postcolonial Narratives in Mongolia*. Routledge.

Nash, B. L. (2024). Love and learning in the age of algorithms: How intimate relationships with artificial intelligence may shape epistemology, sociality, and linguistic justice. *Reading Research Quarterly, 59*(4), 624-631.

Neale, M. (2021). First Knowledges: An introduction. In B. Pascoe & B. Gammage (Eds.), *Country: Future Fire, Future Farming*. First Knowledges Vol. 2, (pp. 11–14). Thames and Hudson Australia.

Neale, M., & Kelly, L. (2020). *First Knowledges Songlines: The Power and Promise*. Thames & Hudson Australia.

Newton, J. (2016). *The Oldest Foods on Earth: A History of Australian Native Foods with Recipes*. NewSouth.

Nguyen, D., & Hajek, J. (2022a). Linguicized subjectivity: Everyday linguicism and the "English-only" ideology. *Applied Linguistics*, 43(1), 1–24. https://doi.org/10.1093/applin/amaf021.

Nguyen, T. T. T., & Hajek, J. (2022b). Making the case for linguicism: Revisiting theoretical concepts and terminologies in linguistic discrimination research. *International Journal of the Sociology of Language*, 275, 187–220.

Nie, P., & Yao, X. (2025). Translanguaging in the linguistic landscape: Creative scripts in Yi ethnicity students' handwritten signs. *Applied Linguistics Review*, 16(4), 1681–1703.

Nikghalb, M., & Cheng, J. (2025). Interrogating AI: Characterizing emergent playful interactions with ChatGPT. *Proceedings of the ACM on Human-Computer Interaction*, 9(2), 1–23.

Noon, K., & De Napoli, K. (2022). *First Knowledges Astronomy: Sky Country*. Thames & Hudson Australia.

Nystrom, G. (2025). "When they speak English, it's normal": The monolingual realities of multilingualism. *Journal of Multilingual and Multicultural Development*, 1–15. https://doi.org/10.1080/01434632.2025.2519566.

Oakley, G., Steele, C., Robinson, C., Dobinson, T., Dovchin, S., & Cumming-Potvin, W. (2025). Towards a playworld translanguaging approach in early childhood education. *Australian Review of Applied Linguistics*, 48(3), 891–911.

Ober, J. (2025a). Playful Englishing: Navigating racialized expectations through linguistic dexterity. *Journal of Sociolinguistic Studies*, 19(2), 134–152.

Ober, R. (2025b). Aboriginal and Torres Strait Islander students' language and learning through a Both Ways approach. In C. Steel, R. Ober & R. Oliver (Eds.), *Celebrating First Nations Languages and Language Learning in Australian Schools* (pp. 199–211). Routledge.

Ober, R., Dovchin, S., & Oliver, R. (2024). "Where you from, who's your Mob?" Ethical considerations when undertaking Australian Aboriginal and Torres Strait Islander applied linguistic research. In Peter I. De Costa, Amr Rabie-Ahmed, and Carlo Cinaglia (Eds.), *Ethical Issues in Applied Linguistics Scholarship* (pp. 192–209). John Benjamins.

O'Faircheallaigh, C. (2023). *Indigenous Peoples and Mining: A Global Perspective*. Oxford University Press.

Oliver, R. (2025). Let them speak: Translanguaging in the classroom. *Curtin University News*. www.curtin.edu.au/news/let-them-speak-translanguaging-in-the-classroom/.

Oliver, R., & Exell, M. (2020). Identity, translanguaging, linguicism and racism: The experience of Australian Aboriginal people living in a remote community. *International Journal of Bilingual Education and Bilingualism*, 23(7), 819–832.

Oliver, R., Wigglesworth, G., & Ober, R. (2024). It "bendy dis one": Recognising and building upon Australian Aboriginal students' linguistic repertoires as educational resources. *Language and Education*, 39(4), 944–964. https://doi.org/10.1080/09500782.2024.2426671.

Oliver, R., Bogachenko, T., & Dovchin, S. (2025). Children learning Mongolian as an additional language through the implementation of a task-based approach. *International Review of Applied Linguistics in Language Teaching*, 63(3), 1715-1738.

Ollerhead, S., Moore-Lister, C. J., & Pennington, G. (2025). Pedagogical translanguaging as "troublesome knowledge" in teacher education. *TESOL in Context*, 33(2), 1–22.

Olszewska, A. I., & Opsahl, T. (2024). "If you don't speak Norwegian well, they think you are stupid": Experiencing and responding to linguistic racism by Polish migrant workers. *Journal of Ethnic and Migration Studies*, 51(9), 2146–2165. https://doi.org/10.1080/1369183X.2024.2444455.

O'Regan, J. P., & Ferri, G. (2025). Artificial intelligence and depth ontology: Implications for intercultural ethics. *Applied Linguistics Review*, 16(2), 797–807.

Otsuji, E., & Pennycook, A. (2010). Metrolingualism: Fixity, fluidity and language in flux. *International Journal of Multilingualism*, 7(3), 240–254.

Otsuji, E., & Pennycook, A. (2024). 4 Precarious assemblages. In S. Dovchin, R. Oliver, & L. Wei (Eds.), *Translingual Practices: Playfulness and Precariousness* (pp. 62–78). Cambridge University Press.

Otheguy, R., García, O., & Reid, W. (2015). Clarifying translanguaging and deconstructing named languages: A perspective from linguistics. *Applied Linguistics Review*, 6(3), 281–307.

Pack, A., & Maloney, J. (2023). Potential affordances of generative AI in language education: Demonstrations and an evaluative framework. *Teaching English with Technology*, 23(2), 4–24.

Pack, A., & Maloney, J. (2024). Using artificial intelligence in TESOL: Some ethical and pedagogical considerations. *TESOL Quarterly*, 58 (2), 1007–1018.

Parini, I. (2025). *Translating playful language in children's literature: Theories and applications*. Stamen.

Parnell, R., & Patsarika, M. (2014). Playful voices in participatory design. In C. Burke & K. Jones (Eds.), *Education, Childhood and Anarchism* (pp. 99–110). Routledge.

Pennycook, A. (2007a). *Global Englishes and Transcultural Flows*. Routledge.

Pennycook, A. (2007b). ELT and colonialism. In J. Cummins & C. Davison (Eds.), *International Handbook of English Language Teaching* (pp. 13-24). Springer US.

Pennycook, A. (2010). *Language as a Local Practice*. Routledge.

Pennycook, A. (2017). *Posthumanist Applied Linguistics*. Routledge.

Pennycook, A. (2024). *Language Assemblages*. Cambridge University Press.

Pennycook, A. & Otsuji, E. (2015). *Metrolingualism: Language in the City*. Routledge.

Pentón Herrera, L. J., & McNair, R. L. (2021). Restorative and community-building practices as social justice for English learners. *TESOL Journal, 12* (1), e00523.

Persaud, J. N., Wannamaker, K., Stark, K., Lambert, C., Harrison, C., & Keller, N. (2025). Decolonizing education: Advancing Indigenous student success through culturally responsive practices in Ontario. *AlterNative: An International Journal of Indigenous Peoples, 21*(2), 11771801251340657, 263-273.

Phipps, A. (2019). *Decolonising Multilingualism: Struggles to Decreate*. Multilingual Matters.

Phyak, P. (2021). Epistemicide, deficit language ideology, and (de) coloniality in language education policy. *International Journal of the Sociology of Language, 2021* (267-268), 219-233.

Piller, I. (2016). *Linguistic Diversity and Social Justice: An Introduction to Applied Sociolinguistics*. Oxford University Press.

Piller, I., Butorac, D., Farrell, E., Lising, L., Motaghi-Tabari, S., & Tetteh, V. W. (2024). *Life in a New Language*. Oxford University Press.

Pistilli, G., Chen, Y., & Ramirez, D. (2024). CIVICS: Building a dataset for examining culturally-informed values in large language models. arXiv. https://arxiv.org/abs/2405.13974.

Prinsloo, M. (2023). Fixity and fluidity in language and language education. *Journal of Multilingual and Multicultural Development, 45*(3), 637-646. https://doi.org/10.1080/01434632.2023.2173215.

Rachmi, R., Atmawinata, M. R., & Arjulayana, A. (2025). The translingual practices in the Indonesian-Spanish family's communication showcased at a digital platform TikTok. *English Learning Innovation (Englie), 6* (2), 217-238.

Rampton, B. (2017). *Crossing: Language and Ethnicity among Adolescents*. Routledge.

Rampton, B. (2006). Stylisation and the dynamics of migration, ethnicity and class. In Braber, N., & Jansen, S. (Eds.), *Stylisation and the Dynamics of Migration, Ethnicity and Class* (pp. 99-120). Springer.

Reagan, T. (2004). Objectification, positivism and language studies: A reconsideration. *Critical Inquiry in Language Studies: An International Journal, 1*(1), 41-60.

Reuter, M., & Schulze, W. (2023). I'm afraid I can't do that: Predicting prompt refusal in black-box generative language models. *arXiv preprint arXiv:2306.03423*.

Ricoeur, P. (2007). *On Translation*. Routledge.

Ridley, K., & Bhowmik, S. (2025). Translanguaging in action: Authentic teaching practices in the high school English as an additional language classroom. *TESOL Journal, 16*(2), e70045.

Roessel, J., Schoel, C., & Stahlberg, D. (2020). Modern notions of accent-ism: Findings, conceptualizations, and implications for interventions and research on nonnative accents. *Journal of Language and Social Psychology, 39*(1), 87-111.

Robertson, B., Demosthenous, H. T., & Demosthenous, C. M. (2005). Stories from the Aboriginal women of the yarning circle: When cultures collide. *Hecate, 31*(2), 34-44.

Robson, J., & LeVoguer, M. (2025). Reflections from the higher education classroom: The role of playful pedagogy in the professional formation of early childhood students. *European Early Childhood Education Research Journal, 33*(2), 275-286.

Romaine, S. (2000). *Language in Society: An Introduction to Sociolinguistics*. Oxford University Press.

Rosa, J., & Flores, N. (2017). Unsettling race and language: Toward a raciolinguistic perspective. *Language in Society, 46*(5), 621-647.

Rosa, M., & Flores, N. (2022). Rethinking language barriers and social justice from a raciolinguistic perspective. *Daedalus, 152*(3), 7-21. https://doi.org/10.1162/daed_a_01999.

Rosiers, K., Van Lancker, I., & Delarue, S. (2018). Beyond the traditional scope of translanguaging: Comparing translanguaging practices in Belgian multilingual and monolingual classroom contexts. *Language & Communication, 61*, 15-28.

Ross, H., & Nursey-Bray, M. (2020). Acknowledging country properly. *Australasian Journal of Environmental Management, 27*(3), 245-248. https://doi.org/10.1080/14486563.2020.1810873.

Rossabi, M. (1994). All the Khan's horses. *Natural History, 103*, 48-48.

Rossabi, M. (2005). *Modern Mongolia: From Khans to Commissars to Capitalists*. Univ of California Press.

Rubin, D. L. (1992). Nonlanguage factors affecting undergraduates' judgments of nonnative English-speaking teaching assistants. *Research in Higher education, 33*, 511-531.

Ruiz, M. J. H. (2025). What is the role of Spanglish in the depiction of Latinidad in an original and in the Spanish dubbed version of a TV series? In R. Attig & R. A. Derrick (Eds.), *Translating Spanglish in US Latinx Audiovisual Stories* (pp.193-217). Routledge. Pp193-217

Russell, E. L. (2022). We should stop anglicising our colleagues' names. *BMJ, 376*, o688. https://doi.org/10.1136/bmj.o688.

Ryu, Y., & Kang, J. (2024). Racism without race in South Korea: Linguistic racism within a curriculum embracing language diversity. *Language, Culture and Curriculum, 38*(1), 77–96. https://doi.org/10.1080/07908318.2024.2416630.

Sabloff, P. L. (Ed.). (2001). *Modern Mongolia: Reclaiming Genghis Khan*. UPenn Museum of Archaeology.

Sah, P. K., KC, M., & De Costa, P. I. (2025). Considering emotions as entanglements in applied linguistics. *International Journal of Applied Linguistics, 35*(3), 959–964.

Sah, P. K., & Li, G. (2022). Translanguaging or unequal languaging? Unfolding the plurilingual discourse of English medium instruction policy in Nepal's public schools. *International Journal of Bilingual Education and Bilingualism, 25*(6), 2075–2094.

Sah, P. K., & Li, G. (2024). Toward linguistic justice and inclusion for multilingual learners: Implications of selective translanguaging in English-medium instruction classrooms. *Learning and Instruction, 92*, 101904.

Sah, P. K., & Uysal, H. (2025). Language ideologies and racial (in)equity in urban multilingual education. *Urban Education*, 00420859251331549. https://doi.org/10.1177/00420859251331549.

Sanduijav, O. (2021). Mentality of Mongolian herders. *Mongolian Diaspora. Journal of Mongolian History and Culture, 1*(2), 105–118.

Sayrafiezadeh, S. (2020). The name on my coffee cup. In K. Whitney & L. Emery (Eds.), *My Shadow Is My Skin: Voices from the Iranian Diaspora* (pp. 97–101). University of Texas Press. https://doi.org/10.7560/320273-014.

Schierup, C. U., & Jørgensen, M. B. (2016). An introduction to the special issue. Politics of precarity: Migrant conditions, struggles and experiences. *Critical Sociology, 42*(7–8), 947–958.

Schmid, U. K. (2025). Humorous hate speech on social media: A mixed-methods investigation of users' perceptions and processing of hateful memes. *New Media & Society, 27*(3), 1588–1606.

Selvi, A. F. (2025). The myopic focus on decoloniality in applied linguistics and English language education: Citations and stolen subjectivities. *Applied Linguistics Review, 16*(1), 137–161.

Shafiee Rad, H., & Roohani, A. (2025). AI language alchemists: Unleashing task-based Chatbots to enhance speaking proficiency, shape attitudes, and foster a translanguaging space. *Journal of Educational Computing Research, 63*(7–8) 1659–1688.

Shah, W. A., & Shah, U. R. (2025). De-centering the anthropocentric world-view in language textbooks: A posthumanist call for discursive reparations for sustainable ELT. *Linguistics and Education, 86*, 101397.

Shahid, F., Elswah, M., & Vashistha, A. (2025). *Think outside the data: Colonial biases and systemic issues in automated moderation pipelines for low-resource languages*. arXiv. https://arxiv.org/abs/2501.13836.

Shi, H., & Cheung, L. M. E. (2024). Storytelling for understanding: A case study of an English-language digital storytelling service-learning subject for refugee children in Hong Kong. *Journal for Multicultural Education*, 18(1/2), 81–97.

Shinjee, B., & Dovchin, S. (2023a). The multilingual landscape of Ulaanbaatar, the capital city of Mongolia. *Multilingualism and Pluricentricity: A Tale of Many Cities*, 20, 249.

Shinjee, B., & Dovchin, S. (2023b). Sociolinguistics in Mongolia. In M. J. Ball, R. Mesthrie, & C. Meluzzi (Eds.), *The Routledge Handbook of Sociolinguistics around the World* (pp. 197–205). Routledge.

Shinjee, B., & Dovchin, S. (2025). Mongolia, English in. In K. Bolton (Ed.), *The Wiley Blackwell Encyclopedia of World Englishes*. Wiley. 1–12. https://doi.org/10.1002/9781119518297.eowe00234.

Shiosaki, E. (2025). First Nations-determined storylines: Noongar story work in the ancestors' words project. *Australian Aboriginal Studies*, 1 (2025), 24–30.

Siffrinn, N., & Coda, J. (2024). A literature review of posthumanist and new materialist research in applied linguistics. *Critical Inquiry in Language Studies*, 22(3), 190–201.

Skutnabb-Kangas, T. (2013). *Linguistic Genocide in Education–Or Worldwide Diversity and Human Rights?*. Routledge.

Smith, P. (2025). Re-/Imagining racialized entanglements of Englishes and peoples: A call for a quantum ethos. In *Entangled Englishes* (pp. 118–137). Routledge. In J. W. Lee & S. Rüdiger (Eds.), *Entangled Englishes* (pp. 99–120). Routledge.

Simpson, J. (2014). *Language and Identity in the Postcolonial World*. Cambridge University Press.

Soma, T. (2025). Traditional ecological knowledge (TEK) of steppe land for Dzud disaster reduction in the mongolian nomadic community. In F. Stammler & H. Takakura (Eds.),*The Benefits of the Cold and Domestication* (pp. 195–226). Routledge.

Song, Y. & Lin, A. (2025). From translanguaging to transknowledging: Decolonizing knowledge production in applied linguistics. *Applied Linguistics Review*. https://doi.org/10.1515/applirev-2025-0157.

Soubutts, E., Singh, A., Knowles, B., Ayobi, A., Dias, N.V., Schulte, B., McDowell, J., Swarbrick, C., Steptoe, A., Fledderjohann, J. & Petrie, H. (2023). Playful, curious, creative, equitable: Exploring opportunities for AI technologies with older adults. In J. Abdelnour Nocera, M. Kristín Lárusdóttir, H. Petrie, A. Piccinno, M. Winckler (Eds.), *Human-Computer Interaction – INTERACT 2023. INTERACT 2023. Lecture Notes in Computer Science*, 14145, 662–667. Springer. https://doi.org/10.1007/978-3-031-42293-5_90.

St Ours, K. (2011). An ecocritical study of the story of the weeping camel. *ISLE: Interdisciplinary Studies in Literature and Environment*, 18(2), 396–412.

Standing, G. (2011). *The Precariat: The New Dangerous Class*. Bloomsbury.

Steele, C., & Oliver, R. (2024). Distraction in Australian language education policy: A call to re-centre language rights. *Current Issues in Language Planning*, 26(3), 345–370.

Steele, C., Dovchin, S., & Oliver, R. (2022). "Stop measuring Black kids with a white stick": Translanguaging for classroom assessment. *RELC Journal*, 53(2), 400–415.

Steele, C., Ober, R., & Oliver, R. (Eds.). (2025). *Celebrating First Nations Languages and Language Learning in Australian Schools: Stories Across Generations of Language Activism, Advocacy and Allyship*. Routledge.

Stewart, N., & Zheng, Y. (2024). Generative AI's recolonization of EFL classrooms: The case of continuation writing. *Australian Review of Applied Linguistics*, 47(3), 383-409.

Sultana, S. (2015). Transglossic language practices: Young adults transgressing language and identity in Bangladesh. *Translation and Translanguaging in Multilingual Contexts*, 1(2), 202–232.

Sun, P., & Sornyai, P. (2025). Mongolian folk songs: Integrating traditional music into contemporary literacy. *International Journal of Education and Literacy Studies*, 13(2), 19–26.

Sun, Y., & Lan, G. (2025). Enhancing critical language awareness in EAL writing education amid the rise of generative artificial intelligence. *System*, 134, 103806.

Tai, K. W., & Wei, L. (2021). Constructing playful talk through translanguaging in English medium instruction mathematics classrooms. *Applied Linguistics*, 42(4), 607–640.

Tankosić, A., & Dovchin, S. (2022). Monglish in post-communist Mongolia. *World Englishes*, 41(1), 38–53.

Tankosić, A., Dryden, S., & Dovchin, S. (2021). The link between linguistic subordination and linguistic inferiority complexes: English as a second language migrants in Australia. *International Journal of Bilingualism*, 25(6), 1782-1798.

Tankosić, A., Dovchin, S., Oliver, R., & Exell, M. (2024). The mundanity of translanguaging and Aboriginal identity in Australia. *Applied Linguistics Review*, 15(4), 1277–1298.

Tankosić, A., Dovchin, S., & Oliver, R. (2025). Educators' reflections in Australian aboriginal translingual classrooms: Entanglement of language, culture, and emotionality. In J. W. Lee & S. Rüdiger (Eds.), *Entangled Englishes* (pp. 218–231). Routledge.

Taylor-Bragge, R. L., Whyman, T., & Jobson, L. (2021). People needs country: The symbiotic effects of landcare and wellbeing for Aboriginal peoples and their countries. *Australian Psychologist*, 56(6), 458–471.

Tavares, V. (2024). Feeling excluded: International students experience equity, diversity and inclusion. *International Journal of Inclusive Education*, 28(8), 1551–1568.

Terbish, B. (2025). *Humans, Dogs and Other Beings: Myths, Stories, and History in the Land of Genghis Khan*. Open Book Publishers.

TheEllenShow. (August 30, 2023). *Modern Family Cast on First Impressions of Each Other and Growing Up on the Show* [Video]. YouTube. www.youtube.com/watch?v=MXtTJVYU3PA.

Theodoropoulou, I. (2021). Humoristic translanguaging in intercultural communication in Qatar: Merits, limitations, and its potential contribution to policy development. In In K. Raza, C. Coombe & D. Reynolds (Eds.), *Policy Development in TESOL and Multilingualism: Past, Present and the Way Forward* (pp. 161-175). Springer Nature Singapore.

Tran, H., & Stell, A. (2024). Beyond borders or building new walls? The potential for Generative AI in recolonising the learning of Vietnamese dialects and Mandarin varieties. *Australian Review of Applied Linguistics*, 47(3), 284-308.

Treffers-Daller, J. (2024). Code-switching and translanguaging: Why they have a lot in common. *ELT Journal*, 78(1), 82-87.

Tri, D. H. (2025). "Tuesday, the mistress": English relocalization by Vietnamese Facebook users. *Asian Englishes*, 27(1), 89-104.

Tsing, A. L. (2015). *The Mushroom at the End of the World: On the Possibility of Life in Capitalist Ruins*. Princeton: Princeton University Press.

Tugjamba, N. (2025). Dancing with cranes: The relational values of the open pasture steppes of Mongolia. *Landscape Research*, 50(6), 927-938. https://doi.org/10.1080/01426397.2025.2461533.

Tuck, E., & Yang, K. W. (2012). Decolonization is not a metaphor. *Decolonization: Indigeneity, Education & Society*, 1(1), 1-40.

Tupas, R. (Ed.). (2015). *Unequal Englishes: The Politics of Englishes Today*. Springer.

Uekusa, S. (2019). Disaster linguicism: Linguistic minorities in disasters. *Language in Society*, 48(3), 353-375.

Upton, C. (2010). Living off the land: Nature and nomadism in Mongolia. *Geoforum*, 41(6), 865-874.

Vaughan, J. (2019). The ordinariness of translinguistics in Indigenous Australia. In In J. W. Lee & S. Dovchin (Eds.), *Translinguistics* (pp. 90-103). Routledge.

Venegas, M., & Leonard, W. Y. (2023). Engaging indigenous language learning through relational accountability: A commentary on "undoing competence: Coloniality, homogeneity, and the overrepresentation of Whiteness in applied linguistics." *Language Learning*, 73(S2), 333-336.

Verdon, S., & McLeod, S. (2015). Indigenous language learning and maintenance among young Australian Aboriginal and Torres Strait Islander children. *International Journal of Early Childhood*, 47(1), 153-170.

Vitebsky, P. (2006). *The Reindeer People: Living with Animals and Spirits in Siberia*. Houghton Mifflin Harcourt.

Waluyo, B., & Rouaghe, F. (2025). Beyond teacher-led approaches: Student-initiated translanguaging with artificial intelligence tools in foreign language acquisition. *SAGE Open*, 15(3), 21582440251362998.

Wang, D. (2024). Translanguaging as a decolonising approach: Students' perspectives towards integrating Indigenous epistemology in language teaching. *Applied Linguistics Review*, 15(4), 1385–1406.

Wang, M., & Dovchin, S. (2023). "Why should I not speak my own language (Chinese) in public in America?": Linguistic racism, symbolic violence, and resistance. *TESOL Quarterly*, 57(4), 1139–1166.

Waring, H. Z. (2013). Doing being playful in the second language classroom. *Applied linguistics*, 34(2), 191–210.

Washington, J. A., & Iruka, I. U. (2025). Linguistic justice: Addressing linguistic variation of Black children in teaching and learning. *Linguistics and Education*, 85, 101382.

Watt D. (2025). Dialectism. In Setter J., Dovchin S., Ramattan V. (Eds.), *Oxford Handbook of Linguistic Prejudice* ( pp. 315–337). Oxford University Press

Weenie, A. (2025). Nihtotamowin: Listening, language and land-based pedagogies. In S. Styres & R. Neepin (Eds.), *The Bloomsbury Handbook of Indigenous Education and Research*, 162–182.

Whyte, K. P. (2017). Indigenous climate change studies: Indigenizing futures, decolonizing the Anthropocene. *English Language Notes*, 55(1–2), 153–162.

Wigglesworth, G., & Oliver, R. (2024). "Because I growed up ... Big Martu ways." In S. Dovchin, R. Oliver, & L. Wei (Eds.), *Translingual Practices: Playfulness and Precariousness* (pp. 165–181). Cambridge University Press.

Williams, Q. (2017). *Remix Multilingualism: Hip Hop, Ethnography and Performing Marginalized Voices*. Bloomsbury.

Williams, Q., Deumert, A., & Milani, T. M. (Eds.). (2022). *Struggles for Multilingualism and Linguistic Citizenship*. Bristol: Multilingual Matters.

Windle, M., Tuvshinjargal, T., Zhang, C., Li, Y., Brandišauskas, D., Piezonka, H., Ochirg, Y., Ariunzul,G., Kertanish, R & Taylor, W. (2025). Understanding the origin of reindeer riding in Northeast Asia through animal paleopathology and collaborative archaeology. *Arctic, Antarctic, and Alpine Research*, 57(1). 1–16. https://doi.org/10.1080/15230430.2025.2493391.

Wong, C. Y. C. (2025). Creating a meaningful summative assessment in a Chinese immersion context: A translanguaging perspective. *Applied Linguistics Review*, 16(4), 1731–1758.

Wong, C. Y. C., & Gallagher, M. (2025). From uncertainty to advocacy: A teacher's journey in translanguaging pedagogy. *System*, 134, 103827.

Wong, N., & García, O. (2025). Expandability and temporality in translanguaging spaces: A space-centred systematic observation of Kongish Daily. *Applied Linguistics Review*, 16(5), 2217–2245. https://doi.org/10.1515/applirev-2024-0372.

Xu, W. (2025). Linguistic racism and micro-aggressions in everyday encounters of African migrants in China: A challenge to the nation's strategic vision for Africa? *Ethnicities*, 25(1), 69–84.

Yazdzik, E. (2011). The Mongolian Horse and Horseman. Independent Study Project (ISP) Collection. 1068. https://digitalcollections.sit.edu/isp_collection/1068.

Yoon, S. (2019). Mobilities, experienced and performed, in Mongolia's urtyn duu tradition. *Asian Music, 50*(1), 47-77.

Zappavigna, M. (2025). "I'm sorry Dave, I'm afraid I can't do that": Moral regulation in refusals by LLM chatbots. *New Media & Society*, 14614448251356686. https://doi.org/10.1177/14614448251356686.

Zhao, J., & Gómez Fariñas, B. (2023). Artificial intelligence and sustainable decisions. *European Business Organization Law Review, 24*(1), 1-39.

Zhao, Z. (2025). Marks of the grassland: Spatial cognition and perception in Mongolian nomadic life. *Journal of Arts and Humanities, 14*(01), 23-35.

Zhao, X., & Biernat, M. (2018). "I have two names, Xian and Alex": Psychological correlates of adopting Anglo names. *Journal of Cross-Cultural Psychology, 49*(4), 587-601. https://doi.org/10.1177/0022022118763111.

Zhu, H., Dai, D. W., Brandt, A., Chen, G., Ferri, G., Hazel, S., Jenks, C., Jones, R., O'Regan., J., & Suzuki, S. (2025). Exploring AI for intercultural communication: Open conversation. *Applied Linguistics Review, 16*(2), 809-824.

Zhu, H., Li, W., & Lyons, A. (2016). Playful subversiveness and creativity: Doing a/n (Polish) artist in London. *Working Papers in Translanguaging and Translation* (WP. 16). (www.birmingham.ac.uk/generic/tlang/index.aspx).

# Index

Aboriginal
  children, 32
  communities, 51
  dreaming stories, 57
  English, 29, 47, 48, 49, 56, 58, 95, 108, 109, 110, 145, 149
  identity, 107
  knowledge, 51
  language, 48, 49, 50, 53, 150
  languages, 29, 59
  learners, 32
  people, 43, 45
  students, 44, 45
  way, 43
  young people, 47
*accentism*, 27, 97
AI-mediated languaging, 117, 119, 133, 137, 140, 142, 148
*AIsplaining*, 132
*algorithmic colonialism*, 131
ally, English as, 86
anglicised names, 99
artificial intelligence (AI), 117, 154
Australian Aboriginal
  background, 62
  people, 43, 44, 45
  school, 32, 43

bi/multilingualism, 145
bush tucker, 51, 57

ChatGPT, 117, 121, 122, 123, 124, 125, 129, 130, 134, 135, 136, 137, 138, 139
*codeswitching*, 13, 14, 15, 16, 17
concept of fluidity, 19
creativity, 15, 19, 25, 30, 31, 32, 33, 34, 40, 60, 78, 97, 98, 120, 121, 122, 128, 130, 136, 137, 147, 148, 149, 153, 156
*crossing* and *style-shifting*, 108
crying, 28, 113
cultural sovereignty, 59, 72, 87, 89
cursing, 28, 82, 113

decolonial turn, 67, 68
displacement, 67, 80, 81, 154
Dukhan, 40, 41

eating disorders, 28
Ellen Show, The, 92
ELT, 68
emotional labour, 103, 111, 112, 113, 114
English, 1, 2, 3, 6, 11, 15, 17, 18, 21, 29, 32, 40, 52, 56, 68, 83, 84, 88, 90, 93, 97, 104, 105, 106, 107, 109, 110, 114, 131, 134, 137, 138, 139, 147, 149, 150, 151, 152, 156
  "proper", 108
  "pure", 27
  AAVE, 97
  accented, 97
  borrowings, 126
  dominance, 59
  fluency in, 93
  hegemony of, 77
  language, 6
  language abilities, 105
  language education, 66, 67
  mispronunciations of, 112
  name, 98
  phonetics, 123
  playful, 101
  proficiency in, 96
  role of, 14, 64, 65

speaker, 33, 94
spread of, 85
Standard, 118
standard American, 104
terminology, 150
translation, 136
translingual, 22
user, 24
varieties, 94, 109
English Medium Instruction (EMI) classroom, 22
English-centric
  schooling, 52
  systems, 141
English-dominant
  societies, 24
English-dominated
  AI frameworks, 142
*Englishes*
  unequal, 27
epistemic justice, 59, 68
epistemic resources, 34, 149
epistemology
  nomadic, 64
equity, 122, 130, 144
ethics of herding, 88

fluidity, 65, 72, 78, 87, 88, 150
  linguistic, 17, 77, 88
  nomadic, 64

Chinggis Khan, 65, 72, 84, 139
*giingoo*, 73, 74, 75, 76, 77, 78, 79, 80, 89
Gija, 152
globalisation from below, 26
Gobi, 79
grief, 27, 82
grotesque. *See grotesque voices*
*grotesque voices*, 28

horse race, 73
humility, 32, 64, 86, 87, 88, 90, 91
hybridity, 5, 17, 19, 31, 41, 87, 150

identity negotiation, 20, 98, 147
ideology, 94, 119
inclusive pedagogy, 121
Indigenous epistemologies, 61
Indigenous knowledge, 37, 45, 61, 68
instability, 27, 29, 30, 60, 156

integrated communicative repertoire, 17
*interactional design*, 148
intercultural communication, 119
*intercultural ethics*, 134, 135
intergenerational transmission, 29, 49, 50, 51, 59, 71
international students, 96, 99, 101
*Intruder, English as*, 83, 87, 88

*kaarda*
  goanna, 56, 57
*khoos*, 79, 80, 82, 89
  khooslono, 79
Korean, 14, 15, 22, 77, 78, 96, 145, 150
Kriol, 11, 46, 47, 51, 95, 107, 145, 149
Kununurra, 28
Kutja School, 44, 46

land-based knowledge, 68
language from below, 26
language ideologies, 5, 6, 22, 24, 113, 115, 132
language loss, 29, 54, 58, 59
language reclamation, 50, 54, 55, 58, 61
language revitalisation, 49, 60
language teacher education, 151
*languaging*, 9, 10, 11, 12, 13, 14, 16, 17, 18, 20, 23, 26, 28, 29, 30, 48, 122, 124, 127, 152, 153
  de-, 141, 142
  enactments of, 145
  evolution of, 25
  example of, 128
  forms of, 135
  human specific, 137
  human-induced, 134
  mediated, 127
  models of, 87
  nature of, 130
  nomadic, 32, 64, 65, 68, 71, 72, 73, 76, 77, 78, 79, 80, 81, 82, 87, 88, 89, 90
  pedagogical, 34, 149, 150, 151, 153, 155
  playful, 23, 25, 30, 76, 92, 101, 125, 130, 147, 156
  playfulness in, 156
  playfulness of, 75, 147

languaging (cont.)
  practices, 9, 25, 33, 41, 44, 123, 143, 144, 149, 154
  precarity of, 142
  racialised, 33, 94, 95, 96, 97, 98, 99, 101, 110, 112, 115, 116
  repertoire-based, 17
  sophisticated, 152
  space, 59
  strategies, 61
  understanding of, 26, 31, 33, 148
  unequal, 27
*Latina*, 93
life without the promise of stability, 26
*linguascaping*, 8
linguistic
  assimilation, 72, 103
  biases, 62, 155
  boundaries, 6, 7, 12, 20, 25, 26, 29, 32, 64, 75, 95, 101
  categories, 4, 14
  code, 13
  codes, 13, 15, 19
  competence, 89, 97
  criteria, 4, 5
  expression, 32, 42
  features, 19, 96
  forms, 9, 19, 149
  identities, 6, 7, 62
  ideologies, 24, 109
  inferiority complexes, 27
  injustice, 5, 28, 82, 113
  innovation, 21, 153
  innovations, 22
  landscape, 4, 6, 9
  marginalisation, 50, 113, 141
  norms, 23, 107, 136, 154
  play, 20, 41
  practice, 1, 15
  practices, 5, 33, 38, 65, 71, 94
  precarity, 103, 142
  purity, 2, 3
  racism, 27, 29, 104, 116
  realities, 5, 7, 146
  resources, 1, 12, 15, 17, 19, 21, 30, 56, 68
  subordination, 25, 109
  suppression, 52, 53, 55
  violence, 96
linguistic diversity, 5, 24, 34, 44, 61, 68, 77, 88, 99, 116, 118, 133, 143, 145, 148, 155, 156
linguistic hierarchies, 5, 23, 97, 99, 110, 115, 119, 120, 131, 147, 151, 155
*linguistic hospitality*, 88
linguistic justice, 6, 91, 141, 148, 149, 154, 157
*linguistic play*, 18, 19, 21, 22, 23, 24, 25, 29, 30, 31, 40, 41, 43, 47, 56, 71, 78, 97, 98, 103, 124
linguistic purity, 1, 3, 17, 89, 145, 149
linguistic, spheres of, 5
linguistics, 7, 10
  applied, 2, 12, 13, 25, 67
  structuralist, 8

*Malchid*
  nomadic herders, 70, 74, 84
Māori, 62, 95
*metrolingualism*, 9, 31
mining, 67, 84, 85
Miriwoong, 28, 29, 46, 47, 48, 49
*Miriwoong Dawang*, 46
Mongol Empire, 40, 65, 83
Mongolian, 1–3, 14–15, 17–19, 127, 135, 136, 145
  accent, 29
  child, 97
  cultural context, 83
  culture, 139
  Cyrillic, 123
  dinner, 64
  discourse, 127
  dress, 45
  ger, 64
  heritage, 45, 69, 122, 125
  history, 139
  horse, 134, 135
  horse rider, 74
  horses, 72, 73, 74
  identity, 72, 86
  lady, 102
  lexical practices, 128
  mother, 124
  mum, 124
  musical instrument, 80
  name, 101, 102
  nomadic communities, 69
  nomadic epistemologies, 69

# Index

nomadic epistemology, 64
nomadic herders, 67, 72
nomadic herding culture, 66
nomadic herdsmen, 88
nomadic knowledge, 80
nomadic masculinity, 83
nomadic tradition, 66
nomadic way, 63
nomads, 65, 73
orthographic system, 66
pastoral life, 88
pastoralism, 66
people, 69, 86
phonology, 123
phrase, 63, 125, 138
proverb, 70, 83, 86
school, 122, 125
script, 66
society, 40
speaker, 125
speech, 124
steppes, 70, 74
swear words, 128
taiga, 35
Tengrism, 69
traditions, 122
*urtiin duu* (long song), 74
varieties, 72
woman, 103, 104
words, 137
young people, 135
Mongolian language, 1, 17, 40, 48, 65, 88, 122, 125, 130, 139
Mongolian nomadic herders. *See malchid*
Mongolian People's Republic, 65
Mongolians, 66, 74, 79
monolingualism, 4, 5, 14, 15, 95
*morin khuur*
   horse-headed fiddle, 79, 80, 137
*multilingualism*, 4, 5, 21, 88, 116

*Naadam*, 73
naming practices, 99, 101, 103
NAPLAN, 53
Native American tribes, 69
*native speakerism*, 94, 97
New Zealand, 62, 95
nomadic
   knowledging, 32, 64, 65, 68, 70, 71, 72, 73, 81, 85, 87, 88, 89, 90

nomadic culture, 69, 72, 79, 85, 138
*nomadic reminiscing circle*, 32, 63, 64
Noongar language, 55, 57, 60
*Nutag*
   land, 63, 70, 73, 84

oral traditions, 38, 51, 53, 71, 72, 73, 87, 90
orality, 42

paralinguistic, 28
   resources, 15
*perceived playfulness*, 120
perceptions of race, 105
performative expression, 21
play-based learning, 20, 58
*playful Englishing*, 108, 110
playful voices, 17, 18, 19, 22, 23, 24, 29, 45, 47, 56, 59, 75, 76, 79
playfulness and precarity, 30, 31, 32, 33, 42, 60, 61, 65, 72, 78, 85, 97, 119, 147, 156
*polylanguaging*, 8
posthumanist applied linguistics, 76
precarious
   assemblages, 26
   dimensions, 145, 147
   grounds, 24, 25, 26, 28, 41, 48, 50, 58, 60
   voices, 24, 28, 82, 113, 114, 115
psycholinguistic, 39

Qing Dynasty, 40, 65

racialised emotions, 111
*racialised English*, 108, 112
Reindeer people, 37, 71
relational epistemology, 70
repertoire, 23, 107, 149, 150
   communicative, 16, 127
   everyday, 127
   existing, 123
   interwoven, 16
   linguistic, 5, 9, 13, 15, 17, 20, 29, 40, 53, 56, 59, 62, 72, 78, 123, 126, 131, 143, 151, 152
   Mongolian, 141
   multilingual, 30, 53
   non-Western, 141
   oral, 71

repertoire (cont.)
  semiotic, 44, 124, 145, 148
  semiotic and spiritual, 40
  spiritual, 40
  verbal, 78
resistance, 21, 32, 42, 43, 58, 60, 95, 108, 110, 147, 156, 157
respect, 7, 32, 37, 38, 44, 48, 51, 64, 66, 71, 79, 83, 88, 90, 100, 101, 102, 130, 143, 144, 146
rootedness, 32, 53, 64, 65, 88
*rubbish talk*, 109
Russian, 1, 2, 3, 14, 15, 35, 40, 72, 84, 85, 125, 126, 127, 128
Russian Cyrillic, 66
Russian language, 1, 125

*Secret History of the Mongols*, 139
self-harm, 28
semiotic
  complexity, 26
  landscapes, 7
  markers, 30
  mobility, 15
  modes, 153
  practice, 7
  practices, 31
  precarity, 30, 31
  resources, 15, 16, 19, 20, 21, 31, 40, 119, 124, 143
shaman
  shamanism, 35, 38, 40, 41, 45, 65
shamanic rituals. *See shaman:shamanistic*
shamanistic practice. *See shaman: shamanism*
*shame*, 28, 29, 48, 49, 50, 103, 108, 109
social justice, 60, 62, 100, 116, 119, 144, 155
sociolinguistic
  histories, 44
Sofia Vergara, 92
Spanish, 3, 92, 93

Standard Australian English, 11, 49, 51, 95, 96, 106, 107, 108, 110, 149, 152
Story of Weeping Camel, The, 79
storytelling, 20, 32, 39, 40, 42, 47, 51, 57, 60, 63, 73, 87, 89, 121, 152, 154
strength-based approaches, 90, 152
*style-shifting*, 108
substance abuse, 28
suicidal ideation, 28, 112
surveillance, 147
symbolic violence, 103, 112
systemic nature of racism, 111

traditional *gers*
  portable round dwelling, 66
transformation, 24, 25, 41, 54, 85
*transknowledging*, 89
*translanguaging*, 8, 9, 20, 22, 25, 26, 30, 61, 62, 89, 153, 154
*translingual practice*, 8, 82
transliteration, 123, 124
trauma, 28, 45, 54
Tsaatan people. *See reindeer people*

uncertainty, 23, 28, 30, 32, 43, 53, 65

*Verlan*, 136
vulnerability, 24, 27, 28, 30, 31, 54, 60, 82, 85, 98, 113, 115, 147, 149, 156

weeping, 28
Western Australia, 32, 43, 44, 50, 55, 107, 122, 125
White listening subjects, 97, 105, 109
White Mainstream English, 95
wording types, 9, 10

yarning, 32, 42, 63
*yarning circle*, 63

*zud (dzud)*
  severe winter disasters, 37, 67, 84, 85

For EU product safety concerns, contact us at Calle de José Abascal, 56–1°, 28003 Madrid, Spain or eugpsr@cambridge.org.

www.ingramcontent.com/pod-product-compliance
Lightning Source LLC
LaVergne TN
LVHW012018060526
838201LV00061B/4354